Politics and Society
in the Southwest

Westview Replica Editions

The concept of Westview Replica Editions is a response to the continuing crisis in academic and informational publishing. Library budgets for books have been severely curtailed. Ever larger portions of general library budgets are being diverted from the purchase of books and used for data banks, computers, micromedia, and other methods of information retrieval. Interlibrary loan structures further reduce the edition sizes required to satisfy the needs of the scholarly community. Economic pressures (particularly inflation and high interest rates) on the university presses and the few private scholarly publishing companies have severely limited the capacity of the industry to properly serve the academic and research communities. As a result, many manuscripts dealing with important subjects, often representing the highest level of scholarship, are no longer economically viable publishing projects--or, if accepted for publication, are typically subject to lead times ranging from one to three years.

Westview Replica Editions are our practical solution to the problem. We accept a manuscript in camera-ready form, typed according to our specifications, and move it immediately into the production process. As always, the selection criteria include the importance of the subject, the work's contribution to scholarship, and its insight, originality of thought, and excellence of exposition. The responsiblity for editing and proofreading lies with the author or sponsoring institution. We prepare chapter headings and display pages, file for copyright, and obtain Library of Congress Cataloging in Publication Data. A detailed manual contains simple instructions for preparing the final typescript, and our editorial staff is always available to answer questions.

The end result is a book printed on acid-free paper and bound in sturdy library-quality soft covers. We manufacture these books ourselves using equipment that does not require a lengthy make-ready process and that allows us to publish first editions of 300 to 600 copies and to reprint even smaller quantities as needed. Thus, we can produce Replica Editions quickly and can keep even very specialized books in print as long as there is a demand for them.

About the Book and Editors

Politics and Society in the Southwest:
Ethnicity and Chicano Pluralism
Z. Anthony Kruszewski, Richard L. Hough, and Jacob Ornstein-Galicia

This book is an assessment of the changing status of the border Southwest's Spanish-speaking population, the largest foreign-language-speaking minority in the United States. Reflecting the results of very recent research, it reveals two opposing forces at work in the Chicano community--one toward assimilation into the Anglo mainstream, the other toward maintenance of Mexican-American social and linguistic identity within the U.S. "mosaic." The authors consider the language, culture, and ethnic identity of Chicanos in Southwestern society, as well as patterns of interethnic contact in the region and the emerging sociopolitical order. The editors' "pluralism assessment" model is used to define the relative degrees and dimensions of assimilation and pluralism explored in the individual chapters.

The consensus of the authors is that the close proximity of the Mexican border and the increasing flow of Hispanic immigrants make full assimilation unlikely, and they cite examples of strong impulses toward preserving the Spanish language and Mexican-American identity. They also note, however, increasing Mexican-American participation in the economic, educational, occupational, and political spheres of mainstream culture, an interesting counterpoint to the pluralistic trends.

Z. Anthony Kruszewski is professor of political science and director of the Cross-Cultural Southwest Ethnic Studies Center at the University of Texas, El Paso. *Richard L. Hough*, coordinator of the Brentwood-UCLA Health Services Research Center, teaches in the Department of Psychology and Behavioral Sciences at the University of California, Los Angeles. *Jacob Ornstein-Galicia* is professor emeritus of modern languages and linguistics at the University of Texas, El Paso.

To fellow ethnic Americans
justly proud of their heritage and their
enormous but largely unsung contributions
to the future of this great country and
our multicultural nation

Politics and Society in the Southwest

Ethnicity and Chicano Pluralism

edited by Z. Anthony Kruszewski,
Richard L. Hough, and
Jacob Ornstein-Galicia

Westview Press / Boulder, Colorado

A Westview Replica Edition

Published in 1982 in the United States of America by
    Westview Press, Inc.
    5500 Central Avenue
    Boulder, Colorado 80301
    Frederick A. Praeger, President and Publisher

Library of Congress Catalog Card Number: 82-7070
ISBN 0-86531-908-1

Printed and bound in the United States of America

Contents

Preface

This book is one of a series of books, monographs, and articles which have resulted from the activities of the Cross Cultural Southwest Ethnic Center at The University of Texas at El Paso over the past eleven years. The Center was organized under a grant from the Spencer Foundation of Chicago and co-directed in 1971-75 by Professor Jacob Ornstein-Galicia of the Departments of Modern Languages and Linguistics and Professor Z. Anthony Kruszewski of the Department of Political Science at The University of Texas at El Paso. It has been directed by Dr. Kruszewski since 1977.

The grant enabled us to bring together a team of researchers from The University of Texas at El Paso, other Southwestern universities, and a large group of scholars from many other universities across the nation who were pursuing cross-cultural and interdisciplinary ethnic research in the humanities, social sciences, and education. Other grants obtained from the Gulf Oil Education Fund (funding research on sociolinguistics and communication problems), the University of Texas at El Paso Excellence Fund (Bilingual/Bicultural Education Symposia), and Texas Colleges Bicentennial Program, Inc. (Interinstitutional Bicentennial project) resulted in an extensive program of workshops and meetings held at The University of Texas at El Paso. Likewise, a four-year project funded by the National Endowment for the Humanities to develop courses for the Humanities Border Studies Program at the University of Texas at El Paso resulted in a series of conferences and symposia organized by the Center.

Most of the chapters of this book are revisions of the conference papers presented under the aegis of the Cross Cultural Southwest Ethnic Study Center; others were either commissioned by the Center or written for this volume. They all share one focus: ethnic relations along the United States-Mexico border, obviously dictated by the location of the Center in El Paso/Ciudad Juarez metropolis--the unique and largest bilingual/bicultural

city on any international border. The selection of the
papers was largely dictated by that common theme. The
individual contributions do not, however, share a common
approach or philosophy. They were, rather, selected for
their particular intrinsic value, point of view, and/or
provocative analysis of a peculiar aspect of politics and
society in the Southwest and its ethnic dimensions. They
aim at the understanding of Chicano pluralism of the
1970s in the context of interethnic relationships, and by
charting some problems, they hope to bring a wider knowledge of future societal trends and amelioration of tensions, if not possible solutions.

In regard to style, certain determinations were made
by the editors in the interests of consistency throughout
the book. The use of the hyphen in the word "Mexican
American" has been determined as follows: when used as a
noun there is no hyphen; when used as an adjective, there
is a hyphen. Spanish words have been italicized with the
exception of titles (such as La Raza Unida) and the word
"Chicano," which has become a part of American usage.

The editors would like to acknowledge the help of
several dedicated friends who have been instrumental in
bringing this long-drawn project to fruition. We owe
thanks to the following:

Dr. J. Lawrence McConville, the former Research Associate of the Cross Cultural Ethnic Study Center and its
spiritus movens for the selection, assessment, and evaluation of the original series of the Center's papers prepared for inclusion in this volume. Without his contribution, this book could not have taken its initial shape.

Ms. Maria Elisa Vasquez, the former Administrative
Assistant of the Cross Cultural Ethnic Study Center, for
her part in preparation of numerous symposia, conferences
and workshops from which most of these chapters originated. Her contribution and her able direction of the
Center's staff are well-remembered and appreciated.

Dr. C. Richard Bath, Chairperson of the Department
of Political Science at The University of Texas at El
Paso, for his help at a crucial time in putting the
facilities of his department at the disposal of this
publishing project.

But first and foremost to Rosalind Federman--whose
professionalism, superb editorial instinct and skills,
patience with the need to prepare several earlier versions
of the book as dictated by the book market, and endur-
ance when drastic changes in profile required total re-
casting of the manuscript-- was in the final analysis
undoubtedly responsible for completion of the project,
which at times seemed full of unending frustrations.

Last, but not least, our thanks go to President
Haskell Monroe and the Office of the Vice President for
Academic Affairs of The University of Texas at El Paso,
and Charles Elerick, Acting Director of the Center of Latin
American and Border Studies at the University of Texas (El
Paso), who made the preparation of the final draft possible

through the Faculty Mini-Grant Award, and expedited this publishing venture at the time when the need for additional resources and the scarcity of support is at its peak.

Now it will be for the readers to judge if all the efforts put into this enterprise were worthwhile.

Z. Anthony Kruszewski
Richard L. Hough
Jacob Ornstein-Galicia

Introduction
A Model for the Assessment of Pluralism
Among Chicanos of the Southwest

Z. Anthony Kruszewski
Richard L. Hough

Despite attention focused on minority groups in the
United States during the late 1960s and early 1970s, relatively little serious social scientific research has
been reported on the Spanish-speaking population of the
border Southwest. Certainly little has been published
assessing the changing status of this population as a
consequence of major societal changes during the 1960s
and 1970s.

Lack of published research is particularly notable
given the unique character of the Mexican American, and
the constant increase in the Mexican-American population
by both legal and illegal immigration makes full assimilation very unlikely. Add the strong impulses toward preservation of the Spanish language and Mexican-American
identity and growth of a number of new Mexican-American-
oriented social organizations and activities in the last
decade, and full assimilation appears even less likely.
The recent trend toward bicultural and bilingual education makes it more reasonable to assume that the Southwest will remain a culturally pluralistic geographical
area and that Mexican Americans will continue to exist as
a distinct subcultural element.

However, it is fascinating to note that despite apparent maintenance and strengthening of unique subcultural orientations among Mexican Americans, substantial
gains have been recorded in terms of participation in
the dominant economic, educational, occupational, and
political structures. Such participation provides an interesting counterpoint to the pluralistic model.

Lack of published research on assimilative and pluralistic trends among Mexican Americans in the Southwest
does not result from lack of research effort. A large
number of scholars across the country have maintained an
active research interest in the subject over the past
decade. This volume accumulates original papers representing a wide range of that research activity. Many of
the papers were originally commissioned by the Cross Cultural Southwest Ethnic Study Center at the University of

Texas at El Paso. However, the editors added papers from
other sources when commissioning activities did not produce materials to gain a well-rounded impression of the
research produced concerning Mexican-American status in
the Southwest.

The editors encountered a significant problem when
we sought the most effective format in terms of which to
organize the available papers. Although the theoretical
literature on assimilation and pluralism is tremendously
broad and complex, we found no theoretical perspective
which yielded an immediately usable framework in terms of
which the relative degree of pluralism or assimilation of
a particular group could be assessed. Therefore, we have
developed the pluralism assessment model discussed below.

A PLURAL ASSESSMENT MODEL

The following model does not pretend to solve the
very difficult social scientific theoretical problems of
how best to conceptualize and predict the course of
majority-minority relations in the United States. All
that is attempted is to provide a theoretical mapping of
possible dimensions of majority-minority group interaction along which degrees of difference and/or similarity
between groups can be assessed. To create such a model,
we have elected to utilize the notions of "assimilation"
and "pluralism." Unfortunately, there has been such emo-
tion-laden debate concerning these concepts that they now
carry more meaning than the current writers would prefer.
However, we have found two alternative terms which serve
our purpose as well, and they are employed in the following model. We also provide our own definitions of the
terms and hope the reader will keep them in mind.

Previous Models of Assimilation and Pluralism

The most popular interpretation of interaction between varying ethnic, racial, and national origin groups
in American history has been the "Anglo-conformity" model.[1] This model assumed that English institutions, English language, and English-oriented cultural patterns,
as interpreted during the American Revolutionary period,
form the dominant standard for what American life ought
to be, and that immigrants into American society or subcultures within it will be assimilated into the dominant
structure. This Anglo-conformity idea is still probably
the basic implicit theory honored in American societal
orientations toward minority groups, although that situation has obviously been changing rapidly.

The second major understanding of majority-minority
groups relations in the United States has been the "melting pot" theory. One of the more expressive presenta-
tions of the idea comes in Zangwill's drama, The Melting

Pot:

>America is God's crucible, the great Melting Pot
>where all the races of Europe are melting and re-
>forming! Here you stand, good folk, think I, when
>I see them at Ellis Island, here you stand in your
>fifty groups, with your fifty languages and histo-
>ries, and your fifty blood hatreds and rivalries.
>But you won't be long like that, brothers, for these
>are the fires of God you've come to--these are the
>fires of God. A fig for your feuds and vendettas!
>Germans and Frenchmen, Irishmen and Englishmen, Jews
>and Russians--into the crucible with you all! God
>is making the American.[2]

Newman[3] describes the melting pot theory as an "ideological utopia" since it not only assumes various cultural
groups will be fused into a single new culture, but also
that the new culture will contain only the best elements
of all its predecessors.

Since publication of Beyond the Melting Pot,[4] it has
become fashionable in social science to argue that the
United States exhibits little evidence of becoming a cultural melting pot and seems more likely to remain a pluralistic society. The notion that pluralism might be a
desirable state of cultural group interaction in the
United States, however, long predated the 1960s. Kallen's[5] statement of the pluralistic approach is regarded
widely as classic. He was impressed with the fact that
a significant number of ethnic groups managed to maintain
their identity over time, and that within certain geographical areas, they had preserved their own language,
religion, and some communal values. At the same time,
people in these groups had learned English and had participated in the country's economic and political life.
Kallen therefore developed the notion that America had
become and would continue to be a land of cooperating,
culturally diverse people, not one of strict unification
or complete assimilation. In fact, he argued, pluralism
is an important expression of the democratic ideal which
any imposition of the Anglo-conformity model necessarily
would violate. Equality implies the right to be different. Finally, interaction of culturally distinct
groups within the democratic society would enrich the
society.

Glazer and Moynihan, while noting that the melting
pot theory did not describe adequately interaction between cultural groups in the United States, did not argue
that the cultural pluralism model was any more accurate.
Rather, they suggested that cultural group interaction in
the United States represented a complex combination of
assimilative and pluralistic processes.

A brief description of two attempts to recast

theoretically the debate about cultural group interaction
in the United States will serve perhaps to sensitize the
reader to more recent discussion. Gordon[6] developed a
multidimensional, multistage theory of the assimilative
process, arguing that assimilation tendencies are still
the most important intercultural group interaction phenomena to understand. According to Gordon, assimilation
occurs at different speeds within various primary and
secondary areas of social action. Assimilation is not an
either/or sort of phenomena. Individuals may be assimilated relatively well on some dimensions of interaction
and not as well assimilated or not assimilated at all on
other dimensions.

Newman[7] adopts a different perspective on cultural
group interaction; he does not assume that such intergroup interaction is moving ultimately toward any particular "end state" such as complete assimilation or a stable cultural pluralism. He assumes that change and conflict are ubiquitous to intergroup interactions, and the
job of the social scientist at any given point in time is
to assess relative propensities toward conflict/consensus
and stability/change which are apparent in group interactions, and to develop some predictive hypotheses concerning the probable future course of those interactions.
Further, this analysis may have to be specific to particular types of groups since the experience of different
immigrant and/or resident groups in the United States
with each other may be quite different.

It is not our aim to attempt a resolution of various
theoretical debates implicit in the literature. Rather,
we are concerned with the question of how social-scien-
tific perspectives on group interaction might help us
draw together and interpret various fragments of research
data on the status of Southwestern Mexican Americans.
What is needed is not so much further theoretical elabo-
ration as distillation of theoretical perspectives into
conceptualization of the variables upon which group difference and interaction ought to be examined if some understanding of the data concerning group differences is
to be obtained. We have attempted such a distillation
in the pluralism assessment model.

The Pluralism Assessment Model

Figure I-1 presents the variables employed in the
pluralism assessment model, which most directly builds on
Gordon's assimilation model. The basic difference between Gordon's and our perspectives is that we have tried
to develop an "assessment" model as opposed to a theoretical modeling of an assimilative process. There is no
assumption of an unalterable, relatively unilinear process of absorption of minority groups into the host society. The model does assume that interaction between host

Figure I-1
The Pluralism Assessment Variables

A. CULTURAL PLURALISM--Degree of Variation from Cultural Patterns of Host Society

1. Language--degree of use of language different from that dominant in host society as primary means of communication.

2. Values--degree of adoption of values different from those dominant in host society.

3. Norms--degree of adoption of typical formal and informal norms guiding everyday behavior different from those dominant in host society.

4. Identification--degree of a sense of peoplehood not based on host society.

B. STRUCTURAL PLURALISM--Degree of Participation in Interaction Systems Differing from Those Dominant in Host Society

1. Economic--degree of participation in material exchange systems differing from those dominant in host society.

2. Civic--degree of participation in formal political and informal influence and power structures differing from those dominant in host society.

3. Education--degree of participation in educational systems differing from those dominant in host society.

4. General Social--degree of participation in primary group relationships beyond the family (e.g., cliques, clubs, etc.) differing from those dominant in host society.

5. Religious--degree of participation in forms of religious behavior differing from those dominant in host society.

6. Family--degree of within-group marriage in family systems differing from those dominant in host society.

C. RECEPTIONAL PLURALISM--Degree of Rejection by Host Society

1. Cultural Rejection--degree of negative prejudicial evaluations of language, norms, values, and peoplehood by host society.

2. Structural Rejection--degree of discrimination by host society in economic, civic, educational, general interest, religious, and family patterns of interaction.

D. DEGREE OF CONFLICT--Degree and Intensity of Conflict with Host Society

1. Cultural Conflict--degree of linguistic, valuative, normative, and identificational conflict with host society.

2. Structural Conflict--degree of conflict with host society in civic, educational, general social, religious, and family patterns of interaction.

or majority groups within a society, and minority cultural groups may produce increasing similarity and assimilative interaction in which members of groups participate
in common social and cultural structures. This process
may proceed so far that no distinctions can be found between social and cultural structures of the two groups--
amalgamation. However, it is assumed also that the interaction process may be such that the minority group
maintains its distinct identity, and some considerable
degree of difference in cultural and structural terms may
be maintained. It is assumed further that any movement
toward assimilation into the host society's cultural and
social patterns may be reversed at any point in time and
that minority groups may become more "pluralistic."
    To avoid the notion implicitly underlying most as-
similation models, that there is unalterable progression
toward amalgamation of minority groups, we choose to
think in terms of pluralism. We define that term as participation in cultural patterns and interaction systems
which differ from those of the host society. These two
dimensions of interaction are represented in parts A and
B of Figure I-1.
    Such a perspective on pluralism concentrates on be-
havioral and attitudinal characteristics of the minority
group. A very viable means of assessing the degree of
pluralism of any minority group would be to examine the
reception being given the group by the members of the
host society. Degree of cultural rejection (prejudice)
and structural rejection (discrimination) manifested by
the host society is reflective of the degree of pluralistic status granted a minority group in a particular society. A full assessment of the degree of pluralism of a
given minority group should take these "receptional" variables into account, and we have done so in part C of
Figure I-1.
    Another dimension of minority-majority group inter-
action often ignored by assimilative models is degree of
conflict. Newman[8] points out that both degree and intensity of conflict between such groups varies independently
from degree of participation in common cultural pluralism
assessment models.
    Two caveats are in order. The first qualification
has to do with the notion of "host" culture. As Gordon[9]
notes, the term is not as neutral as desired, and it is
not meant to imply that the contributions of the host society completely overshadow or make insignificant the
contributions of various minority groups. Some term
simply is needed to designate the dominant group which
serves as the standard against which other groups tend to
measure their relative degree of assimilation. A group
attains "host" status by means of being the original settlers of a region or by gaining dominance through power
or simple force of numbers.

Similarly, when we speak of assimilation, we do not intend to suggest the process is <u>entirely</u> that of the minority group adopting the culture of or participating in the interaction structures of the host society. What we refer to is creation of cultural and structural inter-action systems in which both host and subcultural groups participate. By and large, these interaction systems will resemble more closely those originated by the host group than those by the subcultural group. However, it is highly probable that in the creation of common cultu-ral and structural systems, the emerging system also will contain a great number of elements originating in the mi-nority group. Assimilation, as we use the term, conveys more a notion of blending of cultures than the straight-forward adoption of one culture by members of another.

With those qualifications in mind, further compari-son of our model with Gordon's assimilation theory is in order. In the original presentation of his assimilation process, the major distinction drawn was between cultural and structural assimilation. His suggestion was that cultural assimilation generally precedes structural as-similation. He identified cultural assimilation as learning the host culture's language and acceptance of its basic values. However, he argued, cultural assimila-tion does not lead necessarily to structural assimila-tion. Cultural assimilation has been completed virtually for most ethnic groups in America, but a great deal of structural nonassimilation still exists. Gordon suggests that differences between ethnic groups and host society are to be found primarily in the structural area. Pri-mary group relations, particularly in cases of active re-sistance to structural assimilation, may serve to inhibit and even completely halt the assimilative process.

Again, our model differs from Gordon's in that the cultural dimension has been elaborated and the relation-ship between cultural and structural assimilation is not perceived as a necessary time-ordered developmental pro-cess. It ought to be quite obvious from the model that complete cultural assimilation does not precede structur-al assimilation. Identification with the host culture would only be achieved when structural amalgamation is a virtual reality. Rather than a simple one-way time-ordered relationship between cultural and other forms of assimilation, the process is conceptualized here as one of constant interaction between levels. Advances in cul-tural assimilation tend to promote more structural assim-ilation and vice versa. The process also may work in a nonassimilative direction with development of new subcul-tural specific interaction structures stimulating devel-opment of distinctly subcultural identification, norms, values, and language.

However, a time-ordered process <u>is</u> intimated <u>within</u> the cultural and structural components of the model. To the degree that assimilation does take place, adoption of language probably does precede value and normative assimilation which probably precede complete identification with the host culture. Economic, civic, and educational structural assimilation probably do tend to precede social, religious, and family assimilation.

Two other dimensions of majority-minority group interaction included in our assessment model, receptional pluralism and degree of conflict, are also assumed to interact with cultural and structural dimensions. To fully understand the degree of pluralism manifested by any particular minority group at a particular time, it would be fruitful to be able to determine how much pluralism is manifested on all dimensions and subdimensions of interaction posited in the model and assess how changes over time on various dimensions reflect their interaction.

The assessment model lacks a great deal in terms of precision. There is likely to be disagreement over the best means of measuring the status of a particular group on various dimensions. However, the model is introduced here as a means of organizing and interpreting data presented in this volume and for that purpose it will suffice.

The Assessment of Pluralism Among Mexican Americans in the Southwest

The present volume does not attempt full assessment of the status of Southwestern Mexican Americans. Since the papers were not prepared by researchers with knowledge of or commitment to our assessment goals, it could not be expected that their work would represent a precise operationalization of the pluralism assessment model. However, the editors have tried to present a set of original research reports which represent the work currently being done on various dimensions of interaction. From our perspective, Mexican Americans of the Southwest are characterized by a fairly high degree of cultural and structural pluralism, accompanied by a significant amount of rejection from the host society. Despite pluralism and rejection, degree of conflict with the host society has, thus far, been moderate.

We generally view the Mexican American as more "pluralistic" on structural dimensions of interaction than on cultural dimensions. The Mexican American is generally committed to language, valuative, normative, and identificational systems which vary to some significant degree from those dominant in the larger society. At the same time, economic and political structures in which they participate probably vary slightly more from those of the host society. Certainly the general social, religious, and family interaction systems are quite different from those of the larger society. The major exception to the

tendency for structural interaction systems to be more
differentiated from those of the host society than cultural systems is to be found in the educational structure
where there has been increasingly viable participation by
the minority and the majority in a common educational
system. We would argue that there is less "pluralism"
among Mexican Americans on this dimension than any other.
   In terms of reactions of the host society to the
Mexican American in the last decade, the data suggest
there has been a relatively significant amount of both
prejudice (cultural rejection) and discrimination (structural rejection). Generally, structural rejection appears to have been higher than cultural rejection, and
the degree of rejection probably higher at more personal
structural levels of general social/family interaction
than at economic/civic levels. Education is again the
exception, with a relatively high degree of acceptance
being manifested via integration and bilingual education
programs.
   In terms of conflict, a different assessment
emerges; the most conflict has tended to arise over participation in secondary structural arenas of interaction
(economic, civic, and educational). More personal areas
of interaction (general social, religious, and family),
where more pluralism and rejection occur, have not become
focal points for conflict. Similarly, conflict between
valuative, normative, and identificational orientations
have remained somewhat covert. On the cultural level,
only language has become the focal point for much overt
conflict.
   Although we do not directly address the question of
how much change has occurred in the last decade on each
of these dimensions, we would suspect that more change
has occurred on the educational structure than any other.
Other areas of significant change toward more participation in common structures have been economic and civic
structures. These changes on the secondary structural
level have probably been accompanied by a thrust toward
higher degrees of cultural pluralism.

NOTES

   1. Stewart G. Cole and Mildred Wiese Cole, Minorities and the American Promise (New York: Harper and
Brother, 1954), Ch. 6; Milton M. Gordon, Assimilation in
American Life: The Role of Race, Religion and National
Origins (New York: Oxford University Press, 1964), Ch. 4;
William M. Newman, American Pluralism: A Study of Minority Groups and Social Theory (New York: Harper and Row,
1973).
   2. Zangwill, 1908, as quoted in Gordon, Assimilation, p. 120.
   3. Newman, American Pluralism.

4. Nathan Glazer and Daniel P. Moynihan, Beyond the Melting Pot: The Negroes, Puerto Ricans, Jews, Italians and Irish of New York City (Cambridge, Mass.: MIT and Harvard University Press, 1963).

5. Horace M. Kallen, Culture and Democracy in the United States (New York: Boni and Liveright, 1924).

6. Gordon, Assimilation.

7. Newman, American Pluralism.

8. Ibid.

9. Gordon, Assimilation.

Language and Cultural Identity as a Factor in the Evolution of Southwestern Society

edited by Jacob Ornstein-Galicia

1
Bilingual Patterns
of Nonmetropolitan Mexican-American Youth

Victoria P. Morrow
William P. Kuvlesky

THE PROBLEM

The research reported here builds upon and extends
an earlier study of Spanish and English oral language
patterns of Mexican-American youth carried out in 1967.[1]
In 1973 we designed a historical follow-up study to provide answers to two major questions: Are the oral patterns of Spanish vs. English usage of Mexican-American
youth changing? Are patterns of language usage for reading and writing similar to those for speech? Little, if
anything, in the way of research findings has been reported with respect to etiher question, but increasing
interest in bilingualism among Mexican Americans and
among educators concerned with Mexican-American youth
provides a pressing need for such answers.
     Our earlier study was limited to oral language use
over varying social contexts: with parents, with neighborhood frieds, with friends in school (outside class),
and to mass media language usage, radio and newspapers.
The follow-up study provided us with an opportunity to
extend our view to use of English and Spanish in reading
and writing over various social contexts, and we broadened our coverage in several additional ways. We added
use of television to our mass media indicators and added
a social context for speaking, reading and writing--lan-
guage use in school during classes. The 1973 survey
thus provides a fuller picture of English-Spanish language use patterns.
     Our specific research objective was to address these
questions:
     1. To what extent have historical changes occurred
in use of Spanish and English by Mexican-American high-
school boys and girls over the six-year study period in
reference to the following:
          a. Oral speech with <u>parents in the home</u>, with
             <u>friends in the neighborhood</u>, and with <u>friends
             in school outside of class.</u>
          B. Language utilized for mass media in reference

The authors would like to acknowledge the assistance of Dennis
Medina in preparation of this article.

to (1) <u>radio</u> and (2) <u>newspaper</u> and <u>magazines</u>.
2. To what extent are variations in 1973 language
usage patterns by sex and situational context similar or
different for each of the three modes of language use--
oral speech, writing, and reading?

REVIEW OF RELEVANT RESEARCH

In our report of 1967 data, we reviewed the research
to date concerning language usage patterns of Mexican Americans.[2] Briefly, language usage was found by Mahoney[3]
to be directly related to urban v. rural residence, education, American birth, income and occupational level of
household head, and inversely correlated with age.
Skrabanek[4] found Spanish was highly retained and used far
more than English by household heads in a variety of settings, with radio being used equally in Spanish and English, and Spanish television where available. Findings
for children were similar except for the school setting.
Grebler, Moore, and Guzman[5] found Spanish usage directly related to proportion of Mexican Americans in the
neighborhood and inversely related to income. They also
found Spanish-language radio was preferred over English
in largely Mexican-American neighborhoods, regardless of
income, and among poorer residents of mixed neighborhoods. Preference for Spanish television was related to
low income and predominance of Mexican Americans in the
neighborhood. It was also observed that the Spanish-
language press was not a "serious competitor for the
English-language press."
Sex differentials were not investigated in any of
the reviewed research except for our 1967 study. Since
our earlier report we are aware of only two other research efforts into language usage patterns of Mexican-
American youth: a 1969 study of southern Colorado youth
and a 1973 El Paso study done by Venegas.[6] Venegas rep-
licated our 1967 instruments and operations, and his
findings generally indicated a strong comparability to
those of our 1967 investigation of nonmetropolitan
Mexican-American youth in south Texas.[7] Findings from
the southern Colorado study were difficult to compare to
ours because of differences in instruments; however, it
appears that Mexican-American youth in southern Colorado
utilized Spanish much less than the south Texas youth we
studied and the El Paso youth studied by Venegas.[8]
As far as we can determine, no published research
results exist pertaining to the question of whether Spanish use is declining among Mexican-American youth of any
type. Leaders of the Chicano movement have shown concern
about this and have strongly urged the need for Chicanos
to use Spanish. In summary, the scant amount of research
reported on language usage patterns of Mexican-American
youth on oral patterns and utilization of mass media

indicates a high retention rate of Spanish, particularly in Texas and among the poor. Also, evidence exists to indicate that frequency of Spanish use may vary by rural-urban residence, SES, sex, age, nativity, and region of the country. These statements should be viewed as propositions to be evaluated by future research and not empirical generalizations due to limited amount of extant research and difficulty in obtaining good comparability of findings across studies as a result of variations in time of study, research operations, and instruments.

COLLECTION OF DATA

The analysis reported here is based on an original survey of Mexican-American high school sophomores carried out in the south Texas border region in spring 1967 and a restudy survey completed in spring 1973.

The process began in 1967 with selection of four south Texas counties adjacent to or in close proximity of the United States-Mexico border[9] that exhibited the following characteristics: (1) location in rural and nonmetropolitan area, (2) high frequency of family poverty, and (3) proportionately high concentration of Mexican Americans.[10] In 1967, interviews were conducted in seven schools located in these counties. The 1973 effort could not enlist cooperation of two of these schools, including the only one in Maverick county, and these schools were deleted from the 1967 data set for this analysis.[11]

Extensive efforts were made to duplicate 1967 field procedures in the 1973 study. All high school sophomores present on the day of the study were given questionnaires and assured of the confidentiality of their responses. A trained graduate student read each item aloud, giving students enough time to complete responses before proceeding. Questionnaires were identical with respect to variables involved in the historical analysis and in most other respects.[12] The 1973 questionnaire differed from the 1967 one mainly in respect to additional sets of items. One of these was the extended section on language patterns, reading and writing patterns. No efforts were made to contact students not present on the day of the interview. In 1967 about 85 percent of those reported to be enrolled were present and completed the questionnaire; the 1973 figure was 80 percent.

The 1967 data netted 341 Mexican-American respondents as compared with 379 for 1973. Students who did not identify themselves as Mexican Americans were deleted from this analysis (Table 1.1). Surveyed portions of the sophomore class in the schools involved ranged from a low of twenty-two to a high of 168 in the 1967 effort and from twenty-five to 181 in 1973.

Table 1.1   High School Sophomores Interviewed in Rural South Texas
Study Area in 1967 and 1973 by Ethnicity and Sex

Ethnicity	1967			1973		
	Male	Female	Total	Male	Female	Total
Mexican American	169	172	341	178	201	379
Anglo American	4	9	13	15	15	30
Other	0	0	0	5	2	7
Total	173	181	354	198	218	416

HISTORICAL CHANGE

Obviously any changes observed in language patterns
of the youth studied could be influenced by patterns of
historical change taking place in their communities,
schools, and families. A description of such patterns
should have utility for interpretation of these findings.[13] The general study area involved demonstrated the
following patterns of historical change between 1960 and
1970, according to U.S. census data:[14] (1) increase in an
already proportionately large majority of Mexican Americans,[15] (2) general rise in level of education, and (3)
apparent improvement of general economic conditions--
fewer families in poverty, fewer people working as unskilled laborers.[16]
No dramatic changes took place in reference to
school facilities. In general it can be presumed that
schools became a bit more crowded and that some exhibited
deteriorating physical facilities and equipment. A
follow-up probe aimed at ascertaining general availability of Spanish-language reading materials in school and
communities and attitudes of school administrators toward
bilingual patterns in schools was made by Michael
Miller.[17] It was generally observed that little in the
way of written Spanish was in evidence in the schools,
outside of that used in formal Spanish classes, or in the
communities, i.e., newspapers or magazines. Also, it is
safe to conclude that most school administrators were not
strongly encouraging bilingual patterns and a few even
felt that to do so would be harmful to the students.
Information obtained from the students indicates
little change took place in reference to families of the
respondents over the study period. A slight increase in
parental education was noted and there was a tendency for
fewer fathers to be gainfully employed in 1973 than in
1967.[18]

FINDINGS

Analysis findings are presented in three parts. The first deals with results of historical comparison of data collected in 1967 and 1973. The second presents new data, gathered only in 1973, expanding examination of language use in reading and writing. The third reports new data concerning respondents' perceptions of language usage patterns of parents and friends. Language usage is examined by social context and sex in all three. Chi Square tests were used to determine statistical significance of differences observed throughout the analysis.

Historical Change, 1967-1973

Speaking Patterns. Almost every Mexican-American teenager studied in 1967 and 1973 indicated they could speak Spanish: only four in 1967 and two in 1973 indicated they could not. Yet ability to speak Spanish does not ensure it will be used or used to the same extent in all social settings. Findings in 1967 indicated that boys used Spanish in oral speech more often than girls and use of Spanish declined markedly for both in informal settings away from the home.[19] Have things changed since 1967?

Language Use With Parents. In 1967, Mexican-American boys claimed to use mostly Spanish with parents more often than girls, who tended to claim equal amounts of both English and Spanish. Only small proportions of either males or females claimed using mostly English. In 1973, that pattern had not changed significantly. The pattern of strong Spanish dominance persisted, with males somewhat more Spanish-dominant than females (Table 1.2)

Table 1.2 Language Pattern Predominantly Used in Speaking with Parents by Sex for 1967 and 1973 Respondents

Language Pattern	Male 1967		Male 1973		Female 1967		Female 1973		Total 1967		Total 1973	
	N	%	N	%	N	%	N	%	N	%	N	%
English	8	5	17	10	15	9	13	6	23	7	30	28
Both	33	21	39	22	70	50	97	49	105	31	136	36
Spanish	126	74	120	68	87	41	90	45	213	62	210	56
Total	169	100	176	100	172	100	200	100	341	100	376	100
No. info.	0		2		0		1		0		3	

Language Use With Close Friends in the Neighborhood. In 1967, males claimed use of mostly Spanish more often than females in talking with friends in the neighborhood, while females again preferred "equal amounts of both." In 1973, females again report being less Spanish-dominant than males. The difference between the 1967 and 1973 responses for females are statistically significant but not large enough to be sociologically meaningful. However, there is a discernable pattern in changes from 1967 to 1973 for both males and females; the "both" category decreased while mostly English and mostly Spanish categories increased (Table 1.3).

Table 1.3   Language Pattern Predominantly Used in Speaking with Close Friends in Neighborhood by Sex for 1967 and 1973 Respondents

Language Pattern	Male				Female				Total			
	1967		1973		1967		1973		1967		1973	
	N	%	N	%	N	%	N	%	N	%	N	%
English	19	11	23	13	30	17	51	26	49	14	74	20
Both	61	36	49	28	112	66	107	53	173	51	156	41
Spanish	89	35	104	59	30	17	42	21	119	35	146	39
Total	169	100	176	100	172	100	200	100	341	100	376	100
No Info.	0		2		0		1		0		3	

Language Use With Close Friends in School-Out of Class.   In 1967, males preferred "mostly Spanish" significantly more often than females, while females more often chose "mostly English." The two groups chose "both" at about the same rate. In 1973 there were significant changes for both sexes. Males continue to be more Spanish-dominant than females, but preference for "mostly Spanish" increased significantly for both sexes while "both" decreased for males and "mostly English" decreased for females (Table 1.4).

Use of Mass Media.   In 1967 about a fourth of the respondents claimed to listen mostly or only to Spanish-language radio, and well over three-fourths of both groups claimed to listen to at least some Spanish radio (Table 1.5). There were no sex differences. The 1973 data reveal no notable pattern changes.
    In 1967 very small proportions of either males or females reported doing "more than half or all" of newspaper and magazine reading in Spanish (Table 1.6). However, significantly more males than females claimed to read "none" in Spanish, and more females than males claimed "some" reading in Spanish. In 1973 these English dominant patterns persist, although there is a significant decrease in proportion of females who claim "none."

Table 1.4   Language Patterns Predominantly Used in Speaking with
Close Friends in School, Outside of Class, by Sex for
1967 and 1973 Respondents

Language Pattern	Male 1967 N	%	1973 N	%	Female 1967 N	%	1973 N	%	Total 1967 N	%	1973 N	%
English	34	20	34	19	63	37	57	29	97	20	91	24
Both	86	51	45	26	97	56	107	53	183	54	152	41
Spanish	49	29	97	55	12	7	36	18	61	10	133	35
Total	169	100	176	100	172	100	200	100	341	100	376	100
No Info.	0		2		0		1		0		3	

Table 1.5   Frequency of Use of Spanish Language Radio Programs by
Sex for 1967 and 1973 Respondents

Use of Spanish	Male 1967 N	%	1973 N	%	Female 1967 N	%	1973 N	%	Total 1967 N	%	1973 N	%
None	28	16	37	21	42	24	49	24	70	20	86	23
Some	99	59	95	53	91	53	102	51	190	56	197	52
Over ½	30	18	32	18	30	18	36	18	60	18	68	18
All	12	7	14	8	9	5	14	7	21	6	28	7
Total	169	100	178	100	172	100	201	100	341	100	379	100
No Info.	0		0		0		0		0		0	

Table 1.6   Frequency of Use of Spanish Language Newspapers and
Magazines by Sex for 1967 and 1973 Respondents

Use of Spanish	Male 1967 N	%	1973 N	%	Female 1967 N	%	1973 N	%	Total 1967 N	%	1973 N	%
None	116	69	118	67	96	56	91	45	212	62	209	55
Some	48	28	53	30	71	41	89	44	119	35	142	38
Over ½	4	2	3	2	5	3	15	8	9	3	18	5
All	1	1	2	1	0	0	6	3	1	0	8	2
Total	169	100	175	100	172	100	201	100	341	100	377	100
No Info.	0		2		0		0		0		2	

Patterns Across the Various Settings. 1967 data indicated a consistent pattern, for both males and females,
of substantial reduction in Spanish as home setting is
compared with neighborhood and school. One-third as many
spoke "mostly Spanish" with friends in school as with
parents; the reverse was true for English. In 1973,

decrease in Spanish in moving away from home setting persists, although the pattern is not quite as strong.
About half as many speak "mostly Spanish" with friends in
school as with parents. Increase in English persists but
is not quite as strong.
Greater Spanish dominance of males existed in all
three oral language settings. However, the reverse is
true for use of written language; in reading of magazines
and newspapers, females are more Spanish-dominant and
males more English-dominant.

Males and Females Compared. A summary comparison of
findings on differences in these situational patterns by
sex for 1967 and 1973 indicate clearly there was no marked change over the study period. Males indicated using
Spanish more often than females in all oral situations,
and females used Spanish in reading mass literature more
than boys. No sex difference was observed in listening
to radio programs in Spanish.

Summary of Results on Change (Table 1.7)

A summary presentation generally indicates that little changed in bilingual patterns. Among oral patterns
the only change noted was an increase for both boys and
girls in use of Spanish with friends in school (outside
of class). The only other change was a slight increase
in reading mass literature in Spanish. A look at the
actual percentage change in use of Spanish to any extent
and use of mostly Spanish for the two contacts gives a
clearer picture of the magnitude of changes taking place.
Boys demonstrated very little change in either regard
except for talking with friends in school--a dramatic increase of 26 percent using mostly Spanish. Girls demonstrated more uneven patterns of percentage change. However, the most marked change was in reference to talking
with friends in school; the percentage more than doubled
from 7 to 18. This is the only case for girls where a
substantial change in use of only Spanish took place.
One cannot but observe the almost totally consistent
patterned increase in percentage change across all settings for both boys and girls in predominant use of Spanish. Only in one case was there a percentage decrease in
predominantly using Spanish--for boys in speaking to
parents.

1973 STUDY: MODES OF LANGUAGE USE

The great majority of both males and females reported that they speak, read, and write Spanish. Nearly all
speak it with decreasing numbers claiming reading and
then writing skills, but the proportion even in that
latter category is over 75 percent for the sample as a

whole (Table 1.8).[20] Females claim to be able to read
and write Spanish more often than males. More than half
have taken a Spanish course in school with no significant
differences between males and females in this regard
(Table 1.9).

Table 1.7 Summary of Patterns of Historical Change by Sex in Use
of Spanish to Any Extent and in Using Mostly Spanish,
1967-1973

Language Patterns	Percent Using Spanish To Any Extent			Percent Using Only Spanish		
	67	73	Change in %	67	73	Change in %
A. Boys						
Parents	95	90	-5	74	68	-6
Friends in Neighborhood	89	87	-2	53	59	+6
School (Out of Class)	80	81	+1	29	55	+26
Radio*	84	79	-5	7	8	+1
Newspaper & Magazines*	31	33	+2	1	3	+2
B. Girls						
Parents	91	94	+3	41	45	+4
Friends in Neighborhood	83	74	-9	17	21	+4
School (Out of Class)	63	71	+8	7	18	+11
Radio*	76	76	0	5	7	+2
Newspaper & Magazines	44	55	+11	0	3	+3

*Figures represent proportions using only Spanish in these cases.

Table 1.8 A Comparison of Self-Indicated Ability to Use Spanish in
Speaking, Reading and Writing by Sex, 1973

Use of Spanish	Male	Female	Total
	----% indicating use of Spanish-----		
Speaking	98	100	99
Reading*	80	88	84
Writing*	69	82	76

*Differences by sex are statistically significant at the .05 level.

12

Table 1.9 Have You Taken a Spanish Course in School?

	Male		Female		Total	
	N	%	N	%	N	%
Yes	100	56	123	62	223	59
No	78	44	76	38	154	41
Total	178	100	199	100	377	100
No Info.	0		2		2	

Oral Patterns

Oral patterns were treated above in comparison with data on the same items from the 1967 study. In 1973 boys indicated use of Spanish more frequently in all settings than girls and, for both, frequency of Spanish use decreased from home to neighborhood and then to school. One new item on oral patterns was included in 1973--language used in most school classes. Consistent with findings concerning other oral patterns, males were significantly more Spanish-dominant than females, reporting use of "mostly Spanish" in class five times as often as females (Table 1.10). The group is, nonetheless, fairly English-dominant with more than half indicating "mostly English," most of the rest indicating "both," and only a small proportion indicating "mostly Spanish." Also, use of mostly Spanish is the lowest in this setting, the only formal context of language use studied. Only 9 percent of the total sample used mostly Spanish in school classes. One might ask how they managed to do this.

Table 1.10 Language Used in Speaking in Most Classes in School by Sex, 1973

Language Pattern	Male		Female		Total	
	N	%	N	%	N	%
Mostly English	78	45	112	56	190	51
Mostly Spanish	27	15	6	3	33	9
Both	69	40	82	41	151	40
Total	174	100	200	100	374	100
No Info.	3		1		4	

Reading Patterns

Both males and females are highly English-dominant in reading patterns, with the proportion reporting "mostly English" ranging from 60 percent to over 90

percent across the settings: at home, school outside
class, and school in class. Only very small proportions
claim "mostly Spanish" in any of the settings, never more
than 8 percent. Male/female differences are statistically significant in the latter two cases but are too small
to be of sociological significance. Although less than
half the respondents were involved, English dominated
reading "on the job" for those who had ever worked.
Differences by sex were not significant (Tables 1.11,
1.12, 1.13, and 1.14).

Table 1.11 Language Used in Reading at Home by Sex

Language Pattern	Male N	%	Female N	%	Total N	%
Mostly English	97	65	101	56	108	60
Mostly Spanish	4	3	10	6	14	4
Both	47	32	69	38	116	36
Total	148	100	180	100	328	100
No Info.	30		21		51	

Table 1.12 Language Used in Reading in School, Outside of Class by Sex

Language Pattern	Male N	%	Female N	%	Total N	%
Mostly English	112	76	126	69	238	72
Mostly Spanish	12	8	4	2	16	5
Both	23	16	52	29	75	23
Total	147	100	182	100	329	100
No Info.	31		19		50	

Table 1.13 Language Used in Reading in Class by Sex

Language Pattern	Male N	%	Female N	%	Total N	%
Mostly English	134	91	170	94	304	93
Mostly Spanish	6	4	0	0	6	2
Both	7	5	11	6	18	5
Total	147	100	181	100	328	100
No Info.	31		20		51	

14

Table 1.14   Language Used in Reading on Job for Those Ever
             Employed by Sex

Language Pattern	Male N	Male %	Female N	Female %	Total N	Total %
Mostly English	60	64	56	73	116	68
Mostly Spanish	9	9	4	5	13	8
Both	25	27	17	22	42	24
Total	94	100	77	100	171	100
No Info.	35		21		56	
Never Employed	49		103		152	

Writing Patterns

Writing patterns parallel those for reading. Male/
female differences are negligible, statistically significant in only "at school-outside class," and even there
still too small to be meaningful. "Mostly English" is
claimed by over 60 percent for writing at home, 83 percent for school outside class, 84 percent for on the job,
and 95 percent for school in class, so writing patterns
are clearly English-dominant. Proportions reporting
"mostly Spanish" are higher than for reading but still
never exceed 14 percent (Tables 1.15, 1.16, 1.17, and
1.18).

Table 1.15   Language Used in Writing at Home by Sex

Language Pattern	Male N	Male %	Female N	Female %	Total N	Total %
Mostly English	81	62	101	60	182	61
Mostly Spanish	18	14	15	9	33	11
Both	32	24	52	31	84	28
Total	131	100	168	100	299	100
No Info.	47		33		80	

Table 1.16   Language Used in Writing in School, Outside Class by Sex

Language Pattern	Male N	Male %	Female N	Female %	Total N	Total %
Mostly English	110	84	139	82	249	83
Mostly Spanish	10	8	3	2	13	4
Both	11	8	27	16	38	13
Total	131	100	169	100	300	100
No Info.	47		32		79	

Table 1.17   Language Used in Writing in Class by Sex

Language Pattern	Male		Female		Total	
	N	%	N	%	N	%
Mostly English	126	96	158	94	284	95
Mostly Spanish	3	2	2	1	5	2
Both	2	2	9	5	11	3
Total	131	100	169	100	300	100
No Info.	47		32		79	

Table 1.18   Language Used in Writing on Job by Sex

Language Pattern	Male		Female		Total	
	N	%	N	%	N	%
Mostly English	66	80	55	89	121	84
Mostly Spanish	5	6	1	1	6	4
Both	12	14	6	10	18	12
Total	83	100	62	100	145	100
No Info.	49		34		83	
Never Employed	46	36	105	63	151	51

Mass Media Use

Although radio listening patterns are English-dominant, most listened to some radio in Spanish. The same
pattern exists for reading but females are significantly
more Spanish-dominant than males. Relative to watching
television in Spanish, there are no sex differences.
About half of both groups indicate watching at least some
television in Spanish; if the "more than half" and "all"
categories are added to that, two-thirds watch some television in Spanish. This approaches closely that observed
for listening to Spanish-language radio (Table 1.19).

Table 1.19   How Many of the TV Programs You Watch are in Spanish?

Spanish Programs Watched	Male		Female		Total	
	N	%	N	%	N	%
None	59	33	66	33	125	33
Some	92	52	103	51	195	51
Over ½	20	11	18	9	38	10
All	7	4	14	7	21	6
Total	178	100	201	100	379	100

Summary of Findings--1973 Study

Sex Differences. The most widespread and most substantial differences in language patterns between boys
and girls were in reference to oral patterns; males indicated more frequent use of Spanish in all settings. In
reading and writing, males and females differed only
slightly or not at all in language usage patterns. When
differences did exist, females tended to use Spanish
slightly more often. Only in reference to magazines and
newspapers did males and females differ markedly; females
used more Spanish.

Situational Variation in Language Patterns. Findings clearly indicate a consistent pattern of decreasing
Spanish use in speaking as one moves through informal
social contexts of interaction with significant others
from home, through neighborhood, to out-of-class school
situations, to school classes. The least Spanish was
used in the only formal social context included: school
classes. Similar progressive increases in use of English
in informal situations away from home to formal contexts
can also be observed for reading and writing. Always,
most frequent use of Spanish was in the context of family
and home. Conversely, least use of Spanish always was
indicated to be in school classes.

Variation by Language Usage Mode. Results clearly
indicate that the most use of Spanish was in oral situations. Similar patterns of predominant use of English
over all situations existed in reference to both reading
and writing. Few used mostly Spanish in these ways; only
small proportions used both languages equally in writing
and reading, except for reading at home.

PERCEIVED USE OF SPANISH BY OTHERS--1973

It is important to know the subjects' perception of
other people's behavior in order to gain understanding of
how their own behavioral patterns relate to their social
context. We attempted to get at this through use of two
questions eliciting perceptions of language patterns used
by two groups of significant others (parents and friends)
in informal social contexts.

Use of Spanish by Parents

There are no significant sex differences in response
to the three items concerning parents' language patterns.
Speaking patterns of parents were reported to be largely
Spanish-dominant; 64 percent reported "mostly Spanish,"
and 95 percent "mostly Spanish" or "both" for parents.
Few indicated parents used "mostly English." This

Spanish dominance decreases substantially in reading with only a 9 percent difference between "mostly English" and "mostly Spanish," although the latter is still the larger. Likewise, in parents' writing, the difference between the two categories is about 10 percent, although both are a little higher and "both" is smaller (Tables 1.20, 1.21, and 1.22).

Table 1.20 Parents Language Pattern Used When Speaking by Sex of Respondent

Language	Male		Female		Total	
Pattern	N	%	N	%	N	%
Mostly English	11	6	9	4	20	5
Mostly Spanish	120	68	119	60	239	64
Both	45	26	72	36	117	31
Total	176	100	200	100	376	100
No Info.	2		1		3	

Table 1.21 Language Used by Parents in Reading by Sex of Respondent

Language	Male		Female		Total	
Pattern	N	%	N	%	N	%
Mostly English	54	31	50	25	104	28
Mostly Spanish	67	39	72	36	139	37
Both	52	30	77	39	129	35
Total	173	100	199	100	372	100
No Info.	5		2		7	

Table 1.22 Language Used by Parents in Writing by Sex of Respondent

Language	Male		Female		Total	
Pattern	N	%	N	%	N	%
Mostly English	62	36	56	28	118	32
Mostly Spanish	74	43	81	41	155	42
Both	37	21	61	31	98	26
Total	173	100	198	100	371	100
No Info.	5		3		8	

Use of Spanish by Friends

In writing letters to personal friends, both males and females were highly English-dominant, though males were more so than females. More males claimed "mostly English," and more females claimed "both." "Mostly

Spanish" was reported by only small numbers of both boys and girls. There is a strong sex difference relative to language spoken by friends. While "mostly English" is about the same for both sexes, a much higher proportion of males than females chose "mostly Spanish," and a much higher proportion of females chose "both." It seems that females described friends as less Spanish-dominant than males did. In reading and writing outside class, friends were described as clearly English-dominant. Two-thirds claimed "mostly English" reading patterns and over three-fourths reported "mostly English" writing patterns for firends. There are significant sex differences, however. Relative to reading, males chose "mostly English" more than females, while females chose "both" more than males. Relative to writing, differences are smaller but the same pattern occurred, suggesting that males see friends as more English-dominant in writing and reading than females do (Tables 1.23, 1.24, 1.25, and 1.26).

Table 1.23   Language Used by Respondents in Writing Letters to Personal Friends by Sex of Respondent

Language Pattern	Male		Female		Total	
	N	%	N	%	N	%
Mostly English	107	84	128	76	235	70
Mostly Spanish	11	9	11	6	22	7
Both	10	7	30	18	40	14
Total	128	100	169	100	297	100
No Info.	50		32		82	

Table 1.24   Language Used by Friends in Speaking by Sex of Respondent

Language Pattern	Male		Female		Total	
	N	%	N	%	N	%
Mostly English	28	16	40	20	68	18
Mostly Spanish	72	41	34	17	106	28
Both	76	43	127	63	203	54
Total	176	100	201	100	377	100
No Info.	2		0		2	

Table 1.25   Language Used by Friends in Reading Outside of Class
             by Sex of Respondent

Language	Male		Female		Total	
Pattern	N	%	N	%	N	%
Mostly English	124	71	123	61	247	66
Mostly Spanish	19	11	15	8	34	9
Both	31	18	63	31	94	25
Total	174	100	201	100	375	100
No Info.	4		0		4	

Table 1.26   Language Used by Friends in Writing, Outside of Class
             by Sex of Respondent

Language	Male		Female		Total	
Pattern	N	%	N	%	N	%
Mostly English	141	81	151	75	292	78
Mostly Spanish	16	9	11	6	27	7
Both	17	10	30	19	56	15
Total	174	100	201	100	375	100
No Info.	4		0		4	

Summary

    Quite clearly respondents' perceptions of parents' and friends' language patterns are quite comparable to their own self-reported behavior patterns. Sex differences in language usage of respondents are paralleled in their perceptions of parents' and friends' language usage. Parents are perceived as highly Spanish-dominant by both males and females; friends of females are more English-dominant than friends of males.

DICUSSION

Limitations of the Study

    Several crucial limitations of this data should be kept in mind in analysis of this study. First, it is based upon self-report of a politically sensitive and emotionally charged phenomenon. Even under the best of conditions, valid and reliable data are difficult to obtain. Exploration of the methodological problems involved remains to be accomplished.

    Second, our categories remain very crude. Fishman[21] warns of the complex ways in which language usage varies even within a particular setting, such as home or school. He recommends that we alert ourselves to that complexity and take note not only of who is speaking what language to whom, but of what variety of a particular language they are utilizing, for what purposes, in what specific setting within home or school, with what consequences, and so on. We need to know more about the "whoms" and settings, the when and why of switching between English and Spanish, and the specific characteristics of the English and Spanish being used.

Finally, the crudeness of our language-usage measure implies there would probably have to be rather marked changes in language behavior for it to be reflected in our data. That is, all other considerations aside, change may be occurring but it is not reflected in our gross response categories of "mostly English," or "mostly Spanish," or "both."

CONCLUSIONS AND IMPLICATIONS

Data in all three areas of concern have been summarized after each of the three sections of the findings above; it will not be recapitulated here. Major conclusions of our analysis are presented and discussed below.

Historical Change: 1967-1973

Patterned decrease in Spanish usage observed for both males and females, from home setting to neighborhood and school, was repeated in 1973 but with an interesting twist. Decrease is less dramatic than before with both males and females using more Spanish with friends outside class in 1973. This is difficult to explain. We could speculate that schools are simply being less repressive about use of Spanish, but no evidence suggests this. However, there was much more Chicano movement acitivity in the study area in 1973 than in 1967. That might have led to this finding in one of two ways. The school probably was pressured to be less repressive about use of Spanish outside of class, or heightened ethnicity might have led students to use more Spanish regardless of school conditions. Or, greater politicization might have had another effect; while not necessarily affecting language behavior, it might have affected the way respondents chose to characterize language usage patterns on a questionnaire. As the rhetoric of the movement is generally supportive of use of Spanish and its value, students might have been influenced by ideology to overestimate or, in fact, to estimate more accurately than before the amount of Spanish used at school, even though forbidden. Patterned increase observed in use of "mostly Spanish" in almost all settings for males and females may also spring from change in political orientations leading to change in the way respondents perceive language usage patterns. We cannot say there were no politics in the earlier study; there clearly were, simply different ones, which involved devaluation of Spanish and stigmatization of it. It is difficult to know which set of responses are more realistic as both have doubtless been influenced by political ideology. More attention should be given to this phenomenon of how language usage patterns are characterized as separate from what those patterns might actually be and the influences upon those characterizations.

It was noted above that the greater English dominance of girls in oral language usage persists in 1973; also, the greater English dominance of boys in use of written mass media persists in 1973 as in 1967. We speculated on the reason for that difference in our earlier report on the 1967 results, supposing it might lie with the alleged strong sex-role differentiation of the Mexican-American culture, with females trained to be docile and obedient, and males to be more independent. This socialization difference might lead to females being more conforming in school, where spoken English is a focus of great concern. That explanation should be broadened, however, to take into account academic performance differences of males and females in this society as a whole. Females in general, probably due to dependence training, are more verbally skilled than males.[22] If that training difference and its likely effect operate on Mexican-American females in the same way as upon Anglo females, and there is no reason to expect otherwise, then it might explain the greater tendency of females to read in Spanish. Although about half of the females and males studied Spanish in school (as noted in the 1973-only data), females might be more likely to utilize their training with written Spanish due to greater competence with verbal skills.

1973 Study

Oral language usage patterns were largely English-dominant in class, to be expected as the instruction language is English, but even here males used Spanish more than females, and 9 percent of the total group claimed to use mostly Spanish anyway. We wondered how that might come to pass. It may be that students are generally quiet in terms of speaking out before the whole class, an effective political tool for a subordinate group, as Dumont[23] points out in a study of how Sioux and Cherokee children use silence to maintain control of the classroom. At the same time, there may be substantial whispered conversation going on among students, as any teacher will testify, which could well take place largely in Spanish; in fact, there could be good reason for it to be in Spanish rather than English for the sake of privacy.

1973 data indicated that although the great majority

of both sexes claimed to speak, read, and write Spanish, more females than males claimed reading and writing skills. This explains the finding that females read more magazines and newspapers in Spanish than males, observed in both 1967 and 1973. They simply have greater skill, which may be due to the general tendency for American women to have greater verbal skill. By the same token, males were more English-dominant in letter writing than females; learning to write in English and be comfortable in it is a major goal of the schools, and most males have accomplished it. Spanish writing receives much, much less attention, thus fewer have accomplished it. If females are more verbally skilled and more intent on success in school, they may be generally dominating that skill, in spite of the scanty attention it receives.

Perceived language usage patterns of parents and friends closely paralleled those reported by respondents for themselves. Thus, these youth see themselves to be in harmony with their contexts of interaction, using more or less Spanish in accordance with situational norms they perceive for language usage. If this inference is valid, then it follows that different role definitions involved in the status sets of these youth have as elements varying specifications for appropriateness of Spanish use. For instance, most of them are probably expected by the family to use only Spanish in speaking to parents, while, at the other extreme, teachers probably hold rigid expectations for them to use only English in addressing the class or teachers in the classroom.

In closing, we would like to point out the need for more refined and extensive study of language patterns of Mexican-American youth than represented by this investigation. As noted earlier, much remains to be done in resolving basic methodological questions about how best to obtain valid and reliable data in this sensitive area of research and, in obtaining comparable data across a wider spectrum of population types (i.e., age groups and regions), to evaluate the scope of general patterns derived from the few and limited studies carried out so far.

NOTES

1. Victoria Patella and William P. Kuvlesky, "Situational Variation in Language Patterns of Mexican-American Boys and Girls," SSQ (March 1973): 855-64.
2. Ibid.
3. Mary Mahoney, "Spanish and English Language Usage by Mexican American Families in Two South Texas Counties" (Master's thesis, Texas A&M University, 1967).

4. Robert L. Skrabanek, "Language Maintenance Among Mexican Americans," International Journal of Comparative Sociology 11 (December 1970): 272-82.

5. Leo Grebler, Joan W. Moore, and Ralph C. Guzman, The Mexican-American People (New York: The Free Press, 1970).

6. William P. Kuvlesky, "Use of Spanish and Aspirations for Social Mobility Among Chicanos: A Synthesis and Evaluation of Texas and Colorado Findings" (Paper presented at the Annual Meeting of the Rocky Mountain Social Science Association, Laramie, Wyoming, 1973).

7. Ibid., pp. 11-15.

8. Ibid., p. 13.

9. Dimmit, Maverick, Starr, and Zapata counties.

10. Rumaldo Z. Juarez and William P. Kuvlesky, "Ethnic Groups Identity and Orientation Toward Educational Attainment: A Comparison of Mexican-American and Anglo Boys" (Paper presented at the Annual Meeting of the Southwest Sociological Association, Dallas, April 1968).

11. William P. Kuvlesky and Philip M. Monk, "Historical Change in Status Aspirations and Expectations of Mexican-American Youth From the Border Area of Texas: 1967-1973" (Paper presented at the Annual Meeting of the Southwest Sociological Association, San Antonio, March 27, 1975).

12. Patella and Kuvlesky, "Situational Variation."

13. Detailed discussion of observations about historical change in the study area and its schools is presented in Kuvlesky and Monk, "Historical Change." Note that aggregate census data used to determine historical change in selected study counties were obtained from 1960 and 1970 U.S. census reports. This time lapse does not parallel the actual time lapse of the study (1967-1973) very well.

14. Kuvlesky and Monk, "Historical Change."

15. It should be noted that school enrollments across the study period did not reflect an increase in proportion of Mexican-American students; in fact, they demonstrated a slight trend to the converse. This may be due to difference in time frames between the 1960-1970 census data comparison and actual study period.

16. This trend is probably a reflection of the more general improvement in economic conditions across the U.S. during the late 1960s. It should not be interpreted to mean the respondents' families had generally achieved dramatic or long-lasting improvements in life situations. A more accurate judgment would be that general status of these families changed relatively little over the time period examined.

17. Mike Miller informally interviewed administrators, counselors, and students in the study area and specifically looked for availability of Spanish-language reading materials.

24

18. Kuvlesky and Monk, "Historical Change." While
this was a slight trend, it does not fit well with the
observation that general occupational and economic status
of Mexican Americans improved from 1960 to 1970 in the
study area. The most likely explanation of this apparent
incongruence is the difference in the historical time
frame involved in the census vs. the actual study data.
19. Patella and Kuvlesky, "Situational Variation."
The one exception to this general statement is that for
El Paso youth, females tended to use Spanish slightly
more frequently than males, while South Texas respondents
demonstrated a converse pattern.
20. The no response rate to questions on writing
Spanish and reading Spanish in various situations were
relatively high as compared with a very low rate in reference to speaking it. This may indicate lack of full
ability to utilize native language. Probably many who
indicated they could read and write Spanish have very
limited capabilities to do so. This is an area that requires considerable methodological effort to be researched adequately.
21. Joshua A. Fishman, ed., Advances in the Sociology of Language, Volume 1 (The Hague: Mouton, 1971).
22. Eleanor E. Maccoby, "Woman's Intellect," in
S. M. Farber and R. H. L. Wilson, eds., The Potential of
Women (New York: McGraw-Hill, 1963).
23. Robert V. Dumont, Jr., "Learning English and
How to Be Silent: Studies in Sioux and Cherokee Classrooms," in Courtney B. Cazden, Vera P. John, and Dell
Hymes, eds., Functions of Language in the Classroom (New
York: Teachers College Press, 1972).

2
Sociolinguistics and the Chicano Community

Fernando Peñalosa

The interrelationships among theory, ideology, empirical research, and practical affairs represent the very heart of the social sciences. This paper explicitly explores some of these interrelationships, with particular reference to the sociolinguistic nature of the Chicano community. Ever since the rise of the Chicano movement, the keynote has been self-identification and self-determination. The scholarly study of the Chicano community is no longer the exclusive province of outsiders. The relationships between the Chicano community and the social science community have thus taken on a completely different character. While this is clearly evident in the area of empirical research, the relevance of theoretical concerns may not be as apparent.

Those of us who consider ourselves Chicano sociolinguists must decide whether to concentrate on the matter of enlightenment of the general public, work on specific problems of concern to the Chicano community, or sit in ivory towers constructing theoretical models, and we must ascertain the relationships among theory, research, and public responsibility. These questions must ultimately be answered in the spirit of Chicano self-definition and self-determination. We can no longer allow others to define us and determine our fate. Someone quoted Thomas Szasz to the effect that in the animal kingdom it is eat or be eaten; in human society it is define or be defined.

Even though the inclination and interests of Chicano leaders may lie principally in the area of action and change, they ignore the implications, particularly the political implications, of theory to the detriment of the Chicano movement. Gouldner has ventured the opinion that

Radicals who believe that they can separate the task of developing theory from that of changing society are not in fact acting without a theory, but with one that is tacit and therefore unexaminable and uncorrectable. If they do not learn to use their theory self-consciously, they will be used by it.[1]

Chicanos are, by definition, radicals. Not only are we
insisting on self-definition and self-determination, but
we also are insisting on redefinition of the structure
and goals of the broader society of which we are a part.
     Any new area of study like Chicano sociolinguistics
necessarily abounds in typologies. We have typologies of
Chicano language varieties and typologies of Chicano
speakers. But nomenclature and taxonomy are only the
first step. We need explanations, that is, theories.
Theories enable us to predict and thus extend some measure of control over our own destiny. We await the development of a self-conscious Chicano sociolinguistic
theory. Even the lengthy proceedings of the First National Exploratory Conference on Chicano Sociolinguistics
of 1974 disappointingly reveal no concern with developing
theory, despite the presence at the conference of several
first-rate Chicano theoreticians.
     No sociolinguistic theoretical framework appropriate
to the Chicano situation is presently available. Existing models are generally assimilationist and functional.
Even such a champion of the oppressed as Labov accepts
the functionalist interpretation, as Dittmar has shown.[2]
While Marxist models of society abound in Chicano intellectual circles, none has encompassed sociolinguistics as
yet, to the best of my knowledge. To refer to Chicanos
as a speech community, for example, is to assume a consensus among Chicanos as to norms for the choice and use
of speech varieties. Such a consensus cannot be simply
postulated; it must be empirically established. But
whatever norms vary or are shared among Chicanos or which
may overlap with non-Chicano norms, it must still be the
case that there is no overall United States norm system
into which Chicanos might fit. Therefore, the prevailing
consensus model must be rejected in favor of the more realistic conflict model. For example, the Anglo backlash
over bilingual education is best understood in these
terms.

CHICANO SOCIOLINGUISTIC STUDIES

     One of the most popular cliches concerning the Chi-
cano is that he is bilingual and bicultural, but rarely
have the relationships between Chicano bilingualism and
biculturalism been specifically and explicitly examined.
What has been the theoretical orientation of sociolinguistic research so far conducted on the Chicano community?
     Sociolinguistically oriented studies of the Chicano
have focused primarily on three topics: (1) code switching between English and Spanish within the context of a
conversation; (2) typologies of Spanish, English, and intermediate codes in use in the community; and (3) the use
of special Chicano linguistic creations such as *calo* or

Pocho.[3] Studies have stressed the purposefulness and meaningfulness of code choice, that is, what the code does for the individual, the group, and the community. They at least have established that Chicano linguistic behavior is neither erratic nor the product of confused minds torn by culture conflict. Chicanos, furthermore, do not suffer from congenital deficiencies of cognition and conceptualization, despite prevalent stereotypes in social science and educational literature.[4]

Language acquisition is one of the most neglected areas of Chicano sociolinguistic research. How does the child acquire his various codes and the sociolinguistic rules for their use? From a sociological perspective, this topic most likely is discussed within the context of the socialization process. However, there is considerable evidence that the concept of socialization, at least in some sociological circles, is becoming obsolescent. Socialization implies power by the old over the young, and there is increasing evidence of resistance to socialization by the young, much in the same way as assimilation is resisted by many among the ethnic populations. The creative response of children or "minorities" to the cultural influences which impinge upon them has been emphasized by such diverse scholars as Chomsky, Romano, and Skolnick.[5]

It is difficult to understand on linguistic grounds alone why so many Chicano children fail to acquire adequate command of English, given the natural propensity of children to learn a second language with ease and alacrity. Likewise, given the English-dominance profile sketched for a majority of young Chicanos, it may be that the apparent language deficit is one in the academic language area. This is a deficit working-class Chicanos share with many working-class people of all backgrounds and which derives as much from class as ethnic discrimination. Thus, Lopez has pointed out that in Los Angeles, middle-class-raised Chicanos brought up in Spanish average a year more of schooling than lower-class English monolinguals.[6] It has also been observed that middle-class students with prior schooling in Mexico have relatively little problem acquiring English and adjusting successfully to American schools. The effects of classism as well as of racism must be studied. And yet the question remains: Is it Juanito's speech or his skin color which is primarily responsible for his teacher's belief that he is likely to be an underachiever? On the other hand, Chicano announcers (as well as other minority announcers) on English language media invariably speak accent-free standard English. The Chicano and other minority children are being told, in effect, they don't have to be white to be a television announcer as long as they shed all traces of ethnic accent.

As all research has social meaning as well as

scientific interpretation, the question of the meaning, particularly the sociopolitical relevance, of studies must be raised. Chicano behavior clearly departs from norms prevalent in the majority community. How is such a departure evaluated, both by Chicanos and by others? In a racist society, to be different is to be inferior, or at least deficient or deprived. Although progress is being made in bilingual schooling, prescriptive standards are as strongly entrenched in departments of Spanish as they are in departments of English. Spanish departments are almost invariably controlled by non-Chicanos who enforce non-Chicano standards of usage. Our social institutional structure has yet to introduce notions of sociolinguistic relativity into its rigidly dichotomized concept of English-Spanish alternatives.

In bilingual research, one persistent point of concern has been whether the use of Spanish and English features in the same sentence is best conceptualized as interference, code switching, or use of a hybird code. Must this be an either/or question? Perhaps all three phenomena are present. Most extant descriptions assume that only two codes are involved--some type of English and some type of Spanish. There appears to be very strong ideologically motivated attempts to assert the distinctiveness and discreetness of linguistic codes, although as Labov, for example, has amply demonstrated,[7] codes are most fruitfully thought of as variable systems. Discreet dialects may imply linguistic schizophrenia. But if, on the other hand, the Chicano has his own code-- *Pocho*, *Pachuco*, or whatever--then the claim to cultural uniqueness merits more credence. Our more cosmopolitan Chicanos function adequately in three cultural environments: Chicano, Anglo, and Mexican. They use the appropriate linguistic codes with skill. Denial of a unique culture means, among other things, that in bicultural programs, "American" and "Mexican" culture will be taught, but not Chicano. The same is true for the corresponding linguistic codes. Ultimately how one conceptualizes the latter will depend on how one conceptualizes that heterogeneous entity, "Chicano culture."

SOCIOLINGUISTIC THEORETICAL FRAMEWORKS

Most research on Chicano multilingualism and polyglossia was done before the rise of relatively sophisticated and self-conscious sociolinguistic theoretical frameworks, and before a serious concern with linguistic theory on the part of sociologists existed. It is no longer possible to neglect the theoretical insights developed in sociolinguistics. But first a digression regarding the distinction between the two overlapping fields, sociolinguistics and the sociology of language, is in order.

Basically, the sociology of language aims at using linguistic data as an aid in answering questions posed by the social sciences, particularly sociology and social psychology. Sociolinguistics, on the other hand, is conceptually oriented toward using socially organized data to answer questions posed by linguistics. It may be that one day sociolinguistics will develop to the point where it absorbs the rest of linguistics and the latter will truly become a social science. In the meantime, the main foci of interest will continue to be the traditional areas of phenology, syntax, linguistic change, and, more recently, semantics.

The more socially significant questions are likely to be raised by those working from a sociology of language perspective. It is unreasonable to expect theoretical linguists as such to be overly exercised concerning the power struggle. On the other hand, for sociolinguists the point of departure has usually been some version of structural-functionalism, neo-positivism, symbolic interactionism, exchange theory, or ethnomethodology. These approaches also are not particularly concerned with power relationships. To my knowledge, no U.S. social scientist with a Marxist or other conflict-theoretical orientation has yet ventured into sociolinguistics or the sociology of language. Those who come to the field from an applied interest such as education or economics are more likely to have a "development" or "social mobilization" rather than a liberation perspective. That is, the role of language in the so-called developing societies or subsocieties (e.g., those characterized by ethnic subcultures, such as the Chicano) is perceived as assistance in the development of so-called underdeveloped peoples into a reasonable facsimile of the industrial, capitalistic, democratic societies of the Western world.[8] As scholars with these perspectives have moved over into the area of language and society, they have brought with them their traditional concerns and frames of reference in which notions of revolution and self-determination play little or no part.

Most scholars working in the field recognize a conceptual difference between microsociolinguistic and macrosociolinguistic levels of analysis. Fishman explicitly attempts this, primarily in terms of roles and interaction networks.[9] He considers the norms governing linguistic and social behavior at both levels, so that his approach is normative in the structural sense. As a matter of fact, a consensus rather than a conflict model of society seems to underlie almost all theoretical and empirical discussion in sociolinguistics, especially in such areas as language standardization.

There is a very serious question as to whether diglossia is an appropriate model for characterizing the Chicano situation and to what extent there is functional

allocation of varieties. With English now the primary
language of most Chicano homes, but Spanish and English
being used in the home, along with extensive switching
and mixing, and with bilingual education expanding in the
public schools, diglossic allocation seems increasingly
to be a phenomenon of the past. The major allocation appears to be an intergenerational one. These remarks per-
tain to out-diglossia. The concept of in-diglossia may
be irrelevant to the Chicano situation, and perhaps what
we have is something on the order of a social dialect
continuum or variable usage as conceptualized by Labov
and exemplified for Chicano speech by such scholars as
Ornstein and Hensey.[10]

    Fishman has noted that bilingualism without diglos-
sia typically occurs in immigrant communities undergoing
rapid social change. Despite my earlier statement on
this subject, this latter characterization may well apply
to the Chicano situation.[11]

    Lopez and others have clearly shown the attrition of
Spanish use from one generation to the next and that the
primary cause of the extraordinary Spanish language loyalty in the United States is the continuing immigration
from Mexico.[12] If these analyses are correct, what does
this portend for our linguistic future? Will bilingual
education keep Spanish alive and in use? And how can we
justify the future maintenance of two languages without
functional allocation? Clearly, we need to develop a
cadre of Chicano futurologists.

    One area for potential research might be the rela-
tionship among language attitudes, the compound/coordi-
nate distinction, and the phenomenon of covert and passive bilingualism discussed by Sawyer.[13] Yet it seems
to me that the question of the validity of the compound/
coordinate distinction in the study of bilingualism has
not been completely resolved, despite recent studies
such as that of Jacobson.[14] This distinction, undoubtedly better conceptualized as a continuum, needs to be related to social variables. On the other hand, perhaps
it ought to be allowed to die a natural death, as should
perhaps also the Sapir-Whorf hypothesis. Influence of
the latter has led to such logical absurdities as claiming, as does Jaramillo, that because the Spanish-speaking
person, for example, says 'El camion me dejo,' in cases
where the English-speaking person would say 'I missed the
bus,' the former disclaims any responsibility for having
missed the bus since the bus left him behind.[15] This
merely perpetuates the stereotype of the irresponsible,
nonfuture-oriented, fatalistic Chicano.

SOCIOLINGUISTIC STYLES OF ANALYSIS

    Sociolinguistics has developed several principal
models or styles. The "ethnography of speaking"

approach, among the most prominent, has tended to use
linguistic data to analyze the microspeech situation
rather than using the latter as a bridge to understanding
problems at the macrolevel.[16] On the other hand, the
promising methods developed by sociologists such as Sacks
or Schegloff for the analysis of conversation would not
seem to require any a priori normative assumptions regarding the study of Chicano bilingual speech.[17] Also in
current vogue are correlational studies, which may be a
reflection of a positivist or neo-positivist approach.[18]
Such studies do not ordinarily raise cogent theoretical
or ideological questions. Undoubtedly the most relevant
of the current styles focuses on the study of social dialects, which has adopted a difference rather than a defi-
ciency model of dialectical differences.[19] Still, it has
concentrated on microsociolinguistic situations, and the
broader societal context has generally been ignored.

The most important aspect of social dialects, at
least from a sociological perspective, is the social
evaluation of dialects and the use of such evaluation to
enforce continual social subordination of speakers of the
less prestigious forms. Reactions to types of speech are
reactions to the assumed social characteristics of those
who speak.[20] Thus we may hypothesize that the prestige
of the varieties of speech--including so-called nonstandard English and nonstandard Spanish--which are utilized
in the Chicano community will rise as the power, privi-
lege, and prestige of Chicanos rise. Social status defines language status, not vice versa. The Chicano's
problem is not now and never has been primarily a linguistic one. He is not linguistically deficient or anom-
alous; he is economically deprived and politically anonymous.

The notion of social dialects, particularly the notion of nonstandard dialects, implies some standard
against which to match linguistic variants. This is another instance of the normative approach to the discussion of social issues. The question is particularly
crucial when examining the relationship between standard
English and so-called "Chicano English."[21] We certainly
need a more workable definition of standard English.
Kernan believes that

> We need to abandon vague references to network En-
> glish and the language of major affairs. There is
> hardly a case to be made for the homogeneity of
> this language. Should control of a defined stan-
> dard be a goal in writing and in speaking? Compe-
> tence in a written standard may be a far more im-
> portant feedback system to a spoken language than
> any amount of patterned practice. Moreover, the
> correction of written language might circumvent the
> creation of inhibitory responses in children.[22]

In other words, the diglossic dichotomy might well be established between the written language on the one hand
and various vernaculars on the other rather than between
the socially invidious standard and nonstandard categories. The conceptualization, of course, can be applied to
Spanish as well as English. There is, furthermore, no
reason why the special Chicano codes cannot continue to
be utilized as vital sources of literary creativity.
     Sophisticated linguistic analyses of Chicano code
switching are becoming increasingly available. But we
need to understand more about the social correlates of
both switching situations and the code switchers themselves. Obviously the code switcher possesses not only
competence in the two languages, but he also possesses
switching competence as well. Does this type of competence help to maintain coordinate bilingualism and/or
vice versa?
     In a now classic paper, Chacon said in reference to
Pocho, "It is my mother tongue."[23] Should this statement
be taken literally or metaphorically? There is a tendency in some segments of the Chicano community to disregard the technicalities of interference, borrowing, and
code switching and to regard mixed speech as a code with
an identity of its own. There are ideological forces
working both for and against this idea. Creation of a
unique code might be considered a cultural achievement
emphasizing the specialness of the Chicano community,
leading to a de-emphasis of concepts referring to Chicano
marginality. The poetry of people like Alurista is merely the tip of this creative iceberg, a monument to and of
chicanismo.
     Two Chicano creations typical of barrio youth await
definitive study, youth jargon or *calo* and the famous
Chicano wall grafitti. While *calo* is regarded as a
"snarl language" by writers like Alvarez, the grafitti
are commonly referred to in the Anglo press as "juvenile
vandalism."[24] We need to cast aside both insensitive
criticisms and unmitigated admiration and examine these
creative responses to racist pressures in terms of their
social functions, for their sociological dimensions are
as significant as their linguistic ones.
     Phillips asserts that the phoneme (v) occurs less in
the speech of female than of male Spanish speakers in Los
Angeles; the word *frasquito* is more frequently used by
males and *vasija* by females to refer to a small jar in
San Antonito, New Mexico, according to Bowen; women code
switch more than men, according to McMenamin, and *calo* is
a male speech variety.[25] Beyond this, we know very little about sex differences in the language use of Chicanos. To what extent do Chicano men and women speak
differently? We should expect to find differences in
language both by the two sexes and about the two sexes,
but Chicano sociolinguistics has yet to produce a study

of Chicano male/female language.
So much research emphasizes the Chicano as deviant
or marginal. The number of English words borrowed into
Spanish by Chicanos seems to be considerably exaggerated
in existing studies which list words culturally adopted
throughout the Hispanic world or even words that are not
from English at all but which happen to be a Spanish cognate of an English word. For example, even such a careful scholar as Beltramo lists *doctor* (in the sense of
"physician") and *educacion* (in the sense of "schooling")
as loan-shift extensions, but both of these are listed in
standard Spanish dictionaries of four decades ago.[26]
Ornstein claims *borlote* was derived from "brawl" by jocu-
lar metonymy, although the expression is current in the
formal standard Spanish of Mexico.[27] Tzusaki likewise
cites *xol* ("ball"), *sweter* ("sweater"), and *mofle* ("muf-
fler") as local borrowings in Detroit, thereby exaggerat-
ing the extent of cultural assimilation.[28] The extreme
relexification which Chicano Spanish is undergoing, however, suggests that we may be developing a Creole without
having to go through a previous process of pidginization,
if that is not a contradiction in terms.
One problem making needed reforms difficult is the
fact that in general Chicanos do poorly in high school
and college Spanish classes because of the devaluation of
their vernaculr. As a result, at the graduate school
level, even in the Southwest, Chicanos are vastly outnum-
bered by Anglos in M.A. and Ph.D. programs. Spanish departments thus are typically dominated by non-Chicanos:
Anglos, Spaniards, or Latin Americans interested primarily in literature and generally holding narrowly pre-
sciptive attitudes toward language. Chicano self-determination in the linguistic area might well start in
Spanish departments as well as in departments of English
and speech.
It is not the case, however, that *barrio* Spanish
must be taught in the classroom; standard Spanish will be
taught in most instances. What is lacking is teachers'
respect for the local vernacular and enough knowledge of
it to lead the students toward bidialectalism. In some
bilingual programs, Spanish is used for the teaching of
Mexican history and literature, for example, but English
for mathematics and the sciences, thus fostering the misleading impression that English is the language of a modern, scientific, technological society, but Spanish is
suitable only for literary, folkloristic, and other traditional "impractical" purposes. Certainly this is not
the type of diglossia that we wish to promote.
The most obvious discrepancy in the field of Chicano
sociolinguistics is that between the extensive use of English in the community and the paucity of serious studies
concerning the varieties of English used by Chicanos,
just a handful compared to those dealing with Chicano

Spanish. The main theoretical dispute here appears to be whether Chicano English, the fluent kind spoken by many as their first language, is simply English with Spanish interference, or whether it is a societal variety which represents not imperfect learning of standard English but competent learning of a variety of English current and standard in the community. In its origins this variety was, of course, influenced by Spanish. This latter conceptualization would depend to a considerable extent on empirically establishing that this variety, if it exists, is passed on by and to Chicanos dominant or monolingual in English. How is English learned in the majority of Chicano homes where English is now the only or primary language? We obviously need to know a great deal more about this before we can make definitive statements about the nature of Chicano English.

These are not just theoretical questions because some Chicano students taking the speech test required for teacher certification in California have been failed because of their supposed foreign accent. If their accent had been that of Boston or Charleston, they undoubtedly would have passed. A case can certainly be made for ethnic language varieties as well as for social and regional varieties. It would seem that the nature of linguistic differences, rather than their origins, would be the critical factor, especially in the realm of practical affairs.

Undoubtedly the area of most intense concern has been applied sociolinguistics, particularly with reference to schooling. Here the relations of theory to practice--and vice versa--are more patent. Taylor has suggested that "we should not develop language education or research programs in Black communities until full knowledge is available on the language aspirations of these communities. To do otherwise would represent a new kind of paternalism."[29] The same suggestion appears particularly valid for the Chicano community. Perhaps if we knew more about our people's linguistic aspirations, we could conceptualize the Chicano sociolinguistic situation in more practically realistic and theoretically valid ways.

The nature of the relationships between sociolinguistic factors and ethnic conflict might well be a focus of concentrated attention. Inglehart and Woodward argue that "blockage of social mobility has been the chief motivating force behind language group conflicts" and thus they assume that individual assimilation into a system is a more prevalent goal in subordinate groups than group self-determination or societal restructuring.[30] It is apparent that current applications of sociolinguistic theory to the study of subordinate communities have failed to take into account some of the models of ethnic relations now in use, particularly the internal

colonialism model.[31]
    In attempting to relate some of the ideas of socio-
linguistic theory to some of the concerns of the Chicano
community one might ask what is the Chicano community?
It would seem at first blush that if we are anything, we
are a speech community. Grimshaw has defined a speech
community as a "population whose members share the same
set of evaluative norms with respect to language behavior."[32] This definition appears to beg the question, as
it postulates normative consensus prior to any empirical
investigation to ascertain whether or not such consensus
can validly be imputed. One might counter that it remains to be determined empirically whether Chicanos indeed form a speech community. Yet, other than our common
descent, there seems to be no other single factor as
characteristic of our cultural identity as our linguistic
behavior, although I doubt very much whether in fact one
would find complete agreement on linguistic norms. In
this instance, we must again reject the familiarly postulated but nonexistent homogeneity of the Chicano population.

IMPLICATIONS OF LINGUISTIC THEORY

    Besides the broader area of sociolinguistic theory,
there are some aspects of current linguistic theory which
ought to concern those of us who are attempting to conceptualize and organize our knowledge concerning Chicano
sociolinguistic behavior. I make reference to the assumptions of the current generative-transformational model, particularly as developed by Chomsky.[33] Apparently
every normal child is born with the innate capacity, or
universal grammar, to process linguistic data in order
to produce and understand utterances never before heard,
as well as to construct a grammar of his language out of
the fragments of speech which strike his ear. Furthermore, it is apparently very likely that sentences are
generated in a semantic, rather than in a syntactic,
component, and that universal grammar consists essentially of universal human means inherent in the brain for
conceptually processing one's physical and social environment.[34] It is often alleged that the Chicano child is
conceptually different and that he is unable to handle
abstractions. Chomskyan theory might provide political
ammunition for dealing with some of the compensatory programs based on such erroneous assumptions.
    Because of Chomsky's concern with competence to the
exclusion of performance, his ideas have not had the impact on sociolinguistics that we might have expected.
It comes as no surprise that some sociolinguistically
oriented scholars like Halliday have rejected the compe-
tence-performance distinction.[35] Those of us whose interest is primarily in social structure rather than in

linguistic structure must insist on the greater sociological relevance of performance over competence. Another problem is that current linguistic work is concentrated on sentence grammar. The increasing emphasis on
pragmatics and the current development of discourse grammar look promising as sources of relevant theory for the
analysis of Chicano linguistic behavior.

Transformational grammar itself has scarcely made an
impact on Chicano sociolinguistics. Judging from available published sources, contrastive analysis, Hispanist
models, and taxonomic models still predominate. Twenty
years after the publication of Syntactic Structures, we
have yet to see a proposed model for structure rules and
transformations that would generate sentences in a Chicano mixed code, let alone studies done in a generative
semantic framework.[36] Rather, what we have for the most
part is a series of studies contrasting Chicano forms
with their counterparts in standard Spanish and standard
English. While such studies are of much potential practical value, they do not address themselves to the question of the possibility of a single Chicano linguistic
system with an underlying deep structure subject to a
variety of transformations and lexicalizations (including relexification) derived from Spanish, English, and
more unique Chicano sources. One ideological question
here is whether the Chicano is unique and autonomous
or merely marginal, an outsider to two cultures, the
Mexican and the American.

These remarks should not be interpreted to impute
uniformity to Chicano linguistic behavior. The tremendous heterogeneity of the Chicano population is too well
known to require comment, yet many studies lack socioeconomic information regarding subjects and fail to report variations in style. Like all speakers, no Chicano
is a single-style speaker.

The position of cultural and linguistic relativists
is that there are no universal standards with which to
judge the worth of adequacy of cultures or language varieties. All peoples have developed societies and cultures
which they find satisfying and which they are ordinarily
reluctant to change. As part of their culture they have
fashioned language and speech norms fully adequate for
instrumental and expressive communication. In this
sense, no language variety is more adequate than another.
However, Hymes, a self-avowed socialist, has denied this
axiom.[37] Perhaps it should be re-examined. Perhaps
language varieties in use by the Chicano are not adequate
for his needs. If so, he is being shortchanged, and
means need to be developed to overcome whatever inade-
quacies of code may exist. And what are we to make of
the findings of Grebler, Moore and Guzman who claim that
1-4 percent of their adult samples of Chicanos in San
Antonio and Los Angeles could carry on a conversation in

neither English nor Spanish?[38] While we must reject the vile canard of certain school officials and others that some Chicano children are actually "alingual," without language at all, Chicano performance as well as competence must be studied.

SOME METHODOLOGICAL ISSUES

The basis of most studies of Chicano speech is a comparison of Chicano Spanish and English with the corresponding standard language. Yet in any idiolect or sociolect the standard and nonstandard forms together form a system, and it is a moot point whether a given speaker is conscious of which are which and whether this makes any difference except in very self-conscious speech. Chicano speech, particularly Chicano Spanish, needs to be looked at--by somebody--as a self-contained system. Attention to deviant forms only will not give us a balanced picture. We need to relate both standard and nonstandard linguistic variables to their social and social psychological correlates, where such can be established.

Here I would like to put in a plea for Labovian-type studies of Chicano speech in a natural setting. Experimental and interview settings, while necessary, do bias findings, and the practice of having Chicano university students write essays in Spanish beyond the limits of their ordinary vocabulary can lead to exaggerated estimates of the amount of English influence on their normal Spanish lexicon.[39] I say normal because for such students Spanish is predominantly a spoken language, which many speak well, but they are used to expressing themselves on paper in English. The resulting high degree of relexification which takes place as they try to write Spanish is clearly artificial, as artificial as the experiment itself. Extensive training in formal Spanish would, of course, be a prerequisite for utilizing a written exercise as an estimate of the student's competence.

Scattered throughout the literature are correlation studies involving very small samples--such as McMenamin's paper on code switching--which are chosen neither randomly nor which have employed any tests of statistical significance.[40] Linguists are ordinarily not as fussy about such matters as sociologists and hence the latter are likely to accept the reported associations with considerable skepticism. Such findings cannot be regarded as conclusive, only suggestive or impressionistic, unless, of course, a number of such studies are consistent in the same direction. Where studies contradict each other, we have little basis for choice. We don't know whether the contradictory findings are due to different methodology or other bias, or whether the situations studied are

inherently different, such as between Texas and California, between rural and urban, or between middle- and
working-class subjects. This is not to belittle available studies, but rather to plead for larger scale
studies based on probability sampling and standard statistical procedures.

It is next to impossible to generalize concerning
the linguistic behavior of the Chicano. This is an ex-
ceedingly heterogeneous population, and the linguistic
variables are complex and multifarious. Especially we
cannot generalize on the basis of studies of poverty-
level families or of children considered "problems" by
school authorities. Oppression of such people is a
reality, but the behavior of our more affluent Chicanos
is also worthy of study.

PROBLEMS OF APPLIED SOCIOLINGUISTICS

Halliday states that language serves three functions: the expression of content, the establishment and
maintenance of social relations, and the provision of
contextual links with itself and with features of the
situation in which it is used.[41] Oddly enough, the
question of power is not mentioned, that is, the use of
language to control other people's behavior. Yet all
social situations, including micro ones, have a political
aspect.[42] Thus every social theory is political in nature for no theory can explain anything in society without concerning itself with the distribution of power.

Fishman notes that, "As a result of recent studies,
it is becoming increasingly possible for language planning agencies . . . to pinpoint the particular programs,
projects or products that are successful with particular
target populations and those that are not."[43] Even such
an enlightened scholar as Das Gupta regards language
planning primarily as an administrative problem.[44] In
our society, language-planning agencies are Anglo-con-
trolled agencies. With a move from theoretical sociolinguistics to applied sociolinguistics, Chicanos become
one of the "target populations" for the attentions of the
planners. For example, bilingual-bicultural schooling is
not only an involved political issue, but also is a cultural movement in which Chicanos have a vital and continuing interest. But what do we mean by bilingual? What
variety of English are we talking about? What variety of
Spanish? The question may be raised whether we will win
the battle against racism, sexism, and agism only to lose
the fight against languagism.[45] A child may be made to
feel ashamed because he speaks Spanish differently from
his textbook or from his teacher, who speaks Spanish differently from his textbook, or from his teacher, who may
be a Cuban refugee or an Anglo. A child may be taught
archaic notions concerning language purity and that it is

wrong to mix languages because it is a mark of ignorance,
psychological disturbance, or poor manners. The emergent
theory of pidginization and creolization as it is being
developed by Bickerton and others, however, would seem to
be a fertile source of potential insights for viewing the
Chicano sociolinguistic reality.[46] The same can be said
of the related work of variationists such as Labov,
Bailey, Cedergen and Sankoff.[47]

LANGUAGE MAINTENANCE, BILINGUAL EDUCATION, AND SOCIAL
ADVANCE

We need to examine the changing proportions of Span-
ish- and English-dominant Chicano bilinguals. Is English
dominance a step on the road to English monolingualism?
Or, put more appropriately, under what conditions is it
so?
Chicanos are now a language minority by federal law
with their political, educational, and economic disparities officially ascribed primarily to language problems.[48] There was a time when the Chicano's difficulties
were ascribed to biological inferiority--that is, our
part-Indian ancestry--later to cultural deprivation, then
to cultural differences, all racist "explanations" in
disguise. Now they say we have a language problem so
we're being funded for bilingual education. I hope I am
not labeled a heretic or as pessimistic or disloyal for
suspecting that bilingual education will not do the job.
The problem is not the Chicano's language. The problem
is in the racist nature of our society and the racist
attitudes of Anglo teachers and students alike. Some
problems are perhaps better attacked directly than indirectly, and this may be one of them. Bilingual education
is valuable in and of itself but may not solve fundamental problems. Especially now there may be conflict in
some large urban communities between the goals of bilingual education on the one hand and school integration
involving extensive long-distance busing on the other.
Because linguistic goals on the one hand and educational,
occupational, and economic goals on the other may be in
conflict, the Chicano community must order its own priorities.
As Ulibarri has pointed out, students prohibited
from and punished for speaking Spanish at school become
painfully aware that Spanish is the language of devian-
cy.[49] While such prohibitions are becoming a thing of
the past, and even being replaced by bilingual education
programs, the Chicano child may still be made to feel
deviant because of the variety of Spanish which he
speaks.
The U.S. Commission on Civil Rights found that the
higher the proportion of Chicanos in the school and the
lower the socioeconomic status of the population being

served, the more likely the enforcement of a no-Spanish rule.[50] This pattern again suggests class as well as ethnic bias, the solution to which is perhaps school integration and economic advance. In a materialistic society, economic achievement rather than linguistic versatility is prized.

The desire to get ahead is linked in many Chicanos' minds with the learning and use of English. Poverty is linked in the popular mind with Spanish. Militant Chicanos, however, are trying to make people aware of the necessity and desirability of maintaining Spanish, and people in a good economic position appear to have more positive attitudes toward vernacular Spanish.[51] The research evidence, however, consistently reveals a definite negative attitude on the part of both Anglos and Chicanos toward Chicano English, despite the positive attitudes usually found toward standard Spanish and other varieties of Chicano Spanish. Lower-income people are generally less tolerant of nonstandard varieties than are higher-income people.

Published reports showing negative associations between social status and measures of Spanish language use and retention have assumed, without any empirical evidence, that language loyalty is negatively correlated with status and mobility. But as Lopez indicates, "these reports include large proportions of Mexican immigrants who rank low on indicators of social status and, since they were raised in Mexico, were hardly subject to home/ school bilingualism."[52] He has further shown that Spanish language upbringing and loyalty in Los Angeles are positively correlated with upward mobility among working class men, even though both are negatively correlated with years of schooling. Intergenerational occupational mobility was not positively associated with language shift. Thus it would seem retention of Spanish does <u>not</u> impede social mobility, and social mobility in turn promotes linguistic security and favorable attitudes toward popular speech varieties.

Institutional racism, on the other hand, promotes various forms of linguistic insecurity. Chicano children are sometimes put into speech therapy classes when they have trouble with English. There are problems not only with some speech therapy people, but also with the Spanish teachers who recognize but a single standard of "correctness," and also with many school psychologists who label Chicano as slow learners and unable to handle abstraction because of "deficient" language. Identifying and curbing the activity of such ethnocentric languagist functionaries ought to rank high among Chicano political priorities.

It must be emphasized that if a speech pattern is normal in the community, it is normal and adequate for that community, regardless of what the prescriptive

purists in the classrooms may say. But what is normal in
our community? We must find out more and we must see to
it that those who should know, find out. There must be
input to teacher training, whether of credential or in-
service candidates, particularly of those who will be
concerned with bilingual schooling and bilingual populations. In all fairness, we must carefully investigate,
not merely accuse, the attitudes of teachers toward language varieties and language users.

With Gouldner, I believe that theory arises less out
of empirical research than out of the experience of
people.[53] But if theory is to be more than a mere pedantic rephrasing of the tribal wisdom, we must have research that is both sophisticated and based upon the linguistic aspirations of the Chicano community. Current
sociolinguistic theory, like the activity of language
functionaries, is dominated by normative considerations.
The proffered consensus model avoids discussion of power
relationships, focuses on the micro level, and promotes
the ideology of development. Chicano sociolinguists will
have to develop their own theory, which can then be fed
into the mainstream of sociolinguistics to challenge and
enrich it.[54]

In the practical area, even if inequalities due to
language are wiped out, will the Chicano suffer any less
from racist attitudes and practices in education, government, employment, and social life? Yet can we afford to
be as pessimistic as Christian who has written:

The ideal of linguistic democracy, in which the
speech of every citizen is regarded with equal respect by all others, is perhaps the most unrealistic
of all social ideals. Speech is one of the most
effective instruments in existence for maintaining
a given social order involving social relationships,
including economic as well as prestige hierarchies.[55]

Thus, a dilemma manifests itself: whether to attack language policy, which is a secondary symptom of racism, or
to attack directly the political and economic institutions which are themselves the root cause of racism. Political action, research, and soul-searching: all are
needed.

NOTES

1. Alvin Gouldner, The Coming Crisis of Western
Sociology (New York: Basic Books, 1970), p. 5.

2. Norbert Dittmar, Review of William Labov, Sociolinguistic Patterns (Philadelphia: University of Pennsyl-
vania Press, 1972).

3. See for example: George C. Barker, Pachuco, An American-Spanish Argot in a Mexican-American Community (Tucson: University of Arizona Press, 1972); Lurline Coltharp, The Tongue of the Tirilones (Tuscaloosa: University of Alabama Press, 1965); Daniel Cardenas, "Compound and Coordinate Bilingualism/Biculturalism in the Southwest," Studies in Language and Linguistics (El Paso: Texas Western Press, 1970); John J. Gumperz and Eduardo Hernandez-Ch., "Cognitive Aspects of Bilingual Communication," in Eduardo Hernandez-Chavez et al., eds., El Lenguaje de los Chicanos (Washington: Center for Applied Linguistics, 1975); Fernando Peñalosa, "Chicano Multilingualism and Multiglossia," Aztlan 3, 2 (Fall 1972): 215-223.

4. More recently a number of Chicano scholars have written doctoral dissertations in linguistics which indirectly are important contributions to sociolinguistics. Among the most significant of these are Maria Estela Brisk, "The Spanish Syntax of the Pre-School Spanish American" (University of New Mexico, 1972); Ricardo Jesus Cornejo, "Bilingualism: Study of the Lexicon of the Five-Year-Old Spanish-Speaking Children of Texas" (University of Texas, 1969); Gustavo Gonzalez, "The Acquisition of Spanish Grammar by Native Spanish Speakers" (University of Texas, 1970); Anthony G. Lozano, "Intercambio de Espanol e Ingles en San Antonio, Texas" (University of Texas, 1972); Rogelio Reyes, "Language Mixing in Chicano Bilingual Speech" (Harvard University, 1976).

5. Noam Chomsky, Language and Mind (New York: Harcourt, Brace, 1968); Octavio I. Romano-V., "The Historical and Intellectual Presence of Mexican Americans," El Grito 11, 2 (Winter 1969): 32-46; Arlene Skolnick, The Intimate Environment (Boston: Little, Brown, 1973).

6. David E. Lopez, "Language Loyalty and the Social Mobility of Chicanos" (Paper read at the Annual Meeting of the American Sociological Association, New York, 1976).

7. William Labov, Sociolinguistic Patterns.

8. The most distinguished sociologist of language writing from a functional perspective is Joshua A. Fishman. The most easily available summary of his point of view is his The Sociology of Language (Rowley, Mass.: Newbury House, 1972).

9. Ibid.

10. On in-diglossia and out-diglossia, see Heinz Klos, "Bilingualism and Nationalism," Journal of Social Issues 23, No. 2: 39-47. On variables see Labov, Sociolinguistic Patterns; Jacob Ornstein, "Toward a Classification of Southwest Spanish Non-Standard Variants," Linguistics 93: 70-87; and Fritz Hensey, "Grammatical Variation in Southwestern American Spanish," Linguistics 108: 5-26.

11. Joshua A. Fishman, "Bilingualism With and

Without Bilingualism," Journal of Social Issues 2: 29-38; and Fernando Penalosa, "Chicano Multilingualism and Multiglossia," Aztlan 3: 215-222.
12. Lopez, "Language Loyalty."
13. Janet Sawyer, "More on Passive and Covert Bilingualism" (Paper read at Southwest Area Language and Linguistics Workshop, Long Beach, California, April 15, 1977).
14. Rodolfo Jacobson, "Semantic Compounding in the Speech of Mexican-American Bilinguals: A Reexamination of the Compound-Coordinate Distinction" (Paper read at the Annual Meeting of the Rocky Mountain Modern Language Association, Denver, 1975).
15. Mari-Luci Jaramillo, Cultural Differences Revealed Through Language (New York: National Center for Research and Information on Equal Educational Opportunity, 1972).
16. Dell Hymes, "Toward Ethnographies of Communication," in Pier Paolo Giglioli, ed., Language and Social Context (Harmonsworth: Penguin Books, 1972), pp. 21-44.
17. E. A. Schegloff, "Notes on a Conversational Practice: Formulating Place," in Giglioli, Language, pp. 95-135; Harvey Sacks, "The Search for Help," in David Sudnow, ed., Studies in Social Interaction (New York: Free Press, 1969).
18. Roxana Ma and Eleanor Herasimchuk, "The Linguistic Dimensions of a Bilingual Neighborhood," in J. A. Fishman et al., Bilingualism in the Barrio (New York: Yeshiva University, 1968).
19. See, for example, Ralph W. Fasold, Tense in Black English (Washington: Center for Applied Linguistics, 1972); William Labov, The Social Stratification of English in New York (Washington: Center for Applied Linguistics, 1966); Roger Shy et al., A Study of Social Dialects in Detroit (Washington: U.S. Office of Education, 1967).
20. Walt Wolfram, "Social Dialects from a Linguistic Perspective," in Sociolinguistics: A Crossdisciplinary Perspective, Edited versions of papers presented at a conference sponsored by the Center for Applied Linguistics in October, 1969 (Washington: Center for Applied Linguistics, 1971).
21. Allan A. Metcalf, "The Study of California Chicano English," International Journal of the Sociology of Language 2 (1974): 53-58.
22. Claudia Mitchell Kernan, "Response to Social Dialects in Developmental Sociolinguistics," in Sociolinguistics: A Crossdisciplinary Perspective, p. 67.
23. Estelle Chacon, "Pochismos," El Grito 3, 1 (1969): 34-35.
24. George R. Alvarez, "Calo: The 'Other' Spanish," ETC: A Review of General Semantics 24 (1967): 7-13.
25. Robert Phillips, "The Influence of English on

44

the 'v' in Los Angeles Spanish," in Ralph W. Eaton, Jr.
and Jacob Ornstein, eds., Studies in Language and Linguistics, 1972-1973 (El Paso: Texas Western Press, 1974);
J. Donald Bowen, "The Spanish of San Antonito, New Mexico" (Dissertation, University of New Mexico, 1952); Jerry
McMenamin, "Rapid Code Switching Among Chicano Bilinguals," Orbis 22 (1973): 474-487.
     26. Anthony Fred Beltramo, "Lexican and Morphologi-
cal Aspects of Linguistic Acculturation by Mexican Americans in San Jose, California" (Dissertation, Sanford University, 1972); Arturo Cuyas, Appleton's New English-
Spanish and Spanish-English Dictionary (New York: D.
Appleton-Century, 1940).
     27. Jacob Ornstein, "The Archaic and the Modern in
the Spanish of New Mexico," Hispania 34 (1951): 137-142.
     28. Stanley M. Tsuzaki, English Influence on Mexi-
can Spanish in Detroit (The Hague: Mouton, 1971).
     29. Orlando L. Taylor, "Response to Social Dialects
and the Field of Speech," in Sociolinguistics: A Cross-
Disciplinary Perspective, p. 17.
     30. R. Inglehart and M. Woodward, "Language Con-
flicts and the Political Community," in Giglioli, Language, pp. 358-378.
     31. Robert Blauner, "Internal Colonialism and
Ghetto Revolt," Social Problems 16, 4: 398-408.
     32. Allan Grimshaw, "Sociolinguistics," in J. A.
Fishman, ed., Advances in the Sociology of Language, Vol.
1 (The Hague: Mouton, 1971).
     33. Noam Chomsky, Aspects of the Theory of Syntax
(Cambridge, Mass.: MIT Press, 1965).
     34. Manfred Bierwisch, "Semantics," in J. Lyons,
ed., New Horizons in Linguistics (Harmonsworth: Penguin
Books, 1970).
     35. M. A. K. Halliday, "Language Structure and Lan-
guage Function," in Lyons, New Horizons.
     36. Noam Chomsky, Syntactic Structures (The Hague:
Mouton, 1957).
     37. Dell Hymes, "Speech and Language: On the Origin
and Foundations of Inequality in Speaking," Daedalus
(Summer 1973): 59-85.
     38. Leo Grebler, Joan Moore, and Ralph C. Guzman,
The Mexican-American People: The Nation's Second Largest
Minority (New York: Free Press, 1970).
     39. See, for example, Jerry Craddock, "Lexical
Analysis of Southwest Spanish," in Eaton and Ornstein,
Studies in Language.
     40. McMenamin, "Rapid Code, pp. 474-487.
     41. Halliday, "Language Structure."
     42. Skolnick, "Intimate Environment," pp. 263-269.
     43. Joshua Fishman, "The Sociology of Language," in
Giglioli, Language and Social Context.
     44. Jyotirindra Das Gupta, "Language Planning," in
J. A. Fishman et al., eds., Language Problems in

Developing Nations (New York: Wiley, 1968).

45. I have coined the not overly felicitous term "languagism" to denote the denigration and oppression of people not because of their color, sex, or age, but because of the way they speak. Thus a person or group of persons might be ridiculed or denied employment opportunities solely on the grounds that they speak with "incorrect grammar" or with a foreign "accent." A person who uses a double negative in English is a social outcast, and one who speaks English with traces of Spanish intonation is considered "funny." As these lines were first written (December 1974) Chicano candidates for teaching credentials on my own campus were being failed on the obligatory "speech test," if they had a Spanish "accent." Students, however, with regional (New England, Southern, Texas, etc.) rather than ethnic accents were being passed. It is furthermore gratuitous to point out that Spanish is not a "foreign" language in the Southwestern United States; it has been indigenous here much longer than English. By the same token, the linguistic destruction ("languagism" seems too mild a term) vented on the Native American Indian population is almost beyond belief.

46. Derek Bickerton, "The Structure of Polyectal Grammars," Georgetown University Monograph Series of Languages and Linguistics, Monograph 25 (Washington, D.C.: 1972). The work of Rogelio Reyes is, of course, a major breakthrough in this area.

47. Charles-James N. Bailey, "Variation Resulting from Different Rule Orderings in English Phonology," in Charles-James N. Bailey and R. W. Shuy, eds., New Ways of Analyzing Variation in English (Washington, D.C.: Georgetown University Press, 1973), pp. 211-252. Henrietta Cedergen and David Sankoff, "Variable Rules: Performance as a Statistical Reflection of Competence," Language 50 (June 1974): 333-335.

48. Lopez, "Language Loyalty."

49. Horacio Ulibarri, "Bilingualism," in E. M. Birkemaier, ed., The Britannica Review of Foreign Languages (Chicago: Encyclopedia Britannica, 1968), pp. 229-258.

50. U.S. Commission on Civil Rights, The Excluded Student: Educational Practices Affecting Mexican-American Students. Report III (Washington, D.C.: U.S. Government Printing Office, 1972).

51. Lucia Elias-Olivares, "Language Use in a Chicano Community: A Sociolinguistic Approach," Working Papers in Sociolinguistics, No. 30 (Austin: Southwest Educational Development Laboratory, 1976).

52. Lopez, "Language Loyalty."

53. Gouldner, Coming Crises, p. 5.

54. Recently the first two meetings ever held on the topic of Chicano Sociolinguistics took place. One

was a session on the subject chaired by Rogelio Reyes at
the VIII World Congress of Sociology in Toronto, Canada,
in August 1974, and the other, The National Exploratory
Conference on Chicano Sociolinguistics, directed by
Sergio Elizondo, held at New Mexico State University in
Las Cruces, New Mexico, in November 1974. At the World
Conference there was no workshop devoted to theory. A
virtually underdeveloped field thus awaits the cultivation of Chicano scholars. I hope this paper will be a
modest contribution toward spurring the cultivation of
Chicano sociolinguistic theory and that subsequent developments will promote the rapid obsolescence of these
words.
  55. Chester Christian, "Language Functions in the
Maintenance of Socioeconomic Hierarchies," in Eaton and
Ornstein, Studies in Language.

3
The Mexican American:
A Problem in Cross-Cultural Identity

Manuel A. Machado, Jr.

A paucity of scholarly literature on the Mexican American makes the preparation of any study merely an attempt at pathfinding. Cross-cultural identity emerges as one of the most viable areas of study on the Mexican American. Though residing in the United States, the Mexican American retains much of the culture of Mexico to varying degrees. This, however, is conditioned by socioeconomic status and ideological views about what is a Mexican American. The Mexican American can be viewed as tricultural, sharing Indian, Spanish, and Anglo cultures in a borderlands region. Recent attempts to convert the Mexican American into a homogeneous cultural and political unit fail to take into account a series of variables that affect the social unit as well as the greater society. As a consequence, the Mexican-American community remains divided and confused.

Recent onslaughts of ethnicity and minority group consciousness forced the academic community into a recognition of the existence of groups traditionally ignored by researchers in the social sciences and the humanities. Motivation for such recognition emerged not so much from genuine concern as from the thrust to do penance for sins of the past. Consequently, the traditional approaches to academic research suffered from the rush to make the study of ethnic groups--blacks, Mexican Americans, Jews-- relevant. While the search for relevancy partially obfuscated serious research in the area of ethnic group history and development, some glimmers of hope continue to appear. Occasional critiques of ethnic studies make appearances in professional journals, and the possibility of an academic orientation becomes more a reality.[1]

Mexican-American history remains an area as yet underdeveloped because of problems of periodization as well as a paucity of trained scholars in the field. Given the virginal character of Mexican-American history, the researcher needs to study the Mexican American within the context of both the United States and the cultural matrix of Mexico.

47

Areas of cultural transference from Mexico to the Mexican-American enclaves in the United States need careful and detailed examination. Political institutions, religious practices, socioeconomic determinants, and cultural values inherent within Mexican and United States society bear scrutiny. Of necessity, the cultural conflict between recently arrived Mexicans to the United States and the dominant culture require study. Of greatest import, however, is the imperative of historical perspective to the Mexican American in order to evaluate better the current situation confronting that group.

The borderlands area comprising the United States Southwest and northern Mexico emerged, especially after 1848, as a subcultural region. Previously, the Spanish and subsequent Mexican domination of the Southwest and California (1821-48) brought a cultural *mestizaje* blending between Indian and Iberian groups that produced a racially and culturally hybridized society. The introduction into this area of Anglo or "white," northern European elements after 1800 added yet another cultural variant and also almost immediate potential for cultural conflict.[2]

Kulturkampf in the borderlands resulted in part from the long-standing animosity between the Anglo and Iberian worlds. Centuries of religious and dynastic conflicts between Spanish Hapsburgs and English monarchies, usually in alliance with the Dutch, resulted in a barrage of propaganda against the defenders of Catholic orthodoxy in Spain. The flood of anti-Iberian writings that engulfed England at the time of English settlement in North America infiltrated the general culture of these new Anglo dominions. The thrust for United States independence in the eighteenth century, while severing political ties with England, retained a cultural union that included essentially anti-Iberian attitudes. United States westward expansion inevitably carried these views into areas where an Hispanic culture dominated and was subsequently submerged by the more aggressive Anglo values.[3]

Waves of immigration into former Spanish and Mexican territory from Mexico after 1848 encountered a cultural tension that was exacerbated further by reinforcement from south of the Rio Grande. As the immigrants arrived from Mexico to California, Arizona, New Mexico, and Texas they not only faced animosity from the dominant Anglo power structure, but also from Mexicans already resident in the area for one or two generations. In California, for example, during the Gold Rush (1849) and post-Gold Rush period, Mexicans from Sonora made their way to the mines of northern California. Long established *Californio* families viewed the Sonorans as riffraff, attempting to capitalize upon the new found riches of the Golden State. In addition, these new groups subsequently formed enclaves that, in the Anglo conception, belonged with the

older *Californios.* As a result, a triangular tension developed: old *Californio* families, fearful because of
their threatened loss of status, disdained the Sonorans;
these, in turn, reciprocated the animosity toward the
descendants of the original inhabitants. Both Spanish-
speaking groups, however, came into conflict with the
Anglo conquerors of California.[4]
    Thus, a pattern of cultural conflict emerged by
1900. Subsequent events in both the United States and
Mexico presaged an increase in cultural tension in the
former Spanish borderlands. Patterns of behavior would
be brought into question by both sides that, in many
ways, established cultural relations as an area of potential disagreement, violence, and distrust.
    After the inception of the Mexican Revolution in
1910, more Mexican social and cultural institutions were
transferred into the Spanish borderlands as more Mexicans
moved into the United States and mingled with extant
Spanish-speaking groups. Such institutional transfers,
in all probability, punctuated the tensions between the
essentially Anglo-Protestant and Mexican-Catholic groups
of the area. Anglo tendencies to clump together all Mexican Americans clearly indicated ignorance and lack of
perceptivity by members of the dominant culture. The
Mexican American and the more recently arrived immigrants
from Mexico composed a heterogeneous social group. All
members of Mexico's social strata were represented. Only
a portion of this group ended up in the urban *barrios* or
agricultural workers' enclaves throughout the Southwest.
However, the Anglo tendency to group the Mexican American
into a stereotyped *barrio* dweller or migratory farm
laborer blurred the distinctions within the Mexican-
American subculture.[5]
    According to one team of scholars, the present day
Mexican American apparently differs little from his ante-
cedents, especially at the lower social strata. Ethnic
focal values, i.e., familism, *machismo, envidia,* and
compadrazgo, find their strongest and most tenacious refuge in the lower classes.[6] The persistence of these values, according to Carey McWilliams, grew out of a folk
culture that was centered upon the rural life of northern
Mexico.[7]
    While folk culture dominates the lower levels of
Mexican-American society, as Mexican Americans achieved
higher social and economic positions they acquired greater class consciousness. They became aware of marked differences between themselves and their less fortunate
"soul brothers" of the *barrios* in major Southwestern
cities. These more economically mobile Mexican Americans
perceived with greater perspicacity the differences within the Mexican-American social milieu.[8] What is suggested is the clear transfer of a stratified social institution from Mexico. Members of the Mexican-American

community recognized the existence of a pecking order within their own society; yet, as a Mexican-American middle and upper class became more class conscious, it also adopted more of the mores of the dominant Anglo group.

As some Mexican Americans increased in affluence and became more perceptive about social distinctions, some of the more cohesive elements of the Mexican-American family began to disintegrate. Strong familial ties, both to a nuclear and extended family, weakened as second and third generations of Mexican Americans worked their way up the socioeconomic ladder. Meanwhile, back at the *barrio*, these escapees from *barrio* culture received the onus of traitors to their people. What occurred was an incompatability of value systems. The younger Mexican Americans desired a change in their lives uninhibited by a recalcitrant family. Older family members remaining in ethnic enclaves, on the other hand, saw desertions as a serious threat to fundamental social values.[9]

Again, institutional transfer occurred from Mexico. Since the Spanish conquest of New Spain, the family unit acted as the cohesive element of society. In villages and larger urban areas, ties of blood and marriage superseded any other allegiance. Increased urbanization, however, posed a threat to the strong family structure and, consequently, a breakup occurred. Similarly, as Mexicans moved to the United States and began to settle in cities in increasing numbers, the more socially ambitious attempted to break away from the old patterns that offered their parents and grandparents security in an alien land.[10]

However, not all of the old values received rejection by socially mobile Mexican Americans. According to Cecil Robinson, much of the ceremonial aspect of Mexican life remained a viable element of Mexican-American society at all levels. Individual deportment, states Robinson, mandated that a man conduct himself with *dignidad* (dignity). He must act as himself without the self-effacing camaraderie of the Anglo. To the Mexican American who clung to much of the formality of his society, the boisterousness of the Anglo strikes him as bad taste and as a clear negation of individual presence and bearing.[11]

Such individual insularity and aloofness came about because the Mexican attempted to come to grips with his own cultural identity. The violent seizure of Mexico by Spain produced a cultural schizophrenic. The Mexican viewed himself as neither Spaniard nor Indian; such a cultural chasm forced him into a solitude where he could never reveal his innermost feelings for fear of losing what he considered a precarious social equilibrium. Consequently, the Mexican wrapped himself in a robe of *dignidad*, breaking loose occasionally when sufficient alcohol permitted a release of inhibitions. Concomitant with such aloofness came an endemic *desconfianza* (lack of trust) in institutions in general. The Mexican trusted no one except himself, and even then he was aware of his fallibility.[12]

The very aloofness that is considered de riguer for the Mexican or Mexican-American male also forced them into other associations similar to social institutions in Mexico. Usually male socialization occurred, according to Arthur Rubel, along bilateral kinship lines. One joined with cousins, *compadres*, in-laws, and other members of an extended family rather than with associations outside of these social contacts. At differing age levels, young men formed *palomillas*, or gangs, composed, again, of members of a broadly extended family. Women of this extended family, however, maintained a more cloistered closeness and remained dependent upon each other for assistance and counsel in matters ranging from disease to social relations outside the family.[13]

Mexican folk culture and its concept of disease transferred to the borderlands when immigrants from Mexico migrated to the United States. In one city in the Southwest, a land development company brought lands in the lower Rio Grande Valley and precipitated a migratory wave of Anglos and Mexicans to occupy the area. Nine thousand Mexicans from isolated *ranchos* in northern Mexico transplanted their traditions in Meccas, Hidalgo County, Texas.[14] Traditional concepts of disease transferred across the Rio Grande and became an integral part of the new Mexican-American community in Mecca. *Males naturales* (acts of God) included a variety of intestinal disorders, hysteria or fright, and *caida de la mollera* (collapsed fontanel) in infants. *Males artificiales* (illness created by man) became a different problem. *Mal puesto* (sorcery) and *mal de ojo* (evil eye) required the intervention of a *curandero*, a quasi-medicine man prevalent in most rural Mexican communities.[15]

Such a cultural transfer reached ridiculous extremes. Popular medical mythology among Mexican Americans declared that these diseases could not be cured by a physician, be he Mexican, Anglo, or Mexican American. Ancient traditions needed to be invoked against these persistent maladies to which only Mexican Americans were susceptible. In Mecca, Texas, as social mobility infiltrated the Mexican population of that community, the more affluent Mexican Americans viewed such superstition as pure bunk. Such a negation of traditional values caused anxiety within the total Mexican-American community for fear the heretics might become afflicted by a perturbed *curandero*.[16]

Another medical concept to intrude itself into the Mexican-American communities was the persistence of the *curandero*. These individuals possessed a great deal of influence within the traditional confines of the community. They usually wielded influence as a result of a confidence in their own mission within the society. One *curandero* in south Texas, Pedrito Jaramillo, used his inherent charisma as a means of remaining influential.[17] Such charismatic influence resembled the power of *caciques* and *caudillos* in Mexico itself. These individuals, through a complex nexus of personal and family alliances coupled with their own personal magnetism, controlled sufficient power to lead whole areas into revolt or in support of a government or movement.

The heterogeneity of the Mexican-American communities throughout California and the Southwest resulted in inter-*barrio* tensions growing out of differences in relative social positions of the inhabitants. Not unlike *barrio* rivalries in Mexican villages, members of the Mexican-American *barrios* confined their social contacts to local areas and the resultant social relations within them. *Barrio* competition engendered a fierce loyalty from the population. In this regard, the *patria chica* concept that kept Mexican villages intensely loyal to their local areas instead of an inchoate nation became an integral factor in organization of Mexican-American enclaves.[18]

The *patria chica* applies as well to certain rural occupations of Mexican Americans. Mexican *vaqueros* employed by the King Ranch in south Texas held the ranch up as a primary unit of citizenship. The King *vaquero* referred to himself as a *kineno* in the same way a person from Nogales, Sonora, refers to himself as a *nogalense*.[19]

Transference of social patterns and institutions to the Southwest and California before 1940 can be divided roughly between rural and urban areas. The surge of war in Europe, however, forced great migrations of Mexicans into the United States to augment a labor force that was diminished by war. The resultant concentrations in cities like Los Angeles, San Antonio, Phoenix, and Tucson gave Mexicans and Mexican Americans an urban preponderance over rural countrymen. By the early 1960s, 80 percent of Mexican Americans occupied urban areas. In Los Angeles and Long Beach, there are more Mexicans than in any other city with the exception of Mexico City.[20]

Increased urbanization precipitated a mass movement out of *barrio* culture. More established Mexican Americans moved out of traditional neighborhoods as new arrivals from Mexico clamored for space. Urbanization consequently helped the socially ambitious achieve the mobility they sought.[21]

Prior to the 1940s, Mexican-American concentrations in Southwestern cities contained substantial elements of middle- and upper-class refugees who fled from the internal strife of Mexico's chaotic revolutionary period. Generally, these groups considered themselves exiles merely awaiting an opportunity to go back to Mexico.

They formed political groups that attempted to lobby for
their faction in the United States. These loosely joined
political conglomerations roughly paralleled the political factions that sought power in Mexico between 1910 and
1930. During that time, even the most illiterate refugee
maintained an interest in the political developments
south of the Rio Grande.[22]

Since the first waves of refugees arrived in the
Southwest after 1910, the Mexican Americans maintained a
romantic desire to return to the *patria*. Some evidence
exists for the idea that the emotional attachment persisted for one's native state in Mexico rather than the
nation. In Los Angeles, for example, the *barrios* were
often organized along state lines and maintained social
clubs and athletic organizations for those of state af-
filiations.[23]

While loyalty to the *patria* remained a romantic
ideal, a more practical loyalty possesses the Mexican American. Although functional bilingualism accelerated in
the Mexican-American population, there persisted a strong
attachment to the use of Spanish as a means of preserving
the mother culture. Language gave to the Mexican American a cultural cohesiveness that could not be disrupted
by social mobility, the introduction of new arrivals from
Mexico, and the general press of urban life after 1940.
While at variance with an urban milieu, the language
united disparate Mexican Americans from all social
strata. In fact, empirical studies indicate that ethnic
values stressing material achievement seem far less tenacious than the hold of language on the Mexican American.[24]

Mexican-American society and all of its cultural
ramifications remain essentially a carbon copy of social
practices introduced from Mexico. While remaining more
pristine in the traditionally oriented lower classes,
certain values, such as language, act as a force for
unity. There is, however, a breakdown of traditional
values as a Mexican American moves upward. Familial ties
weaken; language, while remaining a force, yields to bilingualism. On occasion Spanish is replaced by English.
With this replacement comes a greater emphasis on Anglo
values, such as a work ethic, that tend to dilute the
Mexican-American culture.[25]

One area of social and cultural concern for the Mexican American requires individual treatment: the influence of religion upon the Mexican American. Religious
practices reaching the United States from Mexico came into conflict with values adopted by Anglo, Irish, Polish,
and Italian Catholics, and caused substantial conflict as
Mexicans crowded into the urban centers and rural areas
of the Southwest.

Religion in Mexico plays a strong role in society
despite official strictures against the Roman Catholic

church. The Mexican Constitution of 1917 struck a particularly anticlerical note when it destroyed the
church's right to hold property and to teach religion
within its regular school curricula; yet the restrictions
imposed upon the church failed to diminish the nearly
mystical piety of the general population. In some respects, official censure of the church probably strenth-
ened individual devotion through the limitation upon the
number of priests in each Mexican state. The paucity of
priests meant that communication with God must be an individual effort, performed without benefit of clergy.

Mexican religious practices emphasize the ceremonial
and personalistic side of faith. In Mexican villages and
in *barrios* in Mexican cities, parish churches achieve a
completeness of character. Local patron saints are venerated not merely as intercessors between God and the
supplicant, but as beings endowed with their own power to
grant prayers. The concept of a universality of faith
rarely becomes a matter of discussion in Mexico. Instead, fiestas are organized for religious holidays and
for local saint's days. The church, in short, serves as
an element of social significance within the Mexican
society.[26] In addition, individual piety becomes a key
to Mexican religion. A religious fatalism invades the
Mexican and grants to him a sense of resignation. The
will of God often becomes the explanation for events and
personal tragedies.

Religious practices from Mexico were never introduced into California and the Southwest; they were an integral part of the area before the United States takeover
in 1848. Subsequent to that event, the Roman Catholic
church in the Southwest never received the impetus of
Americanization that occurred in the East and the Midwest. The clerics who ministered to clusters of the
faithful literally were *padres* on horseback, irregularly
administering the sacraments and tending to the pastoral
needs of their farflung communicants.[27]

As a consequence, the individual piety so prevalent
in Mexico also characterized the religious life of the
Mexican American. In the isolated mountain villages of
northern New Mexico, for example, one observer described
the resigned religious quality of the Hispano inhabitants
of that area. One man, she observed, had a daughter who
suffered from a prolonged illness. When she died, the
man declared, "She no longer suffers. God has taken
her."[28]

The essentially Mexican character of Roman Catholicism in the Southwest and California prompted action in
the archdiocese of Los Angeles between 1920 and 1949.
The church in Los Angeles sought to Americanize the Mexican American. A school-building frenzy struck the archdiocese. As a result, by 1960 practically every parish
in East Los Angeles, one of the heaviest concentrations

of Mexican Americans in California, possessed a parochial
school that not only taught a general curriculum and religious instruction, but also aimed at the acculturation
of its parishioners.
    Attempts to Americanize the Mexican American in Los
Angeles did not have unanimous support. In 1947, two
years before the intensified school-building program began, an anonymous letter was addressed to Pope Pius XII.
Probably written by a priest of Mexican extraction, the
memorandum, entitled "Religious Assistance to the Mexican
People in the United States," outlined four factors that
plagued such help to the Mexican American. First, the
anonymous author noted psychological racial differences
between the Anglo and the Mexican. Secondly, linguistic
barriers would inevitably hamper religious and cultural
homogenization. Third, the Mexicans possessed a strong
attachment to their religious heritage and would be loath
to make changes in their popular traditions. Finally,
the Anglo desired to Americanize ethnic groups residing
in the United States in the hope of forcing some cultural
homogeneity. Such a warning presaged the conflict between Anglo and Mexican-American cultures in the 1960s.
    The church, however, remained steadfast in the pur-
suit of its twin goals. It must first preserve the faith
for the Mexican Americans and keep Protestantism from
gaining a foothold. In an equal sense, however, the
church struggled against the accusations that it was an
agent of Rome. It wanted to demonstrate to the larger
society that it could Americanize its Mexican laity as a
patriotic act.
    The urban church in California was not the only ob-
ject of priestly concern. Migrant laborers throughout
the Southwest and the San Joaquin and Imperial valleys of
California suffered from pastoral neglect. In 1949,
priests began to receive extradiocesan assignments to
minister to migrant Mexican laborers in California. By
1960, however, these peripatetic clerics became socially
oriented and incurred the anger of wealthy Catholic farmers. The recalling of these extradiocesan pastors probably resulted from pressures brought to bear upon the
ecclesiastical hierarchy by wealthy rural communicants.
In addition, the termination of the *bracero* program in
1965 reduced the number of migrant laborers, the raison
d'etre of the entire program.
    Social activism in the late 1950s and early 1960s
replaced the strictly pastoral concerns of the church in
the Southwest and California. Priestly involvement in
the Delano grape strike and in the strike of agricultural
workers in Brownsville, Texas, in 1966, indicated that
the priests operated in a milieu of social protests.
Even the ecclesiastical hierarchy, generally cautious and
conservative, recognized the social pressures that cata-
pulted the Mexican American into prominence as a

potential force.

In San Antonio, Texas, the bishop in 1945 secured the creation of a Bishops Committee for the Spanish speaking. Gradually, cautiously, the committee evolved from a pastoral group into one that supported moderate social reform. In the 1960s, the Bishops Committee came out in favor of the right of agricultural labor to unionize.

Socially motivated clergy gave impetus to the transfer of the *cursillo* movement from Spain in 1957. It attracted individuals who sought religious renewal and dedication. The *cursillo* program drew an action-oriented clergy and laity. For three days, the *cursillistas* received "techniques of group dynamics and old-fashioned frontier revival."[30]

The present state of the church and the Mexican American continues unresolved. Real problems persist. The church failed to make inroads in its bent for Americanization, and, as a consequence, it helped alienate those with a formal allegiance to it as an institution. Mexican-American attendance at mass proved low. There also occurred a decrease in church marriages among Mexican Americans. In part, this could be explained by the Mexican tradition of a civil ceremony being the only legitimate one recognized by the state. Moreover, the socialization of Mexican-American Catholics failed in that the hoped-for Catholic homogenization did not materialize. Church lay groups with an Anglo or Irish bent could not attract Mexican-American parishioners, and few attempts were made by the clergy to draw the Mexican American on his cultural terms. Empirical evidence suggests, however, that a high degree of personal piety exists within the Mexican-American community despite the low attendance figures at mass.

The political tradition inherited from Mexico constituted one element of Mexican-American cultural values that acted both as a hindrance and as an asset to residents of the *barrios* and the small villages throughout the Southwest. Local *caciques* (bosses) manipulated their alliances with other powerful members of a village and exercised virtual control over the area. Often these unions resulted from familial ties, often *compadrazgo* played a role, and at times wealth elevated an individual to power within a village. Like religion, *caciquismo* did not transfer to the Southwest and California. Its existence predated the arrival of the Anglos by 200 years.[31]

Throughout Spain's far-flung empire in North America, *conquistadores* and colonizers controlled indigenous groups through the incorporation of Indian leaders into the Spanish system of government. Such a union of Indian and Spanish leadership led to the perpetuation of a *cacique* class that later became controlled by *mestizos*. In part, the hold of the *cacique* predicated itself upon

the relative geographic isolation between the disparate
villages and the administrative hub in Mexico City. Virtually semiautonomous, *caciques* in the Southwest governed
villages through an intricate system of alliances.

In the evolution of a *cacique* system in Mexico and
the Southwest, a transmutation of the concept of nobility
also occurred. The *Don*, a title of respect generally
applied to the Spanish gentry and to the Indian nobility
that became integrated into the Spanish system, gradually
achieved applicability to any powerful individual who
possessed some political influence in a village. As
such, the phenomenon of "donship" became an integral part
of the political milieu encountered by Anglos when they
reached Spanish and Mexican territories and later acquired them in 1848.[32]

As the nineteenth century waned, the immigration
that augmented the Spanish-speaking population of the
Southwest reinforced the donship concept. Traditional
donship revolved around the *patron* (employer). This relationship had its roots in the widely scattered *hacien-
das* of northern Mexico and was predicated upon an interdependence between the *patron* and his workers. Mexican
immigrants entering the Southwest served to strengthen
the cultural significance of the *don* as they moved into
extant Mexican-American enclaves.[33]

The *patron*, however, was but one element of donship.
In the United States Southwest, the Mexican consul at
various cities also received the title, both out of respect for the office and for the personal qualities of
the individual. Along with the Mexican consul, wealthy
Mexican-American businessmen were granted the designation. Politically, the descendants of the *cacique* tradition were referred to as *dones*. This perpetuation of a
tradition indigenous to the New World and incorporated
into Spanish rule set apart some of the Mexican-American
communities. Moreover, respected *curanderos*, because of
their great power, were usually referred to as *don*. Giv-
en the patriarchal nature of Mexican society, old men
were venerated with the title *don*.[34]

The Mexican-American cultural phenomenon of donship
profoundly, though subtly, affected the evolution of
Mexican-American political organizations. As early as
the turn of the century, some attempts appeared to organize Mexican residents of the United States into ethnic
political clubs in order to give them greater public influence. In the 1920s, the League of Latin American Citizens (LULAC) undertook as a conscious effort the integration of Mexican Americans into the United States political system. LULAC required that its members speak
functional English as a means of assuring a greater
awareness of political phenomena.[35]

Subsequent developments in the 1950s and 1960s saw
the emergence of more militant and nationalistic Mexican-

58

American political organizations. Groups such as the
Mexican American Political Association (MAPA), the
Political Association of Spanish Speaking Organizations
(PASSO), the Community Service Organization (CSO), and
the American GI Forum consciously strove to develop an
awareness among Mexican Americans of a cultural identity
and of their potential as a political force. Consequently, they did not mandate English as a prerequisite for
membership.[36]
More recent Mexican-American political groups differed from each other only in degree. The principal aim
of these groups remained the election of their own people
in political power. For example, PASSO and MAPA differ
in the emphasis placed on alliance with other ethnic organizations. MAPA chose to remain blatantly Mexican
while PASSO moved to alliance with blacks and Puerto Ricans in an attempt to garner political power and influence. In addition, organizations such as CSO and the American GI Forum aimed at political education among Mexican Americans in order to increase voter registration.
An odd contradiction, probably more apparent than
real, within all Mexican-American organizations is the
rhetoric of loyalty to the United States. At the same
time, they declare themselves on the basis of historical
primacy. The "we were here first" idea, based upon Spanish and Mexican occupation of the Southwest and California, is a declaration of cultural uniqueness and of an-
tipathy to the Anglo takeover of former Mexican areas.
Principal among the problems of Mexican-American
political organizations is the split between more moderate elements and those that cry out for total political
power and influence. Social action, of late, has become
the most insistent aspect of organizations like PASSO and
MAPA. Even LULAC and the American GI Forum, both reasonably conservative groups, became involved in the beginnings of social action programs working through federal
agencies such as the Office of Economic Opportunity.
With the exception of infusion of federal monies into social action programs, the Mexican-American political
organizations still suffer from a lack of funding. They
have failed to make moneyraising a sophisticated art, and
financial support remains haphazard. In 1968, however,
the Ford Foundation granted the sum of $2.2 million for
the establishment of a Legal Defense and Education Fund
for the Mexican Americans of the Southwest. It followed
the legal model of a comparable group within the National
Association of Colored People (NAACP). The foundation
granted monies for the legal education of minority group
members and finally supported the formation of a Southwest Council of La Raza.
Within the political system of the United States,
however, the Mexican American remained tied to the Democratic party. Such a tenacious allegiance hampers

organizational effectiveness among Mexican Americans because members of Democratic, and occasionally Republican,
clubs also belong to ethnic political clubs. As a consequence, membership is duplicative, and support remains
narrowly based.

Mexican-American political leaders also face problems of validation of their leadership. To become acceptable leaders of their group, they need the acceptance
of the dominant Anglo community, yet they cannot appear
as *vendidos* (sellouts) to the Anglo. They must have a
command of English, be elected to office by both Anglos
and Mexican Americans, and remain essentially loyal to
the interests of their ethnic group without being rejected by the Anglo. In short, they perch precariously on a
political tightrope. Moreover, leadership fragmentation
and parochialism militate against the emergence of a re-
gionally acceptable political leadership among the Mexican Americans.

The political system which the Mexican American op-
erates and the apparent disunity among the diverse Mexican-American groups work against political effectiveness.
The gerrymandering of political districts throughout the
Southwest costs the Mexican Americans influence in the
marshaling of votes. Internal political juggling by Anglo political machinery consequently receives reinforcement from unsophisticated migrants from rural areas who
move into urban districts. Finally, the low naturalization rate among Mexican citizens reduces the political
effectiveness of Mexicans residing in the United States.

The Mexican American, therefore, possesses little
political clout. Unlike the black, no one ostensibly
fought a war over them nor were they enslaved. The Mexican American lacks a central form of organization that
would coordinate disparate activities and grant them a
more effective channeled political voice.[37]

The Mexican American began on a traditional Mexican
political base. *Dones* and *caciques* wielded a powerful
influence over the political destinies of a vast population. However, in the recent past, increased Mexican-
American political activity forced adoption of Anglo
political values and systems in order to maintain a precarious effectiveness. This "working within the system"
did not, however, have unanimous support from all Mexican
Americans. Militancy grew in the 1960s and sought to
polarize Mexican-American culture and politics.

A nationalistic movement is afoot in the United
States that possesses traditions predating the arrival of
settlers in Virginia in 1607. The Mexican American discovered a sense of nationality somewhat removed from the
allegiance to the predominantly Anglo culture of the
United States. However, the movement has failed to grip
the majority of Mexican Americans, many of whom settled
comfortably into the Anglo society that ultimately

accepted them. To the militant Mexican American, the act
of acceptance by the Anglo society symbolized a rejection
of autochthonous culture by the Mexican American. In so
doing, he became labeled with the pejorative of *Tio Taco*
or *Vendido*.

In part, the lack of cohesion in the recrudescent
Mexican-American nationalism emerged from the very difference within the Mexican-American community. While
language acted as a force of maintaining contact among
disparate elements of that group, semantic disagreements
also separated its various elements. Essentially, the
Mexican Americans disagreed over exactly what their ethnicity entailed. Were they Spanish-speaking, Mexican
Americans, Latin Americans, Hispanos, or Chicanos? The
degree of adherence to one particular sobriquet clearly
indicated the view of the individual toward the dominant
Anglo society and toward the emergent Mexican-American
movement.[38]

To the militant, the term Chicano, formerly a pejorative applied to Mexicans in general, became a symbol of
uniqueness from the Anglo society. In March 1969, at the
First National Chicano Youth Liberation Conference, held
in Denver, Colorado, the delegates presented the Plan
Espiritual de Aztlan. The document declared the solidarity of the Chicano people. It drew, in part, from the
raza cosmica idea presented by the Mexican philosopher
Jose Vasconcelos, wherein he saw a solidarity between the
mestizo peoples of the Western Hemisphere. The very name
Aztlan was the Nahuatl or Aztec term for what is now the
Southwest. In this declaration, *indigenista* elements
emerged to extol the Indian over the Spanish side of
Mexican-American and Mexican culture. It was, in short,
a carry-over from the *indigenista* "binge" in which Mexico
indulges sporadically.[39]

The Plan Espiritual de Aztlan railed against the
brutal *gringo* invaders of the *patria*. In a declaration
of historical primacy, the plan laid principal claim to
the Southwest. Its call was nationalistic, extolling the
existence of a Chicano nation. The Chicano goals, as
enunciated in the Plan de Aztlan, were clearly activist.
It demanded a mass commitment to Chicano control of their
own economic lives and education. Because of the essentially racist tendencies of Anglo society, the Chicano
would have to defend his own community. Cultural values
of *la raza*, declared the plan, such as family and home,
would "prove as a powerful weapon to defeat the *gringo*
dollar system . . ." It also decried working within the
two-party system.[40]

Such a commitment to traditional values and such a
rejection of the dominant Anglo culture clearly emerged
as an attempt to set the Chicano apart from the society
in which he resided. The use of a political plan became
a symbolic act of retreat to the Mexican expedient. The

call for a social value of the family and the home again reaffirmed tradition. Implicit within such a familial retreat was *compadrazgo*. All Chicanos were *compadres*. Each committed himself to a betterment of *la raza*. *Chicanismo* based itself upon the individual's awareness of his culture and upon the responsibilities inherent in *compadrazgo*.[41]

Some Mexican Americans, however, recognized the reality of existence within the Southwest. A more moderate position was enunciated before the United States Congress on February 26, 1970, when a declaration for cultural pluralism was made.[42]

Rodolfo "Corky" Gonzalez, the Chicano leader of Denver, Colorado, recognized extant political realities. Though a Chicano nationalist, he nonetheless saw that only through effective political organization could the Mexican American exert a powerful influence on his own life and political destiny. To achieve this, Gonzalez advocated the nationalist pride of being a Chicano. *La raza*, to Gonzalez, was a large family in which its individual members had pride. He declared: "Liberation comes from self-determination . . ." This, however, could only emerge when the Mexican Americans took pride in their existence.[43]

Political and cultural militancy made itself felt in predominantly Mexican-American schools throughout the Southwest and California. In Texas, for example, Mexican-American students argued they suffered from discrimination because of their ethnic background. They demanded college prepatory classes, counseling on academic financial assistance and grants, and equal opportunity to attempt things other than industrial arts and home economics. In one instance, a teacher wanted to know what the turmoil was all about. The teacher declared, "You're all Americans." One girl responded with a strident negation: "I am a Mexican American." A sense of brown pride manifested itself. The girl cited the example of the Virgin of Guadalupe appearing as a brown virgin to an Indian boy on December 12, 1531.[44]

Militancy in the schools throughout the Southwest and California resulted in an increase of emphasis upon the Mexican American as a cultural entity. Chicano militants successfully brought about curricular changes in various cities throughout the land of Aztlan. In one example, Crystal City, Texas, Mexican Americans swept the school board elections on April 4, 1970. The school board takeover resulted from a joint political effort between the Mexican American Youth Organization (MAYO) and the Raza Unida party of Crystal City. Voter registration drives on the part of Raza Unida workers brought Mexican Americans to the polls and gave the Raza Unida party a resounding victory.[45]

Chicano militancy, while strident and disruptive,

addressed itself to specific issues. A prime example of
this is the land grant controversy, still unresolved, in
which Rejes Lopez Tijerina emerged as the spokesman for
Alianza Federal de Pueblos Libres. Lopez Tijerina and
his followers have consistently argued that the Treaty of
Guadalupe Hidalgo of 1848, which granted New Mexico to
the United States, guaranteed the protection of extant
Mexican lands and Mexican culture. The gradual dispos-
session of New Mexicans by both private and public forces
became the focal point of the struggle. Violence and
litigation have characterized the long struggle for res-
titution of allegedly alienated lands.[46]

Another long, grueling problem, finally settled in
1968, appeared in the grape strike in Delano, California.
Essentially a labor-management dispute, the strike became
a focal point of Chicano activism. In addition, Anglo
sympathizers, as well as ecclesiastical supporters, declared for Cesar Estrada Chavez and his union. Political
leaders scurried to be photographed with Chavez. Establishment liberals sang his praises at cocktail parties
and supported his boycott of stores that continued to
sell table grapes. Chavez and his supporters used traditional labor tactics to achieve their ends. The major
variant, however, was the ethnic overtone given to the
strike. Cesar Chavez soon took on characteristics of
Benito Juarez, Emiliano Zapata, and Pancho Villa.
Chavez, as the charismatic *caudillo,* operated in a milieu
of labor-management relations and ultimately succeeded in
gaining labor contracts for his union.[47]

The Chavez grape strike became a symbol of one element of the Mexican-American population in California and
the Southwest. His movement generated a cultural boom
spearheaded by Luis Miguel Valdez. Valdez founded the
Teatro Campesino in Del Rey, California. Valdez, poet,
occasional college teacher, and alumnus of the San Francisco Mime Theater, saw in the grape strike a chance for
Mexican-American culture to achieve a renascence. To
Valdez, the Mexican Americans need an organized cultural
tradition in order to articulate their needs. The Teatro
Campesino provides an outlet for cultural experimenta-
tion. The Teatro, moreover, is based upon old Spanish
traditions but set in the context of migrant labor in the
United States, and its productions are part morality
plays and part social commentary. To be viable as a
peasant or worker theater, the staff of the Teatro is
composed wholly of agricultural workers. Agustin Lira,
a grape picker, is resident guitarist and poet, and
writes *corridos* based on the Mexican folk songs about the
migrant laborers in the agricultural belt of California.
Through Valdez' inspiration, other Chicano theaters
merged in the Southwest in an attempt to find an autochthonous art style for *la raza.*[48]

Mexican-American militancy aimed at both political

and cultural birth. Through the medium of politics, Chicano militants hoped to achieve power and a sense of separation from the dominant Anglo culture. At the same
time, a sense of nationalism and pride in one's *chicanismo* has manifested itself among the militant. Pride,
however, circumscribes certain elements of Mexican culture. Iberian influences are denigrated and the barbari-
ties of the Aztecs are upheld. Such an unhistorical position perpetuates a perverse *indigenismo* that tends to
alienate moderate and conservative Mexican Americans and
to thus weaken the thrust for solidarity.

Despite the militant upsurge, Mexican Americans remain a heterogeneous social group composed of varying
social strata and possessing disparate aspiration. Popular attempts at cultural homogeneity tend to disregard
the tripartite nature of the Mexican American. Indian
and Spanish elements blended to produce a Mexican that
shared both cultures. With the transference of the
Southwest to the United States, the Anglo culture infiltrated an essentially Mexican one. As a consequence,
Mexican Americans who aspired to social betterment adopted, at least superficially, some of the dominant mores of
their Anglo countrymen. The result of such an adaptation
was the abandonment of traditional cultural values as the
Mexican American moved out of the *barrio* and the rural
villages.

The militant, however, claimed a homogeneity that
rejected Anglo values entirely. Chauvinistic elements
attempted to arouse an entire people against their fellow
citizens. While some Mexican-American organizations
sought to work within an extant political and social system and at the same time disseminate pride in their Mexican heritage, others became stridently militant. In
their militancy, they alienated moderate Mexican Americans who had succeeded within the dominant political and
social system. Congressman Henry B. Gonzalez of San
Antonio perhaps put it best: "I am against hate and the
spreaders of hate. . . ."49

NOTES

1. For a critique of ethnic studies vis-a-vis the
Mexican American and some of the problems that arise from
Mexican-American history, see two articles by Manuel A.
Machaco, Jr., "Chicano Studies: A Mexican American Dis-
sents," University Bookman (Fall 1970); and "Mexican-
American History: Problems and Prospects," Western Review
(Winter 1971).

2. Cecil Robinson, With the Ears of Strangers: The
Mexican American Literature (Tucson: University of Arizona Press, 1963) offers an excellent analysis of the
borderlands subculture that emerged since 1848. For a

geographer's approach to the borderlands, see D. W.
Meinig, Southwest: Three Peoples in Geographical Change,
1600-1970 (New York: Oxford University Press, 1971). W.
Eugene Hollon in his The Southwest: Old and New (Lincoln:
University of Nebraska Press, 1968), offers an excellent
cultural history approach to the Southwest.
    3. An excellent analysis of anit-Hispanic attitudes
can be found in PhillipW. Powell, Tree of Hate: The Effects of Anti-Spanish Propaganda on United States Relations with the Hispanic World (New York: Basic Books,
1971). A good case study of this *kulturkampf* is Leonard
Pitt, The Decline of the Californios: A Social History of
the Spanish-Speaking Californians, 1848-1890 (Berkeley:
University of California Press, 1970).
    4. Pitt, Decline of Californios.
    5. Fernando Penalosa, "The Changing Mexican Ameri-
can in Southern California," Sociology and Social Research (Septermber 1967): 408-410.
    6. Leo Gebler, Joan W. Moore, and Ralph C. Guzman,
The Mexican-American People: The Nation's Second Largest
Minority (New York: The Free Press, 1970), p. 296.
    7. Carey McWilliams, North From Mexico: The Span-
ish-Speaking People in the United States (New York:
Greenwood Press, 1968), p. 213.
    8. Fernando Penalosa and Edward C. McDonagh, "Edu-
cation, Economic Status, and Social Class Awareness of
Mexican Americans," Phylon (Summer 1968): 119-120, 126.
    9. Cecil Robinson, "Spring Water with a Taste of
the Land," American West (Summer 1966): 12.
    10. For an excellent discussion of family life in
Mexico, see Nathan L. Whetten, Rural Mexico (Chicago:
University of Chicago Press, 1948).
    11. Robinson, "Spring Water," p. 12.
    12. Two excellent philosophical analyses of the Mex-
ican character can be found in Octavio Paz, El Laberinto
de la Soledad (Mexico: Fondo de Cultura Economica, 1957)
and Samuel Ramos, Perfil del Hombre y la Cultura en Mexico (Mexico: 1934).
    13. J. Arthur Rubel, "Concepts of Disease in Mexi-
can-American Culture," American Anthropologist (October
1960): 811ff.
    14. Ibid., pp. 795-796.
    15. Ibid., p. 797.
    16. Ibid., p. 813.
    17. Octavio Ignacio Romano V., "Charismatic Medi-
cine, Faith Healing, and Sainthood," American Anthropologist (October 1965): 1167ff.
    18. Gebler et al., The Mexican American People, pp.
309-311. See also, Oscar Lewis, Life in a Mexican Village: Tepoztlan Restudied (Urbana: University of Illinois
Press, 1951).
    19. Survey Graphic, May 1, 1931, as published in
Wayne Moquin, A Documentary History of the Mexican

American (New York: Frederick Praeger, 1971), pp. 289-292.

20. Ibid., p. 301.

21. Penalosa, "The Changing Mexican American," p. 407.

22. Gebler et al., The Mexican American People, pp. 381-382. Two collections, in addition to the plethora of Spanish language newspapers published in the Southwest, shed light on the role of these refugee groups in the United States. Record Group 59, Papers of the Department of State relating to the Internal Affairs of Mexico, 812.00, contains a profusion of information about the political machinations of the groups. These documents are in the National Archives, Washington, D.C. The Papers of Silvestre Terrazas, a Mexican journalist and publisher who fled to the United States during the 1910-1920 period, are housed in the Bancroft Library, University of California, Berkeley. These contain correspondence between Terrazas and various refugee leaders who sought the support of his newspaper in El Paso. There remained a desire to return to Mexico; at the same time, the documents emit a note of resignation about the probability of stability returning to Mexico and allowing for the repatriation of refugees.

23. Gebler et al., The Mexican American People, pp. 381-382.

24. Ibid., pp. 438-439.

25. Paul M. Sheldon, "Community Participation and the Emerging Middle Class," in Julian Samora, ed., La Raza: The Forgotten Americans (Notre Dame: University of Notre Dame Press, 1966), pp. 125-158.

26. Whetten, Rural Mexico.

27. Gebler et al., The Mexican American People, pp. 451-453.

28. Adelina Otero, "My People," Survey Graphic, May 1, 1931, as published in Moquin, Documentary History, p. 287.

29. Anita Brenner in Idols Behind Altars (New York: Bible and Tannen, 1967) describes the veneer of Catholicity in Mexican religion. What occurred, according to Brenner, was the replacement of indigenous names by Christian names for the extant deities. However, the symbolism and essentially polytheistic character of pre-Conquest religion remained an essential factor in Mexican religious life.

30. Gebler et al., The Mexican American People, p. 467.

31. An excellent discussion of caciquismo can be found in Francois Chevalier, "The Roots of Personalism," in Hugh Hamill, Jr., ed., Dictatorship in Spanish America (New York: Alfred A. Knopf, 1966), pp. 35-51.

32. Octavio Ignacio Romano V., "Donship in a Mexican-American Community in Texas," American Anthropologist

66

(December 1960).
33. Ibid. The *patron-peon* relationship is ably discussed by Chevalier, "The Roots." See also Francois Chevalier, Land and Society in Colonial Mexico: The Great Hacienda (Berkeley: University of California Press, 1963).
34. Romano, "Donship," pp. 968-970.
35. Gebler et al., The Mexican American People, p. 543.
36. Ibid., p. 543. Unless otherwise indicated, the subsequent material is drawn from Gebler et al., The Mexican American People, pp. 543-569.
37. Helen Rowan, "A Minority Nobody Knows," Atlantic Monthly (June 1967): 48-49.
38. Gebler et al., The Mexican American People, pp. 385-386.
39. Documents of the Chicano Struggle (New York: Pathfinder, 1971), pp. 4-6.
40. Ibid.
41. Ysidro Ramon Macias, "The Chicano Movement," Wilson Library Bulletin (March 1970), as published in Moquin, Documentary History, pp. 388-389.
42. Armando Rodriquez in Congressional Record, 91st Congress, Second Session, February 26, 1970, pp. 382-386.
43. Rodolfo "Corky" Gonzalez, "What Political Road for the Chicano Movement," The Militant (March 30, 1970): 378-382.
44. Joe Bernal, "I Am a Mexican American," NEA Journal (May 1, 1969): 367.
45. Mario Compean, Jose Angel Gutierrez, and Antonio Camejo, La Raza Unida Party in Texas (New York: Pathfinder Press, 1970), pp. 3-15.
46. Peter Nabokov, Tijerina and the Court House Raid (Albuquerque: University of New Mexico Press, 1969). See also, Stan Steiner, La Raza: The Mexican Americans (New York: Harper and Row, 1969).
47. Peter Matthiessen, Sal Si Puedes: Cesar Chavez and the New American Revolution (New York: Delta Books, 1969), and Steiner, La Raza, pp. 247-324.
48. Steiner, La Raza, pp. 324-325.
49. Congressional Record, 91st Congress, First Session, April 22, 1969 as published in Moquin, Documentary History, pp. 359-360.

4
Ethnic Group Identity and Occupational Status Projections of Teenage Boys and Girls

William P. Kuvlesky
Everett D. Edington

INTRODUCTION

More than two decades ago, Merton[1] proposed that the aspirational frames of reference of various types of youth in the United States were similar, structured in terms of the "success ethic" and made up of status desires indicative of upward social mobility. To this day, few studies have been designed to test the general validity of this hypothesis as it applies to a range of generally economically disadvantaged ethnic groups. The general purpose of this study is to provide evidence for the evaluation of this hypothesis within the context of comparable data collected during 1972 and 1973 from predominantly disadvantaged rural populations of teenage youth of four ethnic types--Mexican American (south Texas), black (east Texas), Anglo (east Texas), and Navajo (Arizona). More specifically, the analysis reported involved comparative analysis of several aspects of these youths' occupational status projections.

For years, many social scientists and policymakers involved in youth development and education programs attributed the poor success of rural youth and ethnic minority youth to a lack of motivation for social mobility.[2] It was commonly asserted that their social ambitions were lower than that of other youth--they held low level aspirations and expectations for status attainment. It was theorized that this situation resulted from inculcation of subcultural values that produced personality orientations which worked in opposition to a strong motivation to strive for social mobility--strong valuation for family, lack of willingness to experience deferred gratification, local community orientation, and a passive fatalistic orientation toward influencing their own destiny.[3] Also, for example, Talcott Parsons[4] has theorized at a more abstract level that the way of life of Spanish Americans is characterized by particularistic-ascriptive value patterns as compared with the universalistic-achievement patterns of the dominant society. Similar

The authors would like to acknowledge the assistance of Angie Lindley Bain, research assistant in the Department of Rural Sociology, Texas A&M University.

theorizing, speculation, and conclusions predominate in
the literature in reference to blacks and native Americans, particularly those residing in rural areas.[5] This
"self-blame" or "pathological-subculture" explanation of
the relative lack of success of disadvantaged types of
youth in attaining social mobility, particularly through
the normal processes of occupational attainment, tends to
deflect attention away from other factors outside of the
disadvantaged groups that may limit or impede opportunities for social mobility--poor quality education, inadequate job placement information, and social discrimination of one sort or another in initial job placement and
then promotion.[6]
     A thesis offered by Robert Merton sometime ago
stands in direct contradiction to the argument that disadvantaged youth fail to achieve social attainment due to
a lack of ambition or low-level aspirations and expectations. Merton proposed in 1957[7] that most youth of all
types, and of all social classes, have inculcated the
"success ethic" and, consequently, maintain high level
success goals (i.e., occupational and educational aspirations). In other words, Merton proposes that maintenance
of high-status attainment goals in a more or less articulated "aspirational frame of reference" approximates a
cultural universal in our society which cuts across class
and ethnic distinctions.[8] In more recent times, since
the mid-sixties, a number of social scientists have come
to support essentially the current applicability of Merton's thesis as a result of their contention that there
has been a "revolution of expectations" among disadvantaged youth in our society.[9] It is difficult to determine what historical changes have taken place in status
aspirations and expectations of youth due to a lack of
any empirical studies on the subject until very recently.[10] Still, with few exceptions, the extensive body of
research evidence accumulated over the last ten years on
status projections of disadvantaged youth support Merton's general thesis: most disadvantaged youth, including
those from rural areas and ethnic minority groups, do
maintain high aspirations and expectations for status
attainment relative to their families of origin and their
realistic chances for social mobility.[11]
     The relevance of youth's orientations toward future
occupational status is of particular significance for
several reasons. First, in a sociological sense, occupational status is a central consideration in determining
general life style and other social ties, and is considered by most as the central vehicle for obtaining social
mobility.[12] In this latter sense, it has a direct impact
on educational status attainment for many who perceive
education as a means to obtaining a desired type of job
and, in a smiliar fashion, also influences considerations
about place of residence and membership in specific

associations and groups. Secondly, the current emphasis on career education, counseling, etc., has created a need for more information on the vocational aspirations, plans, and orientations of all kinds of youths.

SPECIFICATIONS OF RESEARCH OBJECTIVES

The analysis to be reported is guided by a conceptual scheme taking off from Merton's previously noted idea of an "aspirational frame of reference," and modified and specified further by others as described below. Some time ago Merton proposed that young people maintain a "frame of aspirational reference" composed of personal goals for status attainment as adults.[13] This mental configuration provides them with a cognitive map that serves to guide anticipatory socialization into adult roles. Ralph Turner[14] has presented firm documentation for this assertion.

Merton conceived of only one frame of status projections, that involving aspirations (desires). However, Stephenson[15] has demonstrated the utility of thinking in terms of two types of projections: in addition to aspirations, youth maintain a set of expectations (anticipations) which often differs from their desires. A conceptual scheme presented by Kuvlesky and Bealer[16] begins with this analytical distinction between aspiration and expectation, and provides additional distinctions. The divergence, if any, between the desired and anticipated status objects within a particular area of potential status attainment (i.e., occupation) is labeled "anticipatory goal deflection."[17] While most past research has focused on projected status attainments, Kuvlesky and Bealer call attention to another analytical dimension of status projections which they call the "orientation element." This idea refers to the strength of orientation that a person maintains towards the status object involved in either aspiration or expectation. In reference to aspiration this would be the strength of desire associated with obtaining the status goal specified and is referred to as "intensity of aspiration."[18] The comparable element involved in expectation is labeled "certainty of expectation." This scheme has been reported in detail in a number of publications and papers, along with empirical evidence supporting the utility of the analytical distinctions involved.[19] The analysis of ethnic comparisons to be described here was structured in terms of the elements of status projections differentiated in the scheme described above.

Our specific research objective is to determine, within the context of our data, to what extent ethnic variability exists in reference to each of the following dimensions of occupational status projections of teenage boys and girls:

1. Occupational aspirations
   a. type and level
   b. intensity
2. Occupational expectations
   a. type and level
   b. certainty
3. Anticipatory goal deflection

REVIEW OF RELEVANT RESEARCH LITERATURE

An extensive review of the relevant research literature turned up only four studies involving comparative
analysis of youths' occupational status projections from
as many as three ethnic groups. Two of these involved
tri-ethnic comparisons of metropolitan youth.[20] The
other two involved tri-ethnic comparisons of predominantly rural, nonmetropolitan youth.[21] All of the studies
cited above, except for Antonovsky's, involved either or
both the Texas A&M University and ERIC-CRESS researchers,
and were fully comparable in instruments, data collection
operations, and measurement categories.

Of course, many studies have been reported dealing
with the occupational status projections of white (Anglo)
and black youth[22] and, to a much lesser extent, for Mexican American youth.[23] However, very few have been reported on native American youth.[24] It is often difficult
or impossible to develop valid comparisons across studies
involving one or two ethnic groupings due to problems of
conceptual ambiguity, lack of specification of research
operations, or variability in instruments, measurements,
or historical period of study.[25] Consequently, we will
concentrate our attention in this review on those few
studies cited above involving at least a tri-ethnic comparison of youths' occupational status projections.

The earliest study that we are aware of which was
designed for at least a tri-ethnic comparison of occupational status projections of youth was a 1958 investigation crried out by Antonovsky[26] in a "northern metropolis" involving lower-class black, white, and Puerto
Rican youth. The data he reports indicates little difference by ethnicity. A more recent study involving a
tri-ethnic comparison of metropolitan youth in Galveston,
Texas, was carried out by Crawford[27] in 1974 and utilized
instruments and operations directly comparable to those
utilized to produce the data sets involved in our analysis. Crawford[28] concludes that his "findings indicated
that ethnic groups appeared to be more similar than different relative to their occupational status projections." He reports a total lack of statistically significant differences among the three ethnic groups, regardless of sex, on all dimensions of occupational status
projections examined--aspiration and expectation levels,
anticipatory goal deflection, intensity of aspiration,

and certainty of expectation.[29] Also, the only significant difference by sex that Crawford[30] found was in reference to level of occupational aspirations: girls tended
to have higher aspirations than boys. A study of Mexican-American and Anglo youth carried out by Venegas[31] in
1973 found that the Mexican-American youths had both occupational and educational aspirations significantly lower than Anglo youths. However, there were very few in
either ethnic group that indicated either an aspiration
or expectation for the lower-level occupational categories. Venegas found no significant differences between
Mexican-American and Anglo youth on intensity of occupational aspirations, certainty of occupational expectations, and anticipatory goal deflection.

Let us now examine the two more directly relevant
tri-ethnic studies of nonmetropolitan youth carried out
in Texas in 1966-67 and in New Mexico in 1975. Both of
these studies used directly comparable instruments and
measurements and similar data collection operations. A
very recent study reported by Edington and his associates
involved 550 rural youth in New Mexico: 171 Anglo Americans, 240 Mexican Americans, and 139 native Americans.[32]
For both aspirations and expectations there were more
similarities than differences. The aspirations of the
Anglos were highest, with the Mexican Americans next and
the native Americans lowest. The same order was true for
the occupational expectation; however, the differences
were not statistically significant. Rates of anticipatory occupational goal deflection were similar for both
the Anglo and Mexican-American youth; however, native American youth had a lower rate. In summary, rural native
American youth had both lower occupational aspirations
and expectations than Anglo or Mexican-American youth and
a lower rate of anticipatory deflection than the other
groups.

The earlier Texas comparison reported by Kuvlesky
and his associates[33] involved Mexican Americans from the
"border region" of south Texas, and black and white (Anglo) youth from east Texas--all from predominantly rural,
nonmetropolitan areas. The authors concluded that generally, for both boys and girls, statistically significant
ethnic differences existed on the various dimensions of
occupational status projections. However, they further
state, "In all cases it was judged that the similarity
of the ethnic groups was more significant than the variations existing among them.[34] More specifically, they
describe their findings as follows.

> In summary, the overview demonstrated that the
> three ethnic groups were generally similar in refer-
> ence to aspiration levels, anticipatory deflection,
> certainty of expectation, and intensity of

educational aspiration. On the other hand, substantial ethnic differences tended to occur in reference to level of expectation and for intensity of desire for occupational goals. These differences were due largely to Negros maintaining higher expectation levels and Mexican Americans having a stronger intensity of desire for job goals. Females accounted for most of the marked ethnic variability.[35]

In summary, the studies of metropolitan youth reviewed, ranging in time from 1958-1974 and including several widely separated regions of the United States, generally indicated a lack of substantial ethnic difference in the occupational status projections of teenage youth. The two nonmetropolitan studies reviewed, ranging from 1966-67 to 1974, are particularly relevant for our purposes because they used directly comparable instruments and operations as those used to produce our data sets and deal with youth residing in very similar types of social areas. The findings of these two nonmetropolitan studies generally indicate that rural youth from different ethnic groups in the southwestern United States are more similar than different in their occupational status projections. At the same time, significant interethnic variability was observed as follows:

1. Native American youth tend to hold lower level aspirations and expectation, and to experience more anticipatory goal deflection than do other youth.
2. Blacks maintained higher expectation levels than others, particularly among girls.
3. Mexican Americans, particularly females, had a stronger intensity of desire for job goals than others.

Our study will serve to test the general validity of generalizations that can be drawn from these few past studies. In addition, we can extend the accumulated knowledge as a result of having the first set of directly comparable data--in historical time, research operations, and type of study area--involving rural youth samples of native-American, Mexican-American, black, and Anglo boys and girls.

THE STUDY POPULATIONS AND DATA COLLECTION

The data utilized for this study were collected from high school sophomores as a result of three separate but highly coordinated field efforts as follows: Arizona Navajo youth, spring 1972; east Texas black and white youth, spring 1972, and south Texas Mexican-American youth, spring 1973. While the time lapse of one year between the collection of data on the Mexican-American sophomores and that of the other ethnic groupings might have produced a problem in comparability of the data sets, a recent report presenting findings on historical change in occupational projections of Mexican-American youth from the study area involved here indicated little significant change between 1967 and 1973.[36]

Care was taken to insure that all data collection operations were identical in the three separate field investigations by utilizing standard operations.[37] In each case all high school sophomores present in the schools selected for study on the day of the study were given questionnaires and were immediately assured of the confidentiality of their responses. A trained interviewer read each item aloud, giving students enough time to complete their responses before proceeding. The questionnaires distributed were identical with respect to the variables involved in this analysis. Those students not present on the day of the interview were not interviewed. Detailed descriptions of the study populations and data collection procedures have been reported previously in regard to each of these three field studies.[38] Still, it would be of some use to the reader to have a brief sketch of the study area, study schools, and of the respondents in each case. This is provided below.

Arizona Navajo Youth Study--1972: Data were obtained from 170 Navajo boys and 215 Navajo girls who were high school sophomores in five different high schools located in the Navajo reservation area of Arizona. All of the youth resided in rural, relatively economically disadvantaged areas. In each school almost all students were Navajo. Stout and Edington[39] provide a more detailed description of the socioeconomic conditions prevailing in this area.

East Texas Youth Study--1972: Data were collected from high school sophomores attending ten public high schools in three rural, nonmetropolitan east Texas counties during spring 1972. A total of 493 youths were interviewed (Table 4.1). The three east Texas counties involved in this study--Burleson, Leon, and San Jacinto-- were selected purposefully, using the following criteria: relative high proportion of blacks and low-income families, predominantly or entirely rural, and location in a nonmetropolitan area not contiguous to a metropolitan one. Proportions of blacks in the counties varied from more than one-fourth of the population in Burleson to more than 40 percent in San Jacinto in 1969. The county with the highest median family income in 1969 (Burleson) was $3,000 below that of the state median family income of $8,490 in the same year.[40]

South Texas Youth Study--1973: Data were collected from sophomores attending five high schools in three nonmetropolitan south Texas counties adjacent to or in close proximity to the United States-Mexico border.[41] The counties were purposively selected on the following criteria: proportionately high concentration of Mexican Americans, a high frequency of family poverty, and predominantly rural, nonmetropolitan. We failed to gain the cooperation of two high schools in the study area. The schools' enrollment was predominantly Mexican-American, and only the Mexican-American respondents will be utilized in this analysis (Table 4.2).

Table 4.1 High School Sophomores Interviewed in Rural East Texas Study Area in 1972 by Race and Sex

Race	Male	Female	Total
Black	98	94	192
White (Anglo)	148	153	301
Total	236	232	493

Table 4.2 High School Sophomores Interviewed in Rural South Texas Study Area in 1973 by Ethnicity and Sex

Ethnicity	Male	Female	Total
Mexican American	178	201	379
Anglo	15	15	30
Other	5	2	7
Total	198	218	416

Overview of Study Population

The data sets available from those three field investigations provide us with comparable information on occupational status projections on four different ethnic groupings of teenage boys and girls from three widely separated study areas sharing many important common attributes--predominantly rural, agricultural, nonmetropolitan areas that are relatively disadvantaged economically and which have high concentrations of an ethnic minority group present. Comparability is also enhanced by the short range of historical time involving data collection over the three field investigations---two were done in spring 1972 and the other one a year later. An overview of the study populations by ethnicity and sex is provided in Table 4.3

In conclusion, the high level of comparability of the data, historical period of study, and study areas provides us with the best opportunity that has existed, as far as we know, to investigate broadly interethnic variability in occupational orientations of rural youth.

Table 4.3   Overview of Study Population by Area of Study, Ethnic Identity, and Sex

	Arizona-1972 Navajo	East Texas-1972 Black	Anglo	South Texas-1973 Mexican American	TOTAL
Male	170	98	148	178	583
Female	215	94	154	201	648
Total	385	192	302	379	1,231

Analysis and Findings

Outline of Analysis. The primary objective of this analysis is to determine to what extent the four ethnic groupings of teenage youth involved differ in their occupational status projections by sex.[42] For each of the dimensions of occupational status projections specified earlier, we compared by sex the four ethnic groups involved. Chi Square tests were used in each case to determine whether or not any ethnic differences observed were statistically significant. In reference to all variables utilized, the "No information" category was retained for analysis and included in statistical evaluations because of considerable ethnic variability on this in some cases.

Two measurement schemes were utilized in reference to the status object specified by the respondents for both aspirations and expectations. The initial set of categories, a modification of the Edwards Census scheme, was utilized to provide a basis for discerning variability in qualitative types of occupations and to facilitate comparison with other studies. In addition, these initial categories were collapsed into an ordinal scale made up of three more inclusive "status level" categories (High, Intermediate, and Low) used to approximate social class (SES) distinctions.[43] The initial response categories are listed in Table 4.5, and the broken lines separating these into subgroupings indicate the content of the broader "level" categories derived by collapsing them.

Occupational Aspirations

Level of Status Goals. Several important interethnic differences of significance in the level of status goals exist among the males studied (Table 4.4). Most of these center around the Navajo youth. Substantially

Table 4.4 Interethnic Comparison of Occupational Aspiration Levels by Sex

Level of Aspiration	Males				Females			
	Navajo	Mex-Am	Black	Anglo	Navajo	Mex-Am	Black	Anglo
		%				%		
High	25	42	45	40	34	65	59	53
Intermediate	48	38	28	46	54	27	33	34
Low	19	7	12	7	9	3	6	11
No information	8	14	15	7	3	5	2	3
Total	100	100	100	100	100	100	100	100
Number	170	170	98	148	215	197	94	153

Table 4.5 Interethnic Comparison of Type of Occupational Aspirations Indicated by Sex

Type of Occupational Aspiration	Males				Females			
	Navajo	Mex-Am	Black	Anglo	Navajo	Mex-Am	Black	Anglo
		%				%		
1. High Professional	11	8	7	8	6	6	2	3
2. Low Professional	9	25	11	20	26	51	39	33
3. Glamor	5	9	27	12	2	8	17	16
4. Managerial	10	15	6	26	3	1	0	1
5. Clerical, Sales	0	3	3	1	41	20	23	29
6. Skilled	38	20	18	19	9	6	10	4
7. Operative	18	3	7	4	1	1	2	0
8. Laborer	1	4	5	3	7	2	4	4
9. Housewife	—	—	—	—	1	0	0	7
No information	8	14	15	7	3	5	2	3
Total	100	101	99	100	99	99	99	98

fewer of them had high level job goals and more of them, almost one out of five, had low level goals and intermediate ones as compared with males of other ethnic groups. The other three ethnic groups demonstrated quite similar profiles of goal levels, with about 40 percent of each aspiring to high occupational status and relatively small proportions holding low-level goals. Anglo males were more inclined to hold intermediate goals than blacks or Mexican Americans, and black youth had the second highest percentage of low-level aspiration.

The general pattern of interethnic differences observed among the four female ethnic groupings was quite similar to that noted above for boys (Table 4.4). Navajo girls were markedly less inclined to indicate high-level goals, had by far the highest proportion with intermediate-level goals, and the second highest percentage indicating low-level goals. Again, the Navajo girls obviously demonstrated a clear tendency to have lower-level occupational status goals than the others. The black and Mexican-American groupings of girls had surprisingly similar goal level profiles, with the exception of the fact that Anglo girls were more likely to have low-level goals. The Mexican-American girls had generally the highest-level occupational goals—more than two out of three of them held high goals and very few held low-level goals. In summary, the girls were clearly differentiated on ethnicity in reference to level of occupational status goals, with the Mexican-American girls having the highest level goals, the Navajo girls the lowest, and the other two ethnic types falling between them.

Some patterns of variation by sex are worth noting. Without exception, for every ethnic grouping a higher percentage of girls than boys held high occupational goals; conversely, with only one exception, fewer girls than boys within each ethnic type were judged to have low level aspirations. Also, girls were not as likely to withhold information in this regard as were boys.

Type of Occupational Aspirations. We now turn our attention to a comparison of the ethnic groupings in terms of more specific qualitative types of jobs, which can reveal intralevel variability and patterns of more particular qualitative variation among the four ethnic groupings (Table 4.5). Unquestionably there are significant and substantial interethnic differences observable in the particular types of jobs desired both within and across the more inclusive broad status level categories of jobs examined earlier.

Abstracting the most frequently selected job types aspired to by each ethnic type helps to show most of these patterns (Table 4.6). Among the male groupings, considerable variability exists in the two job types most often desired. Mexican-American boys disproportion-

ately selected the operative and skilled job types.
Blacks were the only ethnic type to frequently select
glamor jobs, and Anglo boys selected the managerial category much more often than others. On the other hand,
skilled blue-collar jobs were one of the two top choices
of every ethnic type. Turning our attention to the other
end of the continuum of selection, jobs least desired, we
again see ethnic variability (Table 4.5). Navajo youth
were less likely than others to desire low professional,
glamor, and laborer jobs. Mexican-American youth were
less likely to aspire to operative jobs than Navajo or
black boys. Black males were less likely to aspire to
low professional and managerial jobs than most of the
others.

Table 4.6   Interethnic Comparison of Types of Occupation Most
            Frequently Aspired to by Sex

	Navajo	Mexican Am.	Black	Anglo
A. Males				
Rank				
1	Skilled Worker(38)	Low Profes- sional(25)	Glamor(27)	Managerial(26)
2	Operative (18)	Skilled Worker(22)	Skilled Worker(22)	Low Professional (20)
				Skilled Worker(19)
B. Females				
Rank				
1	Clerical & Sales(41)	Low Profes- sional(51)	Low Profes- sional(39)	Low Professional (33)
2	Low Profes- sional(26)	Clerical & Sales(20)	Clerical & Sales(23)	Clerical & Sales (29)

Among the girls, much less ethnic variability was
observed than for boys in types of jobs aspired to. This
is due to the fact that two-thirds or more of the aspirations of each female grouping was accounted for by just
two types of jobs, low professional and clerical and
sales. The major ethnic differences observed among girls
are as follows:

1. All ethnic groupings except the Navajo selected
   the low professional category most often.
2. The tendency of certain ethnic groups to disproportionately select or avoid particular types of

jobs as follows:
a. Navajo girls markedly more often selected clerical and sales, and much less often aspired to glamor jobs.
b. Mexican Americans markedly more often selected low professional jobs.
c. Black girls more often selected glamor jobs, similar to what was observed for their male counterparts.
d. Anglo girls were the only ones to indicate a substantial proportion desiring marriage as a career.

Intensity of Aspiration. Intensity of aspiration pertains to the strength of desire associated with the occupational goal specified. Strength of intensity can vary independently of level of aspiration (high- or low-status goals). Due to the proportionately high rate of "no response" evidenced among Navajo youth, boys and girls, on this element of aspirations, comparisons of this ethnic group with others must be made with caution (Table 4.7).

Among the male groupings the Mexican Americans had markedly stronger intensity of aspiration than other ethnic types--60 percent of this grouping indicated strong intensity and only 3 percent demonstrated weak intensity. Black and Anglo youth demonstrated similar group profiles on strength of intensity; however, a substantially larger proportion of Anglo youth indicated strong intensity of desire. As was mentioned before, the Navajo boys differed markedly from others in their failure to respond to this question; 16 percent were classified as giving no response. Assuming this "no response" does not in fact cover respondents having "strong" desires for their occupational goals, the Navajo boys demonstrated, in general, much weaker intensity of aspiration than any other ethnic-sex grouping.

Among the female respondent groupings, the only ethnic difference of major significance centers on the Mexican American girls as compared with the others. The Mexican Americans demonstrated markedly stronger intensity of aspiration than others: 74 percent of the Mexican-American girls had strong intensity of desire for their occupational goals as compared with percentages ranging from 44 to 48 for the other three groupings. Black and Anglo female groupings demonstrated almost identical distributions on intensity of aspirations, and the Navajo differed from them only to the high rate of "no response" they evidenced.

In summary, black and Anglo boys and girls were quite similar in reference to the strength of intensity of their aspirations. Mexican-American boys and girls indicated generally stronger intensity of aspirations

Table 4.7 Interethnic Comparison of Strength of Intensity of Aspiration by Sex

Intensity of Aspiration	Males				Females			
	Navajo	Mex-Am	Black	Anglo	Navajo	Mex-Am	Black	Anglo
		%				%		
Strong (1, 2)	31	60	43	55	45	74	44	48
Intermediate (3, 4, 5)	41	36	43	36	38	20	40	43
Weak (6, 7)	12	3	7	7	5	3	11	8
No information	16	1	7	3	11	4	5	1
Total	100	100	100	101	99	101	100	100
Number	170	170	98	148	215	197	94	153

Table 4.8 Interethnic Comparison of Occupational Expectation Levels by Sex

Level of Expectation	Males				Females			
	Navajo	Mex-Am	Black	Anglo	Navajo	Mex-Am	Black	Anglo
		%				%		
High	26	33	28	25	25	43	33	28
Intermediate	41	32	36	46	63	27	37	29
Low	28	7	17	18	11	17	21	35
No information	6	28	19	12	2	12	9	9
Total	101	100	100	101	101	99	100	100
Number	170	170	98	148	215	197	94	153

Table 4.9 Interethnic Comparison of Type of Occupational Expectations by Sex

Type of Occupational Expectation	Males				Females			
	Navajo	Mex-Am	Black	Anglo	Navajo	Mex-Am	Black	Anglo
1. High Professional	8	5	8	5	2	2	1	2
2. Low Professional	15	21	10	14	22	35	25	21
3. Glamor	3	7	9	5	1	6	7	5
4. Managerial	9	13	6	21	3	1	2	1
5. Clerical Sales	3	1	8	1	46	22	28	21
6. Skilled Worker	28	19	21	24	14	4	7	6
7. Operative	22	2	11	7	2	0	3	1
8. Laborer	6	5	6	10	2	4	4	4
9. Housewife	0	0	0	1	2	13	14	31
No information	6	28	19	12	2	12	9	9
Total	100	101	98	100	98	99	100	101

relative to their counterparts of other ethnic types.
Navajo boys probably have, on the average, a weaker intensity of aspiration than any other ethnic-sex grouping
examined.

Occupational Expectations

Level of Status Expectations. The extremely high
rates of no response evidenced among Mexican-American
youth and, to a lesser extent, among black youth, hinder
valid general comparisons (Table 4.8). In fact, the ethnic variation in "no information" constitutes some of the
most substantial differences noted here. Still, one particular observation of marked ethnic variability stands
out and is not likely to have been influenced by the high
no response rate--the relatively high proportion (28 percent of Navajo boys having low level expectations. The
expected occupational status level profiles of the four
male groupings demonstrate that, as was the case for aspirations, Navajo boys generally anticipated lower-level
attainment than others. However, the differences were
not nearly as substantial in this case and were largely
due to the high proportion of Navajo boys with low-level
job expectations.
     A comparison of Tables 4.4 and 4.6 clearly demon-
strates a general lowering of status level as one moves
from aspiration to expectation. This is reflected in
both lower proportions expecting high-status attainment
and higher proportions anticipating low-attainment levels
as compared to aspirations.
     Ethnic variability in occupation expectation levels
among the girls studied are not as clearly patterned as
was the case in reference to their aspirations. Two-
thirds of the Navajo girls expected intermediate levels
of job attainment, and they had the lowest proportional
rate expecting low-level jobs. As was the case for aspirations, markedly more Mexican-American girls anticipated high-level job status, and, yet, a substantial
proportion (17 percent) expected low-level jobs. Black
girls and white girls again demonstrated similar profiles of expectation levels; however, white girls clearly
held somewhat lower level expectations on the average
than the blacks, or any other grouping for that matter.
The 35 percent of white girls with low-level status expectations stands out as a marked ethnic difference and
is due to the large number of girls expecting marriage as
a career, although they did not aspire to this (Table
4.9). As was the case for boys, expectations were generally lower than aspirations (Tables 4.4 and 4.6).
     Generally speaking, the patterns of sex differences
noted for aspiration level are also observable for expectation level, but they are not as substantial.
     Type of Job Expectations. It is clear that

substantial variability existed among the four ethnic
groupings for each sex in reference to the particular
kinds of jobs they anticipated (Table 4.9). The patterns
of difference observed here for boys are very similar to
those already reported for aspirations as can be seen in
viewing the most frequently anticipated job types (Table
4.10): Navajo boys are more likely to expect to be operatives, Mexican Americans are more likely to expect low-
prestige professional jobs, and Anglo boys to anticipate
managerial positions. Also, as was true for aspiration,
all groupings of boys indicated skilled workers among the
two most frequently expected types. However, for expectations, this tended to be the most frequent job type
mentioned; for aspirations it was more often the second.
Black youth demonstrated a markedly lower indication of
glamor type jobs for expectation than they did for aspiration; while they had the highest percent expecting
glamor jobs, they differed little from most other groupings in this regard. Black males also differed from
others in the following ways: they less frequently expected managerial and low professional jobs, and substantially more frequently expected clerical-sales jobs.
Anglo boys indicated a greater tendency to expect unskilled labor jobs and Navaho youth were less inclined to
expect glamor jobs. Mexican-American boys were markedly
less inclined than others to expect the operative type
and were markedly different from Navajo boys in this regard.

Table 4.10 Interethnic Comparison of Occupational Types Most
Often Expected by Sex

	Navajo	Mexican Am.	Black	Anglo
A. Males				
Rank				
1	Skilled Worker(28)	Low Profes-sional(21)	Skilled Worker(21)	Skilled Worker(24)
2	Operative (22)	Skilled Worker(19)	--------	Managerial (21)
B. Females				
Rank				
1	Clerical & Sales(46)	Low Profes-sional(35)	Clerical & Sales(28)	Housewife(31)
2	Low Profes-sional(22)	Clerical & Sales(22)	Low Profes-sional(25)	Clerical & Sales(21)
				Low Profes-sional(21)

84

As was true for aspirations, the patterns of ethnic
variability in types of expectation tended to be fewer
among girls than boys (Table 4.9). The patterns observed
are quite similar for expectations to those reported earlier for type of aspiration (Table 4.5). There was a
marked increase in proportion of girls anticipating marriage as a career, as compared with those aspiring to
this and, conversely, a marked general decrease in expectations for low professional type jobs as compared to
aspirations.

Certainty of Expectation. Certainty of expectation
represents the equivalent for status expectations of intensity of desire relative to status aspirations. Given
a specification of an occupational status anticipated,
this element represents the respondents' orientation or
feelings of certaintly about actually being able to
attain this job status.

A clear and consistent pattern of ethnic difference
exists in reference to relative certainty of occupation
expectation regardless of sex (Table 4.11). Navajo and
Anglo youth are much more likely to feel relatively certain about attaining their anticipated jobs than are Mexican Americans and particularly blacks. Black youth demonstrated the lowest rates of relative certainty of any
ethnic type, less than 1 out of 3 of the black females
and males felt relatively certain about attaining the
jobs they expected. Mexican-American girls, also,
approached this rate of indicated uncertainty.

Table 4.11 Interethnic Comparison of Proportion of Respondents
Feeling Relatively Certain about Attainment of
Expected Occupation

Ethnic Group	Male	Female
	----% "Very Sure" or "Sure"-----	
Navajo	58	49
Mexican American	45	38
Black	30	31
Anglo	50	54

Anticipatory Goal Deflection. Anticipatory goal deflection is conceptualized as a distinctly separate dimension of occupational status projections, representing
the relationship between status specifications for a subject's aspiration and expectation. Theoretically it is
postulated that a status aspiration is often modified in
light of the subject's realistic evaluation of impediments existing to prevent achievement of his status goal,
producing a status expectation that diverges from aspiration. We are interested in two aspects of this--

frequency of occurrence of anticipatory goal deflection and the direction of the divergence between aspirations and expectations in terms of prestige when it does occur.

Forty percent or more of each of the four ethnic groupings of teenage boys experienced anticipatory deflection from their occupational aspirations: the job they expected to attain was different from the one they desired (Table 4.12). Generally, the deflection was "negative" (expectations were lower than aspirations). Again, the high "no response" rate for occupational expectations is reflected here and seriously hinders making useful comparisons.[44] However, it does appear that Navajo youth experience less negative goal deflection than others. This seems reasonable given the fact that they had markedly lower aspiration levels than the others to begin with.

Among the female ethnic groupings, the Navajo youth experienced less goal deflection than others, only one-third of the Navajo girls as compared with about half of each other grouping experienced goal deflection. Most of the goal deflection experienced by all types of girls was negative in direction, as was observed for males earlier. For the most part, the Mexican-American, black, and Anglo girls were quite similar in the profiles on rate of occurrence and nature of anticipatory deflection, except that the Anglo girls experienced a markedly higher rate of negative deflection. This later observation is due to the large proportion of Anglo girls indicating marriage as a career expectation, while at the same time they aspired to a particular job career (Table 4.9).

In summary, relatively constant high rates of anticipatory deflection were experienced by all eight ethnic-sex groupings, ranging from 37 percent to 58 percent. For most groupings, roughly one out of every two respondents experienced deflection. In general, most of the deflection was negative in nature, meaning that expectations were lower than aspirations. The two substantial ethnic differences observed were the low rate of deflection experienced by Mexican-American girls (and to a lesser extent, their male counterparts) and the relatively high rate of negative goal deflection experienced by Anglo girls.

Male-Female Differences. While it was not our specific objective to examine patterns of sex variability in this analysis, male-female differences have been so striking in reference to some aspects of occupational status projections, we decided to focus on them briefly. Obviously, another perspective on ethnic variability can be gained in the process. Do the ethnic populations examined differ in the nature of the patterns of variability by sex observed?

Table 4.12 Interethnic Comparison of Rate and Nature of Occupational Goal Deflection Experienced by Sex

Type of Goal Deflection	Males				Females			
	Navajo	Mex-Am	Black	Anglo	Navajo	Mex-Am	Black	Anglo
	%				%			
None	58	47	42	59	63	52	48	48
Positive	14	9	10	4	12	7	14	4
Negative	18	15	25	24	22	26	29	39
No information	11	29	23	14	4	15	10	9
Total	101	100	100	101	101	100	101	100
Number	170	170	98	148	215	197	94	153

Table 4.13 Summary Overview of Proportions of Respondents Holding High and Low Level Occupational Aspirations and Expectations by Ethnic Type and Sex

	Males				Females			
	Navajo	Mex-Am	Black	Anglo	Navajo	Mex-Am	Black	Anglo
High Level								
Aspirations	25	42	45	40	34	65	59	53
Expectations	26	33	38	25	25	43	33	28
Low Level								
Aspirations	19	7	12	7	9	3	6	11
Expectations	28	7	17	18	11	17	21	35

The most dramatic patterns of sex variation observed were in terms of the specific qualitative types of jobs selected as the objects for aspirations and expectations (Tables 4.6 and 4.10). Results of Chi Square tests indicate that these differences are statistically significant at the 0 level of P; there is no probability they are due to chance. The pattern of differences is quite similar for both aspirations and expectations and remarkably consistent across all ethnic types. Many fewer girls than boys selected skilled, managerial, and operative job types for either type of status projection. Conversely, almost no boys selected clerical and sales jobs or expected to be housewives. Also, fewer boys than girls were inclined to select lower-prestige professional jobs. In summary, the patterning of differences by sex was very strong and consistent in reference to types of occupations indicated for aspirations and expectations. Some jobs (i.e., clerical and sales and lower professional) were apparently likely to be seen as "female jobs" by the respondents and others (i.e., skilled blue collar) as "male jobs."

In a summary overview of sex differences for each ethnic type relative to the other aspects of occupational status projections examined in our analysis, in only one case was a lack of ethnic variability in sex difference noted--in reference to aspiration level where girls were observed to consistently hold higher goals than boys. In reference to level of expected occupational status, Navajo and Mexican-American girls demonstrated higher levels than boys, Anglo youth demonstrated a converse pattern, and black boys and girls did not differ. Navajo and black boys and girls did not differ in the rate of anticipatory deflection experienced, but Mexican-American and Anglo youth demonstrated converse patterns of sex variability. Pertaining to intensity of aspiration, sex differences were not observed among black and Anglo youth; however, among both Mexican-American and Navajo youth, girls tended to have stronger desires for their specified goals than did boys. For degree of certainty about attaining expectations, only Navajo youth demonstrate a sex difference--males were inclined to be certain more often than were females.

In summary, significant sex differences existed for most aspects of occupational status projection, certainty of expectation being an exception. In some cases--types of jobs desired and expected and level of aspiration--the nature of sex differences were remarkably consistent and did not vary by ethnic type. On all other dimensions of occupational status projection, ethnic variability of some kind was observed. It should be noted that the patterns of sex differences observed to consistently cut across all ethnic types tended to be more substantial than those for which ethnic variability in sex patterning was noted. Also, black youth differed from other ethnic types in that they less frequently exhibited differential sex patterning.

SUMMARY OF FINDINGS

Interethnic Differences

Interethnic differences of considerable magnitude were observed in reference to every aspect examined for both boys and girls where valid conclusions could be drawn from the comparative analysis. A very consistent general pattern of ethnic variability could be observed in reference to the two dimensions of occupational aspirations examined. Navajo youth maintained the lowest level of aspiration and demonstrated the weakest intensity of desire for these among the four ethnic types. Conversely, Mexican-American youth generally had the highest and strongest intensity of aspirations among the groupings. In reference to level of aspiration, the most significant difference centered around the markedly lower level goals of the Navajo youth (Table 4.13). For males, the other three types differed little in this regard and for females, the Mexican-American girls clearly had higher level aspirations than others. Relative to intensity of aspiration, the major differences were centered around the markedly larger numbers of Mexican-American boys and girls having strong desire and, among the boys only, the relatively small proportion of Mexican-American youth with strong desire for their occupational goals (Table 4.14).

As was the case for aspirations, Mexican Americans demonstrated higher-level status expectations than others, and the Navajo youth had generally lower-level expectations. However, in reference to level of expectation, Anglo youth held expectations at a level similar to that of Navajo youth; in fact, Anglo females had low-level expectations much more frequently than any other grouping (Table 4.13). In reference to degree of certainty felt about actually attaining occupations anticipated, a general pattern of ethnic variability cutting across sex existed as follows: Navajo and Anglo youth were markedly more often relatively certain than were black youth and Mexican-American youth in an intermediate position. The most substantial general difference in reference to certainty of expectation was the much higher proportional rate of relative uncertainty experienced by black youth as compared with others (Table 4.14).

In general, except for Navajo youth, ethnic-sex groupings demonstrated divergence between their specific aspirations and expectation (Table 4.14). The one marked ethnic difference that seems clear in this regard is that Navajo youth experienced less anticipatory deflection

Table 4.14 Summary Overview by Ethnic Type and Sex on Proportions of Respondents Having Strong Intensity of Aspiration, Having Relative Certainty for Attainment of Expectation, and Experiencing Anticipatory Goal Deflection

	Males				Females			
	Navajo	Mex-Am %	Black	Anglo	Navajo	Mex-Am %	Black	Anglo
Strong Intensity of Aspiration	31	60	43	55	45	74	44	48
Relative Certainty of Expectation	58	45	30	50	49	38	31	54
Rate of Occurrence of Anticipatory Goal Deflection*	42	53	58	41	37	48	52	52

*Adequate comparison among males is hindered by high, variable no response rate.

than others; however, their rate of anticipatory goal deflection was still high, about 40 percent on the average
(Table 4.14).

Patterned ethnic variability by sex was found to exist in specific types of job careers emphasized or relatively ignored. Each ethnic type, particularly among
boys, seemed to have somewhat unique tendencies of this
sort as summarized in tabular form (Table 4.15).

Table 4.15 Disproportionation in Selection of Job Types Among
Respondents by Ethnicity and Sex

	Disproportionately Selected	Disproportionately Ignored
A. Boys		
Navajo	Skilled Worker	Low Professional, Glamor, Labor
Mexican Am.	Low Professional	Operative
Black	Glamor Jobs	Low Professional, Managerial
B. Girls		
Navajo	Clerical and Sales	Glamor Jobs
Mexican Am.	Low Professional	------------
Black	Glamor Jobs	------------
Anglo	Housewife	------------

These patterns of variability in type of job focus
have obvious implications for educators and youth counselors, which will be discussed later. Also, these particularistic ethnic preferences provide insight into ethnic differences concluded to exist in other respects.
For instance, it seems clear that the lower-level aspirations and expectations of Navajo boys and their lower
rate of anticipatory deflection is due largely to their
strong focus on skilled, blue-collar jobs. Obviously,
this is still a high aspiration of attainment for them
relative to the jobs of their parents; they are still
upwardly mobile. Similarly, the Anglo boy preference for
managerial jobs, coupled with our operational decision to
place this type in the "intermediate" status level rather
than the "high" level, influenced the results. For the
girls, the tendency for Anglo youth to expect to be
housewives largely explains their relatively "low level"
expectations and their high rate of anticipatory deflection.

In summary, the ethnic differences of greatest magnitude observed in the study involved particularistic

Table 4.16 Interethnic Comparison by Sex of Proportion of Respondents Indicating Different Intensity of Aspiration Scores

Intensity of Desire	Males				Females			
	Navajo	Mex-Am	Black	Anglo	Navajo	Mex-Am	Black	Anglo
	%				%			
1. (Strong)	11	18	9	18	8	11	13	14
2.	19	42	34	37	37	63	31	34
3.	19	17	10	20	19	12	15	26
4. (Intermediate)	14	10	17	12	12	5	16	12
5.	8	9	15	5	7	3	10	5
6.	6	2	5	3	4	2	5	5
7. (Weak)	7	1	2	3	2	1	5	7
No information	16	1	7	3	11	4	5	1
Total	100	100	99	101	101	101	100	100

Table 4.17 Interethnic Comparison by Sex of Proportion of Respondents Indicating Different Degrees of Certainty of Attainment of Occupational Expectation

Degree of Certainty*	Males				Females			
	Navajo	Mex-Am	Black	Anglo	Navajo	Mex-Am	Black	Anglo
	%				%			
1. Very Sure	18	14	11	20	18	5	16	24
2. Sure	41	31	18	30	32	33	15	31
3. Not Very Sure	29	39	51	30	44	45	48	28
4. Uncertain	5	9	7	11	5	10	14	12
5. Very Uncertain	2	6	2	1	1	5	3	2
No information	5	9	10	7	1	5	3	2
Total	100	99	99	99	102	101	100	101

*Categories #1 and #2 were grouped into a more inclusive "Relatively Certain" category for analysis and categories #3, #4, and #5 were grouped and labeled "Relatively Uncertain" for more reliability.

ethnic tendencies to select different specific types of
jobs as status objects for their status projections.
Significant differences existed by sex wtihin each
ethnic grouping studied for all aspects of occupational
status projection except certainty of expectation. What
is more, significant ethnic variability existed in the
nature of patterns of sex differences in reference to
occupational expectation level, intensity of aspiration,
and anticipatory goal deflection. On the other hand,
strong differences by sex observed for types of aspiration and expectation and level of aspiration were consistently patterned across all ethnic types: females
demonstrated generally higher level occupational status
projections.

Ethnic Similarities

Given the traditional inclination of sociologists to
look for and give predominant attention to intergroup
differences, and given the potential negative impacts of
easy interpretations of such differences for some groups
involved,[45] we would like to give special attention to
interethnic similarities observed. Often there are abstract patterns of similarity of major significance apparent in comparative analysis even when substantively
significant differences have been observed at more specific levels of analysis. Given the major patterns of ethnic variation that have already been noted, the following
general patterns of ethnic similarity existed:

1. For all ethnic types, a relatively small proportion indicated low-level aspirations and expectations indicative of a lack of desire for vertical
   social mobility.
2. Large proportions of all ethnic types desired
   high-level goals, almost or more than half in
   most cases, indicative of desires for dramatic
   upward mobility for most of these youth.
3. Similar patterns of similarity were observed
   among the ethnic groups in reference to expectations as those just noted for aspiration; however, proportions at the "high level" were smaller and those at the "low level" greater. This
   means that for all ethnic groups, expectations
   were generally lower than aspirations.
4. Very small proportions of each ethnic grouping of
   youth demonstrated weak intensity of aspiration.
   What is more, in almost every case a near majority of each ethnic-sex grouping indicated strong
   intensity of desire for their goals.
5. Large proportions of each ethnic group indicated
   "relative uncertainty" about attainment of their
   occupation expectations, ranging from 42 percent

of Navajo males to 70 percent of black boys and
girls.
6. Very large proportions of all ethnic groupings
   exhibited anticipatory goal deflection, ranging
   from 58 percent of black boys to 37 percent of
   Navajo girls.
7. In every case, most of the anticipatory goal deflection was negative; expectations were lower
   than aspirations.
8. Similar patterns of sex-specific choices for projections of long-term occupational status existed.

In summary, it can be concluded that at a more abstract level of consideration, a number of important general patterns of ethnic similarity existed, even given
the large number of more specific ethnic differences
noted.

DISCUSSION AND IMPLICATIONS

Empirical Implications

     Our findings lend support to and extend the scope of
generalization of the conclusion reached from the two
earlier tri-ethnic studies reported[46]--that substantial
ethnic differences exist in some aspects of the occupational status projections of rural youth. Of particular
importance in this respect is the identical patterns of
native American differences as compared with others observed in this analysis and from the more recent study
reported by Edington and his colleagues; in both cases
the native American youth demonstrated lower-level occupational aspirations and less anticipatory goal deflection than other youth.
     The New Mexico study[46] found that Mexican-American
youth and Anglo youth did not differ significantly in
level of occupational aspiration, while the earlier
(1966-67) Texas study found that Mexican-American youth
tended to have higher occupational aspirations than other
youth. Our results are similar to the earlier Texas
findings, which is not surprising since the data in the
Texas data set used here was collected on youth of the
same age and from the same study areas, as was the earlier Texas study. It may well be that Mexican-American
youth located in different areas do vary to some extent
in the general profiles of occupational projections they
maintain. Only more future research embracing more diverse study populations can provide evidence to determine
this.
     Our research findings are congruent with past re-
search in supporting the following generalizations about
the similarity of occupational projections of different

types of rural youth and metropolitan youth as well:

1. Most youth aspire to jobs indicative of upward
   social mobility; however, some ethnic minorities
   have higher aspirations than the dominant Anglo,
   some have similar levels, and some have lower
   levels.
2. Anticipatory occupational goal deflection rates
   are high and mostly negative in direction, because many--sometimes most--youth have status expectations lower than their aspirations.
3. Intensity of desire associated with occupational
   aspirations is strong, indicative of a high valuation of job goals relative to other life ends.
4. Large proportions of youth are relatively uncertain about actual attainment of the jobs they
   really expect to attain.

Also, although past evidence does not universally support
this, our evidence indicates that for all ethnic types,
sex differences in level and type of aspirations are
marked and persist to a substantial but lesser extent for
expectations as well. Significant sex variation is not
generally evident in the intensity of aspiration, certainty of expectation, or anticipatory goal deflection
relative to occupational status projections.
     Our study providses some relatively unique capabili-
ties for extending the accumulated empirical knowledge
in this problem area as follows:

1. By comparison with the earlier (1966-67) Texas
   study, our findings produce evidence that the
   nature and magnitude of ethnic differences may be
   changing. This certainly should indicate a need
   for caution in utilizing studies done at different points in historical time for interethnic
   comparative analysis.
2. Other studies have not examined interethnic patterns, in particular qualitative job types.
   Usually the responses are transformed into an
   ordinal scale and mean scores are used for interethnic comparison. Our findings clearly indicate
   unique ethnic patterns in aspirations and expectations for particular jobs, especially among
   males. Obviously future research might be reana-
   lyzed in such a way to look for this patterning.
3. Our examination of selection of particular qualitative types of jobs by sex also turned up significant sex-specific patterns of aspirations and
   expectations. Other research has not been analyzed or reported in such a way as to provide a
   basis for evaluating the scope to which this result can be generalized. At the same time, the

fact that the patterns observed cut across all of the four diverse ethnic types studied leads to the inference that this is a very general pattern, at least among rural youth.

The comparison of our findings, along with that of the other two studies of nonmetropolitan youth,[48] with the three studies of metropolitan youth reviewed earlier, suggests that ethnic variability exists to a much greater extent in rural areas and small urban places than in metropolitan areas. This is an intriguing finding, especially since we know from past research that metropolitan youth generally have slightly higher aspirations and expectations than do rural youth. Given the concern for "cultural pluralism" in our society today, future research would do well to examine how general and inclusive this tendency is.

Theoretical Implications

The findings from this analysis indicate quite clearly that both similarities and substantial differences existed among the four ethnic groupings of rural youth involved. It can be concluded that Merton's proposition that all kinds of youth in the United States have high success goals was apparently supported for these youth, if one takes into consideration the fact that most were disadvantaged and were projecting upward intergenerational mobility. At the same time, Navajo youth were clearly not aiming as high as other ethnic types of youth and had substantially more youth with low-level goals. Thus, it can not be concluded that all four ethnic groupings demonstrated similarly high aspirations for status attainment, at least in reference to occupation.

The relatively high rate of negative anticipatory goal deflection existing among all groupings produced expectations that were generally lower than aspirations, indicating support for the notion that many youth were "realistically" lowering their estimates of attainment relative to the status levels they desired. This offers strong evidence in support of the notion that many youth can and do differentiate between aspirations and expectations. Furthermore, it clearly implies that many perceive impediments--in themselves or in their opportunities--to achievement of their hopes and dreams.

The generally high level of intensity of desire these youth indicated for occupational aspirations, relative to other life goals, indicates that they place high personal value on achieving these goals. Yet many do not expect to achieve their aspirations; whether expectations match their aspirations or not, large proportions feel relatively uncertain about the actual long-run attainment of their anticipated lifetime job careers. It would be difficult to see how the cognitive model sketched above could lead to anything other than a rather dismal view of how well these youth are going to adjust as adult citizens in our society. Certainly it would seem to be both substantively and socially productive to begin examining through longitudinal panel studies whether or not, or to what extent, these cognitive orientations toward the future, and the fact of whether or not they are realized, influence personality adjustment, social adaptation, and a variety of aspects of social or antisocial behavior.

The ethnic differences observed here, and to some extent in the few other studies providing interethnic comparisons among rural youth, are very interesting in their potential theoretical significance. Certainly there is no clear linear pattern generally observed in reference to relative disadvantage, as much of the past theoretical reasoning and inferences from much past research (largely done on white youth) have proposed. If there was, Mexican-American youth would not have been equal to or higher than Anglo youth in level of aspiration and expectation as has been consistently found, nor would Anglo girls be more inclined to experience a greater downward modification of aspirations in terms of expectations than others, as we found they did. The fact that both black and Mexican-American youth maintained high intensities of desire for their occupational goals argues against the often proposed notion that ethnic minority youth are exposed to subcultural values different from those in the larger culture in such a way as to inhibit motivations for upward social mobility. This assertion is also challenged by two other observations from our analysis, indicating that the minority ethnic groupings are not exposed to a more traditional "folk" type culture than the Anglo (white) majority: the fact that Anglo females were more frequently oriented to the housewife role as a vocation than the others and the fact that the sex-linked ("sexist") patterns of status object selection for occupational aspirations and expectations cut across all ethnic types.

The strong patterns of ethnic differences observed in our study in reference to almost every dimension of occupational status projection, particularly in reference to the unique ethnic tendencies for selection of specific types of jobs among males, indicates some basis for arguing that ethnically distinct subcultures exist, at least in some respects. The evidence seems clear from our study that the ethnic groupings are apparently being exposed to different socialization influences in reference to vocation and in some ways are getting different estimates of their chances to attain the aspiration and expectations they have. We need a theoretical formulation of this process specifically oriented to variability in socialization processes in perceptions of social reliability that is more refined and elaborate than the simple, gross "subculture" thesis most of us rely on now. The notion of markedly different subcultures (ethnic minorities vs. the majority) does not hold up in light of our findings, at least in terms of the way it has been traditionally formulated. In addition, it tends to ignore the marked variability existing within each ethnic group and the dramatic sex-linked differences common to all ethnic groups.

It can be inferred from a comparison of our findings with those of the interethnic comparisons of metropolitan youth reviewed earlier[49] that metropolitan influences may produce a leveling effect on intergroup variability in occupational status projections. Does this mean that "ethnic distinctiveness" is or can be more easily maintained in rural and small urban settings? If so, why? These are questions requiring theoretical reflection and ones worthy of more research attention given their potential social import.

Policy Implications

It is sometimes hazardous for social scientists to speculate at length on the possible inferences of their research results for practical concerns. At the same time, we are convinced that our research, together with the other research reviewed here, offers some clear general guidelines for those who would set general social or educational policy for rural and minority young people, or for those desiring to assist these youths through educational or social action programs. We will briefly describe the more important of the implications we perceive.

First, it is clear that most of the minority youth studied, regardless of ethnicity, aspire strongly to be upwardly mobile and that many of them perceive this aspiration to be blocked to them. Consequently, most of these youth do not suffer from a lack of motivation for social mobility. Their problem is how to make the connection between their aspirations, a reasonable program for attaining them--including self-development, gaining social skills, and specialized training--and finding opportunities for occupational achievement. At the same time, there are some youth (particularly Navajo boys) who have low-level aspirations. Maybe some of these youth originally had high ambitions and later gave up as a result of perceived bleak possibilities. At any rate, it seems clear that because of the variability within ethnic groups and strong patterns of differences among them in terms of occupational orientations, counselors and teachers need to enlighten themselves on their students' own perceptions of career needs and help them work out individual programs to achieve their goals.

It seems abundantly clear that it would be a

strategic error to try to develop a general all-inclusive
program of career counseling and education to fit all
ethnic types of rural youth. Their orientations, perceived needs, and problems vary in patterned ways. For
instance, it seems clear that special attention needs to
be directed to helping black youth find ways to increase
their feelings of certainty about their future prospects
for occupational attainment. What are the alternatives?
To admit their prospects are bleak and can not be altered
or to have them adapt to anticipated failure in traditional ways? Of course, we might say the same for the
large proportion of all other ethnic groupings of youth
who experience this sense of uncertainty about their job
futures.

Just to agitate the feminists to some thought, we
might suggest that the relatively high proportions of
teenage girls expecting careers as housewives, even
though they desire job careers for the most part, indicates a need to encourage these girls to study home economics in school. Speaking more seriously, we think that
counselors ought to become aware of this patterned tendency for anticipated goal deflection and try to help the
many young women struggling through this problem in personal identification and traditional sex-role patterning.
The clear and consistent sex-specific patterning of occupational choices may indicate a need to open both girls'
and boys' eyes to possible job alternatives they are
apparently excluding almost automatically from consideration.

In summary, the schools, parents, youth workers,
program managers, and policy makers need to become more
sensitive to the subjective orientations of the individual young person if we are in fact concerned with helping
them to develop their full potential as productive human
beings. Labeling of aggregates of any youth--by ethnicity, for instance--will not do away with the complex diversity of any one grouping. It will only serve as a
lazy pretense to cover it.

NOTES

1. Robert K. Merton, Social Theory and Social
Structure, revised enlarged edition (New York: The Free
Press of Glencoe, 1957).
2. William P. Kuvlesky, Dave Wright, and Rumaldo P.
Juarez, "Status Projections and Ethnicity: A Comparison
of Mexican-American, Negro and Anglo Youth," Journal of
Vocational Behavior 1 (April 1971): 138.
3. William P. Kuvlesky and Rumaldo P. Juarez,
"Mexican-American Youth and the American Dream," in
Steven Picou and Robert E. Campbell, eds., Career Behav-
ior of Special Groups (Columbus, Ohio: Charles E.

Merrill, 1975), pp. 243-247; David E. Wright, Esteban
Salinas, and William P. Kuvlesky, "Ambitions and Opportu-
nities for Social Mobility and Their Consequences for
Mexican Americans as Compared with Other Youth," in de la
Garza, Kruszewski, and Arciniega, eds., Chicanos and
Native Americans: The Territorial Minorities (Englewood
Cliffs, N.J.: Prentice-Hall, 1973), pp. 43-44.

4. Talcott Parsons, The Social System (New York:
The Free Press, 1951).

5. Niles M. Hansen, Rural Poverty and the Urban
Crises (Bloomington: Indiana University Press, 1970);
H. Rodman, "The Lower-Class Value Stretch," Social Forces
42 (1963): 205-215; M. J. Yniger, "Contraculture and Subculture," American Sociological Review 25 (1960): 625-
635.

6. Kuvlesky and Juarez, "Mexican-American Youth,"
pp. 280-284.

7. Merton, Social Theory, pp. 131-139, 161-170.

8. Ibid., pp. 131-139, 171.

9. Celia S. Heller, New Converts to the American
Dream? Mobility Aspirations of Young Mexican Americans
(New Haven: College and University Press, 1971), pp. 13-
22; E. C. Hughes, "Anomalies and Projections," Daedalus
94 (1965): 1133-1147; I. Broom and N. D. Glenn, Trans-
formation of the Negro American (New York: Harper and
Row, 1965); J. W. Dyckman, "Some Conditions of Civic
Order in an Urbanized World," Daedalus, 1966.

10. Very recently evidence has been reported indicating ethnic variability might exist in the nature of
historical change in occupational status projections of
the three ethnic youth populations from Texas utilized in
this study. Comparison of results on analysis of patterns of historical change (1967-1973) for Mexican-
American sophomores (William P. Kuvlesky and Philip M.
Monk, "Historical Change in Status Aspirations and
Expectations of Mexican-American Youth from the Border
Area of Texas: 1967-1973," Paper presented at the annual
meetings of the Southwestern Sociological Association,
San Antonio, March 27, 1975) with those of black and
white sophomores over a similar six-year period (William
P. Kuvlesky and William D. Stanley, "Historical Change in
Status Aspirations and Expectations of Rural Youth: A
Racial Comparison," Paper presented at the annual meetings of the Texas Academy of Science, College Station,
March 4-6, 1976) indicate that the Mexican-American youth
changed little while black and Anglo youth experienced
and a marked decline in certainty of expectation. This
evidence should warn against comparison of ethnic types
studied at different points in time. It also indicates
that ethnic differences in status projections might well
be changing over time.

11. Kuvlesky and Monk, "Historical Change";
Kuvlesky and Juarez, "Mexican-American Youth"; Kuvlesky,

100

Wright, and Juarez, "Status Projections"; William P.
Kuvlesky and Katheryn A. Thomas, "Social Ambitions of
Negro Boys and Girls from a Metropolitan Ghetto," Journal
of Vocational Behavior 1 (April 1971): 177-178; Everett
D. Edington, Timothy J. Pettibone, and Jane E.
Heldt, Educational, Occupational, and Residence Aspirations and
Expectations for Rural and Minority Youth in New Mexico
(Las Cruces, N.M.: New Mexico State University, Depart-
ment of Educational Administration, December, 1975);
Harold B. Crawford, Educational and Occupational Aspira-
tions and Expectations of Galveston High School Students
(Dissertation, New Mexico State University, May, 1975).
     12. William P. Kuvlesky and Robert C. Bealer, "A
Clarification of the Concept 'Occupational Choice,'"
Rural Sociology 31 (September 1966): 265-76.
     13. Merton, Social Theory, pp. 132-133.
     14. Ralph H. Turner, The Social Context of Ambition
(San Francisco: Chandler Publishing, 1964).
     15. R. M. Stephenson, "Mobility Orientations and
Stratification of 1,000 Ninth Graders," American Socio-
logical Review 22 (1957): 204-212.
     16. Kuvlesky and Bealer, "A Clarification."
     17. George W. Ohlendorf and William P. Kuvlesky,
"Racial Differences in the Educational Orientations of
Rural Youth," Social Science Quarterly 49 (September
1968): 274-283.
     18. Merton, Social Theory, p. 171.
     19. Ohlendorf and Kuvlesky, "Racial Differences";
Kuvlesky and Juarez, "Mexican-American Youth."
     20. A. Antonovsky, "Aspirations, Class and Racial-
Ethnic Membership," The Journal of Negro Education 36
(1967): 385-393; Crawford, Educational and Occupational.
     21. Kuvlesky, Wright, and Juarez, "Status Projec-
tions"; Edington, Pettibone, and Heldt, Educational,
Occupational, and Residence.
     22. William P. Kuvlesky, "Rural Youth: Current
Status and Prognosis," in David Gottlieb, ed., Youth in
Contemporary Society (Beverly Hills: Sage Publications,
1973); Kuvlesky and Thomas, "Social Ambitions."
     23. Kuvlesky and Juarez, "Mexican-American Youth."
     24. Larry H. Stout and Everett D. Edington, "Navajo
Adolescents' Projections for Status Attainment: Occupation, Education, and Size of Income" (Paper presented at
the annual meeting of the Southwestern Sociological Association, Dallas, March 1974); Edington, Pettibone, and
Heldt, Educational, Occupational, and Residence.
     25. Kuvlesky and Bealer, "A Clarification"; Kuv-
lesky and Juarez, "Mexican-American Youth."
     26. Antonovsky, "Aspirations."
     27. Crawford, Educational and Occupational.
     28. Ibid.
     29. Ibid., pp. 64, 71.
     30. Ibid., p. 66.

31. Moises Venegas, "Educational and Occupational Aspirations and Expectations of El Paso High School Students" (Dissertation, New Mexico State University, 1973).

32. Edington, Pettibone, and Heldt, Educational, Occupational, and Residence.

33. Kuvlesky, Wright, and Juarez, "Status Projections."

34. Ibid., p. 142.

35. Ibid., pp. 142-144.

36. Kuvlesky and Monk, "Historical Change."

37. The south Texas and east Texas studies were carefully standardized and carried out by the same research team led by Dr. Kuvlesky. Larry Stout made several trips to meet with the research team at Texas A&M University to insure that comparability of instruments and data collection procedures existed between his study of Navajo youth and the Texas studies. The Navajo data was processed by the Texas A&M University research team under the co-direction of Stout and Kuvlesky.

38. Stout and Edington, "Navajo Adolescents'"' Kuvlesky and Monk, "Historical Change."

39. Stout and Edington, "Navajo Adolescents'," pp. 1-4.

40. Randall S. Dowdell, "Historical Change in Occupational Frames of Reference of Black and White Southern Youth, 1966-1972" (Paper presented at the Annual Meeting of the Rural Sociological Society, College Park, Md., August 1973).

41. Dimmit, Starr, and Zapata counties.

42. Past evidence on the status projections of the Texas youth involved here from earlier studies indicate that sex differences were often substantial. Kuvlesky, Wright, and Juarez, "Status Projections."

43. We established the "High" and "Low" levels first, utilizing conservative standards (i.e., skilled blue collar was not classified as "Low," and managerial was not classified as "High"). The "Intermediate" level was a residual category, including all other types. An argument can be made that the managerial category should have been placed in the "High" category; it traditionally is in studies of this type. Also, a question can be raised about the reasoning in including "housewife" in the "Low" status level. Questions have been raised before about this decision, and Kuvlesky has vacillated in the past on treatment of these responses. However, it is our judgment that in terms of the subjective meaning of housewife as an occupational career held by the girls studied, it is viewed as an equivalent to "unskilled labor." Note the tendency for the girls studied here to be deflected from aspirations for job careers to expectations to become a housewife.

44. High rate of no response, particularly among black male respondents, may not be simply interview

resistance. The high rate of uncertainty regarding actual occupational attainment (discussed later) may fit with this tendency. It could be that many youth are so uncertain about their actual career prospects or opportunities that they feel completely unable to project themselves a decade into the future.

45. Kuvlesky and Juarez, "Mexican-American Youth."
46. Kuvlesky, Wright, and Juarez, "Status Projections"; Edington, Pettibone, and Heldt, Educational, Occupational, and Residence.
47. Edington, Pettibone, and Heldt, Educational, Occupational, and Residence.
48. Ibid.; Kuvlesky, Wright, and Juarez, "Status Projections."
49. Crawford, Educational and Occupational; Venegas, "Educational and Occupational."

Interethnic Contact and the Emerging Sociopolitical Order

edited by Z. Anthony Kruszewski
and Richard L. Hough

5
Implications for Quality of Life on the Texas-Mexico Border: Interdependence, Inequality, and Sociocultural Diversity

Michael V. Miller

A relatively singular quality of life is said to have evolved within communities on the United States-Mexico border. Whereas Mexican frontier cities are often said to be "not really Mexico," so too are American border cities usually depicted as places far different from urban areas to the north. To a great extent, these notions are prejudicial and are grounded in the presumed "corrupting" influence of the close social, economic, and cultural contact generated with the nation of the other side. Frontier cities, for example, are often derided within Mexico for the role they play in servicing large numbers of American visitors; prostitution (believed to be rampant), a tourist-oriented commercial and night life, and an economy reflecting a "hustle" for American dollars all fuel this stereotype.[1] Conversely, U.S. border cities traditionally have been cast by northern observers as "sleepy little border towns" governed by "The Mexican Way of Life."

Stereotypes sometimes possess a kernel of validity, but they are caricaturizations, distortions which typically hinder the development of less facile yet potentially more useful explanations. Border cities are clearly different. This is due in part to the functions they serve for their respective nations and their physical isolation from national interiors. In light of the uneven level of development between the United States and Mexico, the border region also has attracted large numbers of people in search of economic betterment. Such migration has in turn structured a society marked by a large labor surplus and by extreme sociocultural diversity--and thus, has further underlined the uniqueness of the region.

This essay attempts to temper prevailing stereotypes by providing a broad overview of some of the more salient contemporary processes, patterns, and outcomes that contribute to a distinctive border society.[2]

A Working Definition of the Border

The border region has been defined in a variety of ways, largely dependent on the special focus and design of the definer.[3] One definition, commonly termed the "borderlands," includes all of the American and Mexican states that touch on the international boundary.[4] Still another specifies that the border region extends as far into the United States as the significant penetration of the Mexican people, their customs, and the Spanish languate, and, conversely, as far into Mexico as the everyday influence of the United States is strongly felt.[5] Without considering the validity of either definition, this essay employs a much more limited and traditional frame of reference, defining the border region as those county (in the United States) and *municipio* (in Mexico) jurisdictions lying directly on the international boundary.

Traversing the border region from west to east, one finds a certain amount of variability relative to topography, climate, and patterns of human settlement. The border region as a whole, however, given its prevailing dry climate and limited access to water resources, tends to be sparsely populated. Conurbation generally has arisen only in areas along well-established trade routes and/or in areas that have undergone extensive irrigation for agricultural purposes. This almost 2,000-mile-long corridor, in fact, contains less than thirty U.S. cities having more than 10,000 residents. Most of these are congregated at the extreme ends of the boundary: San Diego County, California, and in the major counties, Hidalgo and Cameron, of the Texas Lower Valley. Furthermore, the region possesses only seven standard metropolitan statistical areas (SMSAs), and four of these are in Texas. Of the remaining three, one is concentrated at San Diego--some fifteen miles removed from the border--and one is centered at Tucson, Arizona--approximately sixty-five miles from the boundary--while the residential community of the other, Las Cruces, New Mexico, is about forty miles from the border. Populations within Texas border SMSAs, on the other hand, are clustered either directly on or in close proximity to the boundary. The remainder of the U.S. border region tends to be characterized by vast amounts of open space in California, Arizona, New Mexico, and western Texas, and by scattered rural towns and villages in southwestern Texas. In light of the distinctive pattern of urban development along the Texas boundary, the remaining discussion will primarily focus on the Texas-Mexico border region.

The northern frontier edge of Mexico is likewise sparsely settled, containing only a few communities of any size. Population patterns here generally mirror those directly to the north, i.e., where significant population centers are found, they tend to be concentrated together along both sides of the boundary. However, there is one important and consistent exception to this pattern of joint dispersal. While common to the region has been the evolution of twin border cities, the Mexican twin in every case is much larger than its American counterpart (see Table 5.1). This imbalance ranges from the relatively small ratio between Ciudad Juarez-El Paso (where the former is only about one-third larger than the latter) to the differential of 40:1 exhibited between Mexicali and Calexico. Uneven patterns of growth, to be discussed later, largely reflect the blockage of northward migration at the border.

FUNCTIONAL INTERDEPENDENCE

Cities along the Texas-Mexico border tend to be isolated by long distances from population centers within their interiors. Laredo, for example, is about 150 miles from the nearest city of size, San Antonio, and over 300 miles from Houston. El Paso, the most isolated community on the Texas border, lies over 200 miles from "nearby" Albuquerque, New Mexico, and is 750 miles from Houston. Mexican border cities, likewise, share this phenomenon of isolation from the interior. Matamoros, the closest border city to the heavily populated central interior, is approximately 600 miles air distance from Mexico City.

Climate, topography, and the lack of stable water supplies have played important roles in structuring the isolation of the border region. Spanish settlement began along the Rio Grande during the late seventeenth and the early eighteenth centuries in the predominant form of colonial military outposts and missions. Literally on the frontier of European colonization, they grew little and held little national significance until the establishment of the border at the Rio Grande with the Mexican-American War (1846-1848) and Treaty of Guadalupe-Hidalgo. With the boundary redefinition, the small Mexican communities, primarily oriented to serving expansive ranching hinterlands, became "border towns" and, in a number of cases, U.S. military forts and villages soon developed across from them. Where no restrictions to trade and human movement had existed prior to this, the river suddenly became an international barrier and the contemporary relevance of the border region was structured.

Most cities having sizable populations in the border region largely seem to exist if for no other reason than that they are on the boundary. This boundary serves as a break in transportation by constituting a barrier to the free flow of products, services, and people. Thus, a major function of border cities lies in the administration of this barrier and the regulation of international

Table 5.1 Populations of Major U.S.-Mexico Twin Cities, 1940-1970

Mexican-U.S. Twins	1940	1950	1960	1970
Matamoros, Tamps.	15,699	45,737	143,043	186,146
Brownsville, TX	22,083	36,066	48,040	52,522
Reynosa, Tamps.	9,412	34,076	134,869	150,786
McAllen, TX	11,877	20,067	32,728	37,636
Nuevo Laredo, Tamps.	28,872	57,669	96,043	151,253
Laredo, TX	39,274	51,510	60,678	69,024
Piedras Negras, Coah.	15,663	27,578	48,408	46,698
Eagle Pass, TX	6,459	7,267	12,094	15,364
Ciudad Juarez, Chih.	48,881	122,566	276,995	424,135
El Paso, TX	96,810	130,485	276,687	322,261
Nogales, Son.	13,866	24,480	39,812	53,494
Nogales, AZ	5,135	6,153	7,286	8,946
Mexicali, B.C.	18,775	64,658	281,333	396,324
Calexico, CA	5,415	6,433	7,992	10,625
Tijuana, B.C.	16,486	59,950	165,690	340,583
San Ysidro, CA*	--	--	--	--

*Separate data are not available for San Ysidro as its population is included with that of San Diego.

SOURCE: Abstracted from Oscar J. Martinez, Border Boom Town: Ciudad Juarez Since 1948. Austin: The University of Texas Press, 1978.

movement for their respective nations.[6]

Due to the functional role of the border coupled with long distances to interior population centers, twin Mexican and Texas border cities have become highly inter- dependent with one another over time.[7] Indeed, they are often accused of being more integrated with one another than they are with their own nation. One basis for in- terdependence is structured on the heavy daily exchange of people.

Texas employers in agriculture, industry, construc- tion, and trade hire great numbers of Mexican border res- idents who commute on a daily or a lengthier periodic basis to work across the river. In fact, Mexican border cities, in large part, serve as vast labor colonies for those communities just north of the boundary.[8] Such workers--green-card commuters, U.S. citizens who choose to live south of the boundary, and illegal aliens (visi- tation pass abusers and those without documents)--find employment which would either be unavailable in Mexico or, if available, would pay considerably much less than that which they earn on the Texas side. On the other hand, Texas employers gain definite advantages from this employment as Mexicans (particularly illegal aliens) re- portedly tend to work harder with fewer complaints and often at significantly lower wages than would American residents.[9]

While Texas border businesses are highly dependent on Mexican workers and such workers, in turn, are keenly dependent on this employment, many commercial establish- ments along both sides of the border rely to an extreme degree on transactions with residents of the other side. Due to such factors as price, quality, and general availability, various goods tend to be purchased on one side of the boundary or the other--although the trading advantage has long been with Texas merchants and has un- doubtedly grown in recent years given Mexico's even higher rate of inflation. Mexicans typically cross to buy certain groceries and a host of manufactured items (appliances, autos and auto parts, clothing, etc.).[10] U.S. residents traditionally have obtained better buys on various agricultural products, crafted goods, and personal services--and more recently, petroleum--in Mexi- can border cities. Tourists from the interiors of both nations form an important sector contributing to the regional economy.

The dependence of Texas commercial interests on in- ternational trade is graphically evident whenever poli- cies serve to sharply curtail border crossings or trans- border spending. Operation Intercept, for example, launched by the Nixon administration in the late 1960s to allegedly stem drug smuggling, accomplished little more than reducing border vehicular traffic to a trickle and outraging border businessmen over the severe loss of trade. Likewise, the Mexican peso devaluations of 1976, which dramatically reduced the buying power of Mexican shoppers in the United States, provoked a general downturn in the local economy and critically affected many regional establishments--causing severe drops in business, layoffs, and in some cases, closings.[11]

Although transborder commerce is voluminous, the boundary importantly divides the natural trading territory which would otherwise be available to border retailers and wholesalers. Tariffs and duties, devised in Mexico City and Washington, D.C., to protect indigenous production and commercial interests, limit the kinds and amounts of goods that can either be imported or purchased and brought back across the river. Much of the important history of this region, in fact, concerns the periodic, and often reciprocal, tightening and loosening of trade restrictions and the concomitant social consequences wrought on border society.[12] In the face of this barrier, smuggling has evolved as a significant border institution allowing for a freer exchange of commerce. Many of the richest families on either side of the river, indeed, owe their wealth to this lucrative practice. Continuing on a grand scale, smuggling is also commonplace, engaged in by much of the local population on a small and everyday basis. Goods subject to duty, either in kind or amount, may be had much less expensively with the calculated and generally minor risk of detection at crossing or with payment of *mordida*.[13]

While life quality in the Texas region is importantly affected by economic interdependence with Mexico, it is also significantly influenced in other ways by virtue of location at the border. Population pressures mounting along the northern frontier invariably tend to spill over and affect local job markets. Many public services and facilities are, in part, employed in behalf of the thousands of Mexican residents who daily commute across the river to work, shop, or visit. Brownsville's current population of 80,000, for example, is augmented during any given weekday by an estimated "floating" population of 30,000. This increment is not incorporated in federal disbursement formulas based on residential census counts. Thus, local services and facilities (such as traffic control and police protection, street maintenance, park development and upkeep, etc.) tend to be grossly inadequate, unless otherwise financed by additional local revenues. On the other hand, from a Mexican point of view, it may be argued that the border serves as a highly selective barrier, allowing Texas economic interests to profit through the largely unidirectional flow of labor and trade, yet, in the main, containing the greatest public costs of this burgeoning labor reserve in Mexican border cities.

Finally, health and environmental problems generally

(to paraphrase an oft-repeated local adage) "do not respect international boundaries." Given the close physical proximity of twin border cities, problems that develop on one side of the river--e.g., disease epidemics, mosquito infestations, air pollution, etc.--will periodically carry over and have similar negative consequences on the other side. Binational planning, policy formation, and implementation, therefore, are crucial for the resolvement of these problems, as well as for such other needs as crime control and bridge construction. However, an integrated approach, coordinating applied programs on both sides of the border, is extremely difficult to effect, at least within the framework of formal authority structures.[14] Border cities, thus, are frequently confronted by problems over which they may have only limited jurisdictional control, and consequently, little hope for resolution.

INEQUALITY, MIGRATION, AND GROWTH

Life along the border is fundamentally shaped by the extreme differences in economic development between the United States and Mexico. Nowhere else in the world do two nations at such disparate levels of industrialization, productivity, and wealth share a common political boundary. Moreover, the border region, in itself, concretely focuses and manifests these rather abstract national inequalities.

Texas border cities and counties rank as the poorest within the United States. Three of the four Texas border SMSAs--Brownsville, Laredo, and McAllen--persistently have fallen at the bottom of U.S. metropolitan areas in terms of per capita income; El Paso has been the lowest among the nation's larger urbanized areas. In 1970, approximately 40 percent of all individuals and families in the three former SMSAs were poor according to federal criteria.[15] Poverty on the rural Texas border was of even greater magnitude.[16] In many respects, the scale of severe conditions existing there--dilapidated housing, bad health, inadequate medical care, etc.--has made the region more comparable to a developing nation than to the United States.

The extreme privation of the Texas side, however, constitutes relative prosperity when compared with the far greater public and human poverty prevailing immediately across the boundary along the Mexican frontier. Per capita incomes in border *municipios* generally are less than half the amount of the already meager average for Texas border counties. Despite this pattern, however, the northern frontier reflects relatively affluent conditions when compared with other places in Mexico. Incomes opposite the Texas border, for example, tend to be approximately twice the national Mexican average.[17]

In addition to higher incomes at the border, the general
quality of life is reportedly better here than for the
nation as a whole. Studies suggest that housing is less
crowded and of higher quality,[18] health conditions are
better,[19] and a greater proportion of the public is oriented to the style of a mass-consumption society.[20]
This does not imply by any means that most residents
share in this relative affluence or that severe inequalities are not present on the frontier. By any standard of
evaluation, poverty remains pervasive and extreme within
these cities.[21]

While the Mexican economy has undergone rapid industrial development and growth since 1940, such expansion
has not kept pace in providing sufficient employment
opportunities either for those attempting to enter the
labor market or for those being displaced from an agrari-
an sector in the process of technical and organizational
revolution. With a yearly birth rate of 50 per 1,000
population during the 1970s, Mexico's annual growth rate
of 3.5 percent was the highest in the western hemisphere.
Extreme growth coupled with extensive changes in agricultural production, which often turned labor-intensive
holdings into scientifically operated and mechanized
agribusiness units, have resulted in serious problems of
widespread unemployment and underemployment. For example, the average number of days worked per year between
1950-1960 among farm workers decreased by about half.[22]
Thus, with severely reduced rural employment, great numbers of people have moved to the cities; this migration
has been primarily directed toward Mexico City and the
cities along the northern frontier.

Recent population growth on the frontier has been
explosive as Mexican border towns increased by over 1,000
percent between 1940-1970 (see Table 5.1). The greatest
growth transpired just south of the California boundary,
although cities across from Texas expanded by 700 percent. Ciudad Juarez, e.g., grew from a city of 49,000 to
one in 1970 of 424,000. Matamoros, a village of 16,000
in 1940 had become thirty years later a compacted metropolis of 186,000 (by 1980, the city contained an estimated
270,000 people). While the most significant growth for
frontier cities occurred between 1940-1960, it continued
at a high rate through the 1960s and appears to have
again skyrocketed over the past decade.[23]

The massive flow of people from the interior to the
border, in great part, reflects the push factors of high
rates of natural increase and agricultural displacement.
Migration to the region, in turn, has been abetted by
certain important pull influences. Improved transportation networks linking the border with the interior have
facilitated movement, and the attraction of presumed
opportunities on the border and in the U.S. interior has

provided the impetus. In addition, two specific programs appear to have played significant roles in stimulating northward movement. The Bracero Program, jointly administered by the United States and Mexican governments in response to a reputed manpower shortage in American agriculture, sponsored the movement of several hundred thousand workers into the Southwest throughout the 1940s, 1950s, and early 1960s. This program served to promote general awareness of the greater economic opportunities available north of the boundary and the potential to be had with migration. An undetermined but significant number of *braceros* chose to settle along the border at the termination of their involvement in the program.

Ostensibly in response to the exorbitant rate of frontier unemployment (estimated in the 1960s at around 40 percent) allegedly caused by *bracero* settlement, Mexico opened up the border region in 1967 to foreign industry. The Border Industrialization Program (BIP) has since provided lucrative inducements for American corporations in terms of extremely low wage scales, high rates of worker productivity, and various other incentives present in Mexican border cities.[24] Materials and parts are crossed over from the U.S. side duty-free, assembled and/or processed, and then sent back north across the boundary with only the value added by this phase taxed. Normally, much smaller plants (for this "twin plant" system) located on the American side of the border stage materials to the south, receive assembled products, and then ship finished goods northward to interior U.S. distribution points. As of 1980, approximately 110,000 Mexican frontier residents (mostly women) were employed in over 500 in-bond plants operating under BIP auspices.[25] Ciudad Juarez, and to a lesser extent, Matamoros, Tijuana, and Nogales, are the primary centers of *maquiladora* production.[26] A very strong component of *maquila* activity is the assembly of electrical machinery and appliances under such firms as RCA, Zenith, and Motorola; shoes and clothing assembly constitute a second major source of employment.

Extensive *maquiladora* proliferation has had important consequences for economic development not only on the Mexican side of the boundary, but also on the U.S. side. Perhaps just as importantly, however, it appears that the expectations for employment generated by the location of these plants have provoked exceptionally high rates of migration from the interior to the border during the 1970s. *Maquiladoras* have heightened the economic disparities between the frontier and the general interior. In so doing, they have further elevated the mystique of the region for the Mexican masses; the northern frontier has come even more to be considered as an area possessing tremendous opportunity wherein one can obtain work and high wages. Unfortunately, the recent rate of job creation along the border, although high, has not been sufficient to absorb more than an infinitesimal amount of these migrants so desperately in search of work.[27] Thus, for many migrants, the "promised land" does not materialize; jobs are too few in number and competition for them is vicious. Some, in failing to find work, return to their homes in the interior. On the other hand, it also appears there are many who do not share the option of return migration; they have sold all property that they might have had to journey to the border for anticipated work.[28] Recent migratory movement to the border has therefore eventuated in large numbers of people piling up along the boundary. For these people (amassed in already congested cities and in suburban squatter settlements) without work, ill-fed, and ill-housed, seeking employment at any wage just across the boundary usually constitutes the only viable alternative.[29]

While Mexican frontier cities registered spectacular population growth between 1940-1970, Texas border cities experienced significantly large increases but in no way as much as that of their Mexican counterparts (see Table 5.1). During this period these cities grew 380 percent--a figure just over half the rate of growth across the river. Up until the 1970s, the most significant decade of growth was 1950-1960; Texas border cities had an average increase of 75 percent. Within that decade, most of the increase was due to the phenomenal growth of El Paso as this community doubled in size. In the following decade, 1960-1970, Texas cities expanded by a rate of only 15 percent. Current estimates suggest, nevertheless, that the 1980 census will show these cities to have attained growth rates since 1970 either commensurate to or behond those of the 1950s. Between 1970-1977, e.g., Brownsville reportedly grew from 52,000 to 80,000; El Paso from 322,000 to 391,000; Laredo from 69,000 to 83,000; and McAllen from 38,000 to 53,000.[30]

Recent population expansion along the Texas border basically reflects emergent industrialization generated through BIP combined with general sunbelt development dynamics. On the Mexican frontier, BIP has significantly expanded consumer demand and has raised aggregate income. More employment in Mexico has meant more Mexican spending on the U.S. side. BIP employees spend approximately half their wages in American border cities, and much of the general frontier income stimulated by BIP development has spilled over to the United States.[31] This multiplier effect has enhanced trade and job creation on the U.S. side. Furthermore, BIP has directly expanded employment north of the border through its American "twin" operations--although they employ proportionately few workers in comparison to the number employed in Mexico. Most importantly, however, has been the indirect role BIP has

played in structuring industrial expansion on the U.S.
side through opening up the border region to the American
business community. Transportation diseconomies and
long-standing prejudices against the region based on its
isolation, proximity to a foreign nation, and assumed
backwardness have been mitigated to an extent in light of
rising utility, labor, and tax costs in the north. Many
firms, after weighing the feasibility of a Mexican location, have established primary operations on the American
side of the boundary. Given the observation of a strong
"business climate"--i.e., large labor surpluses, low prevailing wage levels, Texas "right to work" laws, and the
presence of few effective unions--these corporations discovered they could enjoy many of the benefits of the Mexican frontier without paying many of the possible costs
involved in transborder operations. Still other corporations, prevented from BIP participation by federal trade
regulations, found they could likewise profit by locating
plants near the Mexican border.

Over the 1970s, ratios of manufacturing income to
income derived from all sources increased significantly
in every Texas border SMSA, with the exception of El
Paso.[32] Brownsville has experienced the greatest recent
industrial growth; between 1967 and 1978, approximately
8.000 manufacturing and 5,600 nonmanufacturing jobs were
created.[33]

Historically, Texas border cities have served as key
entry points for Mexican immigrants. First and second
generation Mexican immigrants, according to the 1970 census, constituted half of Laredo's total population, and
across other border cities, 40 percent or more of the
total. Residence for some is tenuous--the border indeed
becomes a highly permeable membrane--whereby their exact
location on either side of it at a given time is determined by any number of circumstances, including legality
of status and detection, and changing economic opportunities and family situations. Fluidity across the border
tends to be facilitated by family relationships spanning
the boundary.[34] While relocation for many has been temporary or has merely involved movement of short distance
from long-standing residence along the Mexican frontier,
increasing numbers of other immigrants have been drawn to
the border from the Mexican interior.[35] For some, these
communities represent, in effect, "Ellis Islands"--only
temporary stopovers along the way to more permanent
points of relocation in the U.S. interior.[36] Several
years' residence or less in these communities may provide
enough time to obtain necessary savings, develop a working understanding of the English language and American
culture, or consolidate family units fragmented by economic or legal problems. Still other immigrants find
stable location in Texas cities.

However, the Texas border region has also been

characterized by two important patterns of out-migration.
One pattern is cyclical and seasonal, while the other involves more or less permanent relocation to the U.S. interior. Regional out-migration, whether it be temporary,
as in the case of agricultural workers, or permanent, has
been generally a direct consequence of employment-related
factors. Historical employment limitations include: a
restricted number of higher-status jobs that would provide for economic mobility, the seasonal nature of most
jobs in the agricultural sector, and a regional employment structure reflecting comparatively depressed wage
scales.[37]
    These structural problems have been exacerbated by a
large surplus labor supply. Border city unemployment
rates are typically twice the national average. This
abundant labor reserve emanates from two phenomena--Mexi-
can work-force participation and high regional fertility
rates.
    Although precise data are not available, nonresident
Mexicans make up a significant share of workers in every
Texas border city. In 1978, approximately 15,000 green-
card commuters and a similar number of U.S. citizens residing in Mexico regularly crossed the river to work.[38]
A minimum of one-fifth of the Brownsville area work
force, for example, resides in Matamoros.[39] These figures for both Brownsville and the region do not include
members of the shadow work force of undocumented aliens--
commuters who commonly work in local agriculture, construction, restaurants, motels, private households, and,
more recently, in electronics and garment assembly
plants.
    Out-migration additionally has been stimulated by
high rates of natural increase. Texas border city birth
rates are much higher than urban Texas and national aver-
ages--typically almost twice as high. Between 1960-1970
young adult males entering the regional labor market out-
numbered available job opportunities by a general margin
of three to one.[40] In the face of such demographic pressures compounded by commuter work-force participation,
out-migration to the north has been a widespread functional necessity for many residents.
    Seasonal migration is one such response. Although
some temporarily leave the region for construction and
industrial work in such cities as Corpus Christi and
Houston, by far the greatest number of seasonal migrants
are involved in agriculture. In 1975, the Texas farm
migrant population was composed of approximately 375,000
workers and family members. The fifteen counties along
the Mexican border contained almost half of this total--
with the highest concentration living in the two counties
of the Lower Valley, Cameron and Hidalgo. These two
counties alone accounted for approximately 30 percent of
all Texas migrants, and about one-tenth of the U.S.

migrant farm population.41

Permanent out-migration from the region has also been of important significance. Between 1960-1970, for example, Texas border SMSAs experienced deficits in net migration, ranging from 30 percent in Brownsville to 9 percent in El Paso. Migration deficits were particularly acute among young Mexican-American men (20-29 years of age) as this group underwent a decline of approximately 50 percent in Brownsville, McAllen, and Laredo SMSAs, and a decline of over 25 percent in El Paso. The study from which these findings were drawn concludes by saying,

> On the Texas side of the border large numbers of men becoming of labor force age by 1970 had moved away from the region during the decade. There is little doubt that many did so because of a lack of employment opportunities . . . The age structure of the Texas-Mexico border region is such that it will be likely to stimulate migration for many years.42

Post-1970 growth dynamics along the Mexican border, on the other hand, suggest the alteration of predominant patterns of demographic movement. With recent industrialization, Texas border cities have experienced far greater in-migration from Mexico and from other regions of the United States, and have probably undergone a decline in their traditionally high rates of out-migration. By 1979 in Brownsville, for example, almost 40 percent of all households were headed by those who had moved to the city during the decade.43 Migration from Mexico has been significant: one-fifth of recent Brownsville in-migrants had come from Mexico, and the number of immigrant children entering border school systems increased by threefold over pre-1970 yearly averages.44 However, far larger populations from the U.S. interior have been drawn to Texas border cities with recent economic growth. Some of these people have been transferred to the border to manage new industries; others, who had left the region in years past to find better employment to the north, have returned with the expansion of local opportunities.

SOCIOCULTURAL DIVERSITY AND INEQUALITY

Given location next to Mexico and the nature of regional migration dynamics, life quality within Texas border cities is importantly influenced by high levels of sociocultural diversity. Ethnicity serves as a general organizing principle for many crucial differences, but numerous intraethnic distinctions contribute as well to the varied social mosaic of border society.

In gross terms, the Texas border region is populated by essentially two ethnic groups--white Americans principally of distant European extraction and people of

Mexican origin or ancestry. Blacks form only a minute minority in all border cities, ranging from a 1970 high of 2 percent in El Paso to a low of .2 percent in Brownsville. White Americans, although derived from a diversity of ethnic groups, are popularly referred to in the region as "Anglo Americans." While border society has homogenized these people into a group of emergent ethnicity, complementary forces have structured a contrasting ethnic category locally referred to as "Mexican" or "Mexican American"--despite differences in national citizenship, tenure of residence, styles of life, and individual preferences for labels of ethnic identification.

People of Mexican origin numerically predominate in the border region. In fact, in no other area in the United States, do Mexican Americans reside in such concentrated proportions. Although comprising approximately 5 percent of the U.S. population and about 20 percent of the Texas total, Mexican Americans are the majority in every Texas border region community. This majority status within the larger cities ranged from a 1970 high of 86 percent in Brownsville and Laredo, to a low of 58 percent in El Paso. Excluding the very small number of black residents, the residual population is composed almost totally of Anglo Americans.

Within the border region, important social class differences are superimposed along lines of ethnicity. Anglo Americans generally tend to be of relatively high educational attainment, middle and higher status occupations, and middle and high incomes. While a number of Mexican Americans are found within the ranks of border city elites and there is now presence of a developing Mexican-American middle class, most Mexican Americans--according to standards prevailing in the United States--are of poverty or near-poverty status. Only in El Paso, where about one-fourth of the 1970 Mexican-American population was poor, is there divergence from this pattern.[45] Mexican Americans thus form a numerical majority along the border but they are, for the most part, a social minority--one grossly overrepresented within the lowest socioeconomic strata. For example, in the poorest area of urban Texas, indeed the poorest area in the United States, Hidalgo (McAllen) and Cameron (Brownsville) counties, Mexican Americans in 1970 constituted 70 percent of all families, yet accounted for over 90 percent of all poor families.[46] Moreover, recent evidence suggests that ethnic inequalities may be widening, although aggregate community income expanded greatly during the 1970s. By the end of the decade, 45 percent of all Mexican Americans in Brownsville were poor, while only about 1 percent of the Anglo population fell below the poverty threshold.[46]

Consequently, the impoverishment of the region commonly has been translated as "Mexican-American poverty,"

with the onus placed on the reputed shortcomings of this
group. Early studies conducted along the rural Texas
border and in rural New Mexico reported that low Mexican-
American socioeconomic attainment was primarily a function of a set of shared cultural traits.[47] Differences
were found among not only the more obvious and superfi-
cial manifestations of culture such as food, housing,
celebrations and rites of passage, but also among fundamental patterns of thought and social organization. Values of local people were said to include fatalism, emo-
tionalism, dependency, familism, traditionalism, etc.
These traits, among many others, were said not only to be
contrary to hypothesized Anglo-American value configurations, but also directly incompatible to the pursuit of
upward mobility in contemporary American society. Accordingly, achievement would only be facilitated if Mexican Americans would reject these traditional folk values
and, instead, embrace Anglo-American ways of thinking and
acting. Acculturation was thus presented as the broad
panacea for poverty.

Over the past decade, such arguments based on culturally deterministic explanations have largely been dis-
credited, at least within academic circles. One line of
attack has been mounted by various scholars arguing that
these early rural studies tended to be ethnocentric,
failed to consider externally imposed factors, and were
inappropriate for deriving generalizations about Mexican
Americans since most live in highly urbanized rather than
rural places.[48] Likewise, they assert that such traits
are generally a consequence of deprivation instead of its
cause. Subsequent research investigating status aspirations among lower-class Mexican-American youth has also
tended to counter cultural arguments by showing that such
youth tend to be even more oriented to American success
goals than are their black and Anglo counterparts.[49]

Furthermore, cultural determinism recently has been
challenged by a perspective which states that the poverty
of Mexican Americans is primarily due to a highly unjust
and racist social system external to the ethnic community. Poor Mexican Americans are thought to be a "colo-
nized people," exploited for their labor power, and vic-
timized in various institutional realms by the dominant
Anglo-American society. Cultural and behavioral aspects
predominantly internal to the ethnic community and potentially impeding group achievement tend to be either ignored or minimized. Rather, the focus is on historical
themes of Anglo-American conquest and discrimination,
and contemporary patterns of social, economic, and political exploitation. Writings based on the "internal colonialism" concept perhaps best exemplify this perspective.[50]

Without further addressing the putative relationship
between culture and poverty, it must be stressed that the

border region is marked by significant variations in language-use patterns and cultural orientations. To a great extent, this heterogeneity is a reflection of the close physical proximity of Mexico and the region's function as a "receptacle" for migrating populations. While normal processes of linguistic and cultural assimilation are operant along the border and thus serve to adapt the generations in varying degrees to the dominant mainstream, border cities undergo a constant infusion of Spanish-speaking people of Latin cultural background. This, according to D'Antonio and Form,[51] in observing El Paso, has led to the creation of a "permanent culture of ethnicity" within border communities.

Language forms common among border people include English, Spanish, and border Spanish. Each tends to predominate among specific subpopulations. Regional Anglos almost universally subscribe to English as their dominant language. Relatively few Anglo Americans, however, are able to speak Spanish beyond a rudimentary level. Less than 20 percent of Anglo adults in Brownsville, for example, reported bilingual fluency.[52] On the other hand, a substantial portion of regional Mexican Americans have little or no English capability (approximately 45 percent of all Mexican-American adults in Brownsville). Thus, Texas border cities contain significant numbers of people who are unable to speak directly to each other. Given their numerical minority status, this presents obvious daily difficulties for Anglo Americans. Yet, their problems are relatively minor when compared to those of Mexican-American residents whose access to, and participation in, dominant economic and political institutions is minimized by language differences.

The picture of cultural traditionalism described earlier clearly has only limited applicability today. While traditionalism may serve as a polar extreme on the cultural continuum, most regional Mexican Americans undoubtedly would not be found at this end point. Indeed, given such factors as socioeconomic status, nativity, and residence origin, as well as current place of residence, value configurations and behavioral patterns should tend toward extreme variation as subpopulations exhibit varying levels of understanding, acceptance, and practice of presumably modern, as opposed to traditional, traits. In border society, nevertheless, such variation is commonly taken to reflect the tension between Anglo and Mexican cultures. For example, Mexican Americans who desire smaller families, greater female independence, and more egalitarian decision-making between husbands and wives typically are viewed by both groups as having become anglicized, rather than prescribing to behavioral modes of greater adaptive relevance to an urban-industrial setting. As to whether this, in fact, represents a shift between class-based cultures, contemporary research tends to be mixed in assessment.[53]

Whichever may be the case, it is clear that the border region is a zone of meaningful social-psychological transition.[54] As various writers have pointed out, the U.S.-Mexico border area is neither distinctively Latin or Anglo--but rather a syncretized form of the two, a border culture. Yet, while acculturative processes operate in both directions, the material hegemony of the United States has the greatest influence in structuring this hybrid. Cultural transition is not only significant on the northern side of the boundary, but also within Mexican border cities. For some observers, this change is evaluated negatively: "If the influence of the United States (in Mexico) is universal, along the border it is overwhelming. It takes the form of myth, of modern production methods, of the social invisibility of poverty, of the socialization of technology.[55] For others, the transition is viewed from a more positive perspective. Martinez,[56] for example, notes the strong tendencies along the northern border toward "demexicanization" and *agringamiento*, and indeed, the creation of "Chicanos *del otro lado*"--whom, he argues, will be adaptively superior to other immigrants should they migrate to the United States given this period of anticipatory socialization.

On the other hand, it appears that local definitions of well-being in Texas border cities, in part, are influenced by Mexican frames of reference.[57] These cities represent partial settlements in the context of the greater urban concentration that includes their Mexican twin. By virtue of location and interdependence, which require daily human movement in both directions across the boundary, observations of the comparatively worse conditions in Mexican communities are easily at hand. Therefore, local standards for evaluating well-being are considerably more complex than are those for American cities removed from the border. If the frame of reference is evoked at a national level, then life quality within Texas border cities should generally fall far short of that in most other American towns. Conversely, a frame of reference based on physical propinquity and set within the border context should suggest that these cities reflect relatively positive conditions. In certain respects, research findings from Brownsville support this hypothesis. Mexican immigrants there, compared to all other residents, were by far the most satisfied in regard to evaluations of a host of local public services and facilities. Likewise, recent in-migrants from other places in Texas and the United States generally ranked among all residents as the most dissatisfied with public conditions.[58]

Differing frames of reference for the evaluation of personal circumstances, nonetheless, may not be pronounced among border people--although it is commonly

argued that the local poor should not feel poor because
the poverty immediately south of the boundary is of much
greater intensity than that within Texas border cities.
This is believed to be particularly the case for poor immigrants; the objective hardship they now face should be
"relative affluence" in comparison to the conditions they
previously endured in Mexico only a short time ago. However, recent survey findings from Brownsville cast serious doubt on these assumptions. Poor people there reported serious problems in obtaining necessary medical
care and enough food for their families, and a majority
(much unlike their nonpoor counterparts) expressed strong
dissatisfaction with the adequacy of present incomes.
Furthermore, data show that reported economic problems
and perceptions of deprivation were no less among the immigrant poor than were they among other poverty-stricken
residents. Indeed, recent in-migrants from Mexico, both
poor and nonpoor alike, expressed the highest rate of income dissatisfaction of all local groups. These findings
indicate that immigrants did not view their existence in
Brownsville as one of relative affluence. Although earn-
ings made in the city were much more than those derived
in Mexico, they still received low wages, often only obtained sporadic work, and faced severe economic pressures
made worse by the growth-inflated cost of local goods and
housing. Public services and facilities, perceived to be
much better than those in Mexico, appeared to compensate
little for the problems immigrants confronted in Brownsville. In all, evidence suggests that their expectations
for an improved life by migrating to the city had not
been appreciably realized.[59]

CONCLUSION: THE BORDER AS A STAGING AREA

As noted, the border region is a zone characterized
by significant patterns of migration. Not only do many
Mexican frontier residents commute to work in Texas border cities, but such cities also serve as primary centers of resettlement for immigrants and constitute key
departure points for Mexican immigrants and Mexican Americans moving further into the United States. Thus, border cities may be conceptualized as migrant staging
areas.
Contemporary patterns of borderland poverty, in my
judgment, must be viewed as being strongly influenced by
this staging function. As shown, the magnitude of regional poverty is to a great extent a consequence of the
region's location as a transitional zone between two nations at highly uneven levels of development. Greater
real and perceived opportunities at the border have stimulated significant migration flows from the Mexican interior. The permeability of the border relative to human
migration defines the special character of the region

wherein an economic system could be constructed that exploits such flows. Recent industrialization reflects the attraction of low-wage labor-intensive industries which specifically take advantage of the large extant labor reserve. However, the persistence of a regional economy primarily structured on minimum-wage employment, even at full employment, provides little potential for aggregate mobility out of poverty for the local working poor. Pressures generated through in-migration, Mexican labor force participation, and high rates of natural increase will continue to reinforce job competition and depress wage rates for most of the working class. However, outmigration to the interior of Texas and the Southwest should continue to serve as an adaptive check, keeping the extent of border poverty far lower than would otherwise be the case.

NOTES

1. John A. Price, Tijuana: Urbanization in a Border Culture (Notre Dame: University of Notre Dame Press, 1973); Oscar J. Martinez, Border Boom Town: Ciudad Juarez Since 1948 (Austin: The University of Texas Press, 1978).
2. Support for research was contributed by TAES Project H-3286 and USDA-CSRS Regional Project NC-128. The author acknowledges the helpful reactions of William P. Kuvlesky, James H. Copp, and Robert Lee Maril to an earlier draft of this manuscript.
3. Ellwyn R. Stoddard, Patterns of Poverty Along the U.S.-Mexico Border (El Paso: Center for Inter-American Studies, University of Texas at El Paso, and the Organization of U.S. Border Cities and Counties), p. 3.
4. Richard L. Nostrand, "The Borderlands in Perspective," in Gary S. Elbow, ed., International Aspects of Development in Latin America: Geographical Perspectives (Muncie, Ind.: Clag Publications, 1977), pp. 9-28.
5. Ellwyn R. Stoddard, "Functional Alternatives to Bi-National Border Development Models: The Case of the U.S.-Mexico Region," Department of Sociology and Anthropology, The University of Texas at El Paso, mimeographed.
6. Niles Hansen, "The Economic Development of Border Regions," Growth and Change 8 (October 1977):2-8.
7. William V. D'Antonio and William H. Form, Influentials in Two Border Cities: A Study in Community Decision-Making (Notre Dame: University of Notre Dame Press, 1965); C. Daniel Dillman, "The Functions of Brownsville, Texas and Matamoros, Tamaulipas: Twin Cities of the Lower Rio Grande" (Ph.D. dissertation, University of Michigan, 1968); Oscar J. Martinez, Border Boom Town: Ciudad Juarez Since 1948 (Austin: The University of Texas Press, 1978).
8. Ibid., p. 155.

9. Daniel S. North, The Border Crossers: People Who Live in Mexico and Work in the United States (Washington, D.C.: TransCentury, 1970); Vernon M. Briggs, The Mexico-U.S. Border: Public Policy and Chicano Economic Welfare (Austin: Bureau of Business Research, University of Texas, Studies in Human Resource Development, No. 2, 1974); Avante Systems, Inc., A Survey of the Undocumented Population in Two Texas Border Areas (San Antonio: U.S. Commission on Civil Rights, Texas Advisory Committee, 1978); Roy Flores and Gilbert Cardenas, A Study of the Demographic and Employment Characteristics of Undocumented Aliens in San Antonio, El Paso, and McAllen, Texas (San Antonio: U.S. Commission on Civil Rights, Texas State Advisory Committee, 1978).

10. During the late 1970s in Brownsville, approximately three-fourths of dollar volume trade within the central business district was with Mexican shoppers. Michael V. Miller, "Poverty, Development, and the Quality of Life in a Texas Border City" (Ph.D. dissertation, Texas A&M University, 1981), p. 107.

11. Ellwyn P. Stoddard and Jonathan P. West, The Impact of Mexico's Peso Devaluation on Selected Border Cities (Tucson: SW Borderlands Consultants, 1977); Gilbert Cardenas, The Manpower Impact of Mexico's Peso Devaluation of 1976 on Border Labor Markets in Texas (Edinburg, Tx.: School of Business Administration, Pan American University, 1979).

12. See, e.g., Leroy P. Graf, "The Economic History of the Lower Rio Grande Valley, 1820-1875" (Ph.D. dissertation, Harvard University, 1942); Paul Horgan, Great River: The Rio Grande in North American History (New York: Rinehart, 1954).

13. Organized smuggling centers on the transport of drugs and undocumented aliens into the United States, and guns, machinery, and electronic goods into Mexico. The border presents special opportunities for law violators aside from smuggling. Those committing crimes on one side of the Rio Grande sometimes take refuge on the other side, free from legal apprehension. The border also structures a convenient and relatively safe market for various types of stolen property. Motor vehicles stolen in Texas, for example, may be driven across the river, where they are either sold or disassembled for sale in the lucrative auto parts business. Miller, "Poverty, Development," p. 304.

14. John W. Sloan and Jonathan P. West, "The role of Informal Policy-Making in U.S. Border Cities," Social Science Quarterly 58 (September 1977): 270-282.

15. Stoddard, Patterns of Poverty.

16. Vernon M. Briggs, Chicanos and Rural Poverty (Baltimore: John Hopkins University Press, 1973); Brian Rungeling, L. H. Smith, V. M. Briggs, and J. F. Adams, Employment, Income, and Welfare in the Rural South (New

York: Praeger, 1977).

17. C. Daniel Dillman, "Urban Growth Along Mexico's Northern Border and the Mexican National Border Program," The Journal of Developing Areas 4 (July 1970): 487-508.

18. Victor Urquidi and Sofia Mendez Villarreal, "Economic Importance of Mexico's Northern Border Region," in Stanley R. Ross, ed., Views Across the Border (Albuquerque: University of New Mexico Press, 1978), pp. 141-162.

19. Ricardo Loewe Reiss, "Considerations on the Health Status Along Mexico's Northern Border," in Ross, Views, pp. 241-255.

20. Oscar J. Martinez, "Chicanos and the Border Cities: An Interpretive Essay," Pacific Historical Review 46 (February 1977): 85-106; Antonio Ugalde, "Regional Political Processes and Mexican Politics on the Border," in Ross, Views, pp. 97-116.

21. Raul A. Fernandez, The United States-Mexico Border: A Politico-Economic Profile (Notre Dame: University of Notre Dame Press, 1977).

22. Centro de Investigaciones Agrarias, Estructura Agraria y Desarollo Agricola en Mexico (Mexico City: Fondo de Cultura Economica, 1974).

23. Ellwyn R. Stoddard, "Selected Impacts of Mexican Immigration on the U.S.-Mexico Border" (Paper presented at the Special Conference on Border Problems, Department of State, Washington, D.C., 1978.

24. Donald W. Baerresen, The Border Industrialization Program of Mexico (Lexington, Mass.: Lexington Books, 1971).

25. Donald W. Baerresen, "Mexico's Assembly Program: Implications for the United States," Texas Business Review 55 (November-December 1981): 253-257.

26. Maquiladora, the Spanish term for BIP assembly plants, is derived from maquila--the payment of grain provided by the farmer to the miller for the milling services. With regard to BIP, wages paid to Mexican workers constitue the maquila.

27. Fernandez, United States-Mexico Border; Martinez, "Chicanos and the Border Cities."

28. Fernandez, United States-Mexico Border, p. 129.

29. In addition to the charge that maquiladoras have drawn a large Mexican hinterland population to the border region, the assumed effectiveness of the BIP strategy in facilitating border economic development has been challenged in other respects as well. For one, the new industries have come to the region for a single purpose--exploitation of a large and inexpensive labor force. Given unfavorable economic or political conditions, such as the rise in Mexican labor militancy in certain border towns during the early 1970s, maquiladoras are highly susceptible to flight to places offering less hampered operations. Many industries did flee, in fact,

126

during this period to Hong Kong, Taiwan, Haiti, etc. Others intending to leave decided to stay in light of the wage savings brought by the 1976 peso devaluations. Thus, it is argued, *maquiladoras* offer little promise for stable long-term developments. Critics further charge that scant evidence exists that *maquiladoras* have upgraded skill-levels. While assembly work is highly exacting, it is extremely tedious, can be learned quickly, and has little transfer value to other types of industry. Technical jobs are said to be primarily filled by recruits trained elsewhere in the United States or Mexico. Claims of industrial socialization to regimentation and precision probably have more validity. Also, observations about relocated asbestos plants in Juarez and Agua Prieta indicate that some corporations may set up operations south of the border to avoid federal safety and health laws. Paul Sweeney, "AMATEX in Juarez: A Squalid Business," Texas Observer (June 9, 1978): 8-10. For general criticisms of BIP, see NACLA, "Hit and Run: U.S. Runaway Shops on the Mexican Border," NACLA's Latin American and Empire Report 9 (July-August 1975): 1-48; Jorge A. Bustamante, "Maquiladoras: A New Face of International Capitalism on Mexico's Northern Frontier" (Paper presented at the Latin American Studies Association, Atlanta, 1976); Cameron Duncan, "The Runaway Shop and the Mexican Border Industrialization Program," Southwest Economy and Society 2 (October-November 1976): 4-25.

30. Arthur Young, An Economic and Demographic Study of U.S. Border Cities (El Paso: Organization of U.S. Border Cities, 1978).

31. Jerry R. Ladman and Mark O. Poulsen, Economic Impact of the Mexican Border Industrialization Program: Agua Prieta, Sonora (Tempe: Center for Latin American Studies, Arizona State University, Special Study No. 10, 1972); Jacquelyn A. Mitchell, "Preliminary Report on the Impact of Mexico's Twin Plant Industry Along the U.S.-Mexico Border" (El Paso: The Organization of United States Border Cities, 1977), mimeographed.

32. Niles Hansen, "Development of the Southwest Borderlands," Texas Business Review 55 (November-December 1981): 247-252.

33. Michael V. Miller, "Industrial Development and An Expanding Labor Force in Brownsville," Texas Business Review 55 (November-December 1981): 258-261.

34. North, The Border Crossers; Linda M. Whiteford, "The Borderland as an Extended Community" (Paper presented at the American Anthropological Association, Houston, 1977).

35. Vernon M. Briggs, "Labor Markets Aspects of Mexican Migration to the United States in the 1970s," in Ross, Views, pp. 204-225; Jorge A. Bustamante, "Commodity Migrants: Structural Analysis of Mexican Immigration to

the United States," in Ross, Views, pp. 183-203;
Stoddard, "Selected Impacts."
    36. Anthony N. Zavaleta, "Substance Abuse in the
Lower Rio Grande Valley of Texas: Causes and Effects"
(Brownsville: South Texas Institute of Latin and Mexican-
American Research, Texas Southmost College, 1979), mimeo-
graphed.
    37. Robert R. Nathan, Industrial and Employment
Potential of the United States-Mexico Border (Washington,
D.C.: Department of Commerce, 1968); Briggs, "Labor Mar-
ket Aspects"; Barton Smith and Robert Newman, "Depressed
Wages Along the U.S.-Mexico Border: An Empirical Anal-
ysis," Economic Inquiry 15 (January 1977): 51-66; Michael
V. Miller and Robert Lee Maril, Poverty in the Rio Grande
Valley of Texas: Historical and Contemporary Dimensions
(College Station: Texas Agricultural Experiment Station,
No. 78-2, 1978).
    38. Data on green-card commuters were obtained
through personal correspondence with the Immigration and
Naturalization Service. Contemporary data on U.S. citizens who live in Mexico and commute to work in Texas are
unavailable. This projection is based on INS counts made
during the 1960s, which found the citizen commuter component roughly equivalent in size to that of the green-
card force.
    39. Miller, "Industrial Development."
    40. Benjamin S. Bradshaw, "Potential Labor Force
Supply, Replacement, and Migration of Mexican-American
and Other Males in the Texas-Mexico Border Region,"
International Migration Review (Spring 1976): 29-45.
    41. GOMA, Migrant and Seasonal Farm Workers in
Texas (Austin: Governor's Office of Migrant Affairs,
1976). Governed by a dilemma, migrants may be seen as
generally attempting to reach a compromise between harsh
economic realities and highly meaningful sociocultural
preference. North, The Border Crossers. Migration is
necessitated due to the absence of sufficient summer agricultural employment in the region, and the limited education and skill levels among migrants which tends to
preclude entry into other local jobs. Paul B. Miller,
"The Role of Labor Market Institutions in the Lower Rio
Grande Valley of Texas" (College Station: Department of
Economics, Texas A&M University, 1970), mimeographed.
While the well-known effects of seasonal migration are
often deleterious to educational achievement, health, and
family organization, migrants tend to be economically
better off than nonmigrating farm workers. Yet, certain
features of the region provide strong incentives for many
militating against permanent out-migration to areas offering better employment prospects. A mild winter climate, the local predominance of the Spanish language,
close proximity to Mexico, and cultural and family affil-
iations are some of the more important impediments to

relocation.

42. Bradshaw, "Potential Labor Force," p. 41. Other findings suggest additional implications for out-migration. First, despite the surprisingly common myth purporting that Mexican Americans will not relocate away from the border, Mexican-American youth are generally cognizant of the historically dismal regional employment situation and view out-migration as a basic requisite for economic mobility. A regional survey, for example, found such youth not only positive toward out-migration, but better than one-half indicated that within five years they would be living outside of the Lower Valley and Laredo. Niles Hansen and William C. Gruber, "The Influence of Relative Wages and Assisted Migration on Locational Preferences: Mexican Americans in South Texas," Social Science Quarterly 51 (June 1971): 103-114.

Secondly, actual movement of long distance has been pronounced. The spread of former agricultural migrants over the cities of California and the Midwest is well known. A Hidalgo County farm worker survey discovered that over three-fourths of the respondents had either siblings or children who had permanently migrated out of the region, with the vast majority settling out of Texas. Miller, "The Role of Labor Market Institutions." Discussions with many regional Mexican Americans also reveal numerous close relatives who, although not farm migrants, had moved to other cities in the state and nation. Houston seems to be a particularly strong magnet for many previous Lower Valley residents.

43. Miller, "Poverty, Development."

44. Jim B. Hensley, Mexican Immigrant-Alien Study, 1975-76 (Edinburg: Region I Education Service Center, Texas Education Agency, 1976). These expanding enrollments did not reflect the presence of the large and growing number of children of illegal alien parentage who, until a 1980 federal court ruling, were prevented by local law from attending public schools.

45. Stoddard, Patterns of Poverty.

46. Miller, "Industrial Development."

47. Florence Kluckhohn, "Los Atarquenos: A Study of Patterns and Configurations in a New Mexican Village" (Ph.D. dissertation, Radcliffe College 1941); Munro Edmundson, Los Manitos: A Study of Institutional Values (New Orleans: Tulane University Press, 1957); William Madsen, The Mexican Americans of South Texas (San Francisco: Holt, Rinehart, and Winston, 1964); Arthur J. Rubel, Across the Tracks: Mexican Americans in a Texas City (Austin: University of Texas Press, 1966).

48. Octavio I. Romano-V, "The Anthropology and Sociology of the Mexican Americans: The Distortion of Mexican-American History," El Grito 2 (Fall 1968): 43-56; Nick C. Vaca, "The Mexican American in the Social Sciences, 1936-1970," El Grito 4 (Fall 1970): 17-51; Miguel

Montiel, "The Social Science Myth of the Mexican American Family," El Grito 4 (Summer 1970): 56-63.
49. William P. Kuvlesky, D. Wright, and R. Z. Juarez, "Status Projections and Ethnicity: A Comparison of Mexican American, Negro, and Anglo Youth," Journal of Vocational Behavior 1 (April 1971): 137-151; David Wright, D. Salinas, and W. P. Kuvlesky, "Opportunities for Social Mobility for Mexican-American Youth," in R. O. de la Garza, Z. A. Kruszewski, and T. A. Arciniega, eds., Chicanos and Native Americans: The Territorial Minorities (Englewood Cliffs, N.J.: Prentice Hall, 1973), pp. 43-60; William P. Kuvlesky and Rumaldo Z. Juarez, "Mexican American Youth and the American Dream," in J. S. Picou and R. E. Campbell, eds., Career Behavior of Special Groups (Columbus, Ohio: Charles E. Merrill, 1975), pp. 241-296.
50. See, among others, Rodolfo Acuna, Occupied America: The Chicano's Struggle Toward Liberation (San Francisco: Canfield Press, 1972); Mario Barrera, Carlos Munoz, and Charles Ornelas, "The Barrio as an Internal Colony," in Harlan H. Hahn, ed., People and Politics in Urban Society (Los Angeles: Sage Publications, 1972), pp. 465-498.
51. D'Antonio and Form, Influentials.
52. Miller, "Poverty, Development."
53. Ellwyn R. Stoddard, Mexican Americans (New York: Random House, 1973); Miller, "Variations in Mexican-American Family Life," Aztlan 8 (Spring 1978): 209-231.
54. Martinez, "Chicanos and the Border Cities"; Miller and Maril, Poverty in the Lower Rio Grande Valley; Stoddard, Patterns of Poverty.
55. Carlos Monsivais, "The Culture of the Mexican Frontier: The Mexican Side," in Ross, Views, pp. 50-67.
56. Martinez, "Chicanos and the Border Cities."
57. Miller and Maril, Poverty in the Lower Rio Grande Valley; Stoddard, Patterns of Poverty.
58. Miller, "Poverty Development," pp. 316-319.
59. Ibid.

6
Changing Patterns of Segregation and Discrimination Affecting the Mexican Americans of El Paso, Texas: An Analysis of Socioeconomic Characteristics

Clark S. Knowlton

The study of the Spanish borderlands encompassing the American Southwest and northern Mexico has, since the pioneering work of Bolton, attracted a growing scholarly interest. The historians, the first to enter the field, focused for the most part on the period of Spanish exploration and settlement with a few side glances at the following Mexican occupation.[1] Until very recently, few historians have been interested in the troubled historical experiences of the Mexican Americans since the American annexation of the Southwest. Sociologists began to study rural Mexican villages and migrant farm workers of the upper Rio Grande Balley and in southwestern Texas during the 1930s and 1940s.[2] It was not until after World War II that the growing Mexican urban concentration received much scholarly attention. Since then, scholars in almost all of the social sciences have created what has come to be called the field of Mexican-American Studies and are analyzing both the history, the culture and the processes of social and cultural change among the various Mexican-American subgroupings.[3] In spite of all this current interest, the majority of even the larger Mexican-American settlements, villages, and urban neighborhoods has escaped scholarly scrutiny.

In this chapter an effort will be made to analyze certain selected aspects of one of the more important, oldest, and significant Mexican-American concentrations in the United States, the Mexican-American inhabitants of the city of El Paso. This group is significant because it was one of the earlier groupings to come into existence in Texas. It is located between the Spanish Americans of New Mexico and the Mexican Americans of western and central Texas. El Paso has been the gateway through which uncounted thousands of Mexicans have entered the United States. From El Paso itself an important stream of Mexican Americans has migrated to metropolitan centers of the West Coast, the Rocky Mountains, and even the Midwest. El Paso is also important because within and near the city are significant Mexican-American groupings that

131

differ from each other in history, rural-urban residence, dialect of Spanish spoken, and in cultural variations. For these reasons alone, the large Mexican-American community deserves the study that it has not received. Virtually all data for this study come from six years spent as a participant-observer in the life of the Mexican-American people of El Paso.

INTRODUCTION

El Paso, with a 1970 population of 322,261, is located on the Mexican border in the extreme southwestern semiarid section of Texas. It is the largest and one of the faster growing American border cities and is even faster growing than its Mexican twin, Juarez, which lies just over the Rio Grande River. The two cities, the New Mexican town of Las Cruces (37,857 residents in 1970), and their dependent smaller towns and villages are integral parts of a large urban and rural oasis separated from other Mexican and American cities by long distances of sparsely populated deserts, mountains, and plateaus.[4]

European settlement in the oasis area began with establishment of a mission and supply point in 1659 on the site of Juarez where the road from the interior of Mexico to settlements in northern New Mexico forded the Rio Grande River. Through the centuries, population gradually increased, and a small series of farming villages came into existence on both sides of the river, of which Juarez was one. After American conquest of the Southwest in 1847, American merchants and cattlemen gathered around an American army post established in 1849 on the north bank of the river. The twin cities of Juarez and El Paso, then known as El Paso del Norte (The Pass of the North), did not grow much until the 1870s and 1880s. Establishment in that period of a strong central government in Mexico; the ending of Indian hostilities; the coming of railroads from the interior of Mexico to Juarez and from points east, north and west to El Paso that articulated the twin cities into the transportation networks of their respective countries; and establishment of a free trade zone in northern Mexico permitting Mexican residents to buy goods without payment of duties in American border towns, brought about an increase in population and commerce that laid the basis for economic prosperity in both communities.

It must be emphasized that political and economic events on one side of the border inevitably have an impact upon economic, political, and social trends and events on the other side. Events that take place in the border regions will also have important impact upon local, state, and federal governments of the two countries concerned. The border area is where Mexico and the United States come together. Tensions or their absence between the two countries are reflected in the daily life of border inhabitants. Quite often federal policies of both Mexican and American governments, designed without any real knowledge of border conditions, may have quite a negative impact upon the welfare of the border regions. The one event that did have the most significant impact on the border was the Mexican Revolution. When the revolution first broke out, large numbers of Mexicans crossed into El Paso and other border towns to escape the violence. Other large numbers crossed seeking refuge from defeat of their faction. Although many did return ultimately to Mexico when peace was restored, a considerable number did not. The Mexican population jumped significantly. What is significant is that many middle-class Mexican merchants and large landowners settled in El Paso, adding to the complexity and diversity of the Mexican and Mexican-American social class system in El Paso.

At the time that the Mexican Revolution broke out, the American Southwest was undergoing economic development. Mines came into production, smelters were built, farming expanded greatly as more and more irrigated projects were developed, and towns began to expand. Mexican refugees found ready employment in the United States. It was during this period that the economic dependency of significant segments of the railroad, construction, mining and smelting, and agriculture industries developed a preference for a dependence on the poorly paid Mexican and Mexican-American workers.[5]

Local Mexican-American farmers living in the Rio Grande Valley from below El Paso to Hatch, New Mexico, were negatively affected by formation of irrigation projects in the El Paso area. Before the 1920s, the majority of farmers in the region were subsistence farmers living in a number of small rural farming villages and cultivating small acreages of land primarily to support their families. Their cash incomes were very low. When the Elephant Butte Irrigation Project was established, covering most of their lands, heavy charges were placed upon the acreage covered by the project to reimburse the federal government for its expenses. Poor subsistence Mexican-American farmers, because of inability to pay these charges plus the land tax imposed upon them, lost their lands through foreclosure. Many migrated to California and elsewhere. The rest were forced to work lands now owned by Anglo-American farmers that once belonged to them and their families. Almost every irrigation project on the Rio Grande River in New Mexico and the El Paso region has driven thousands of small Mexican-American families from their lands. This is a dark side of the history of irrigation projects in the Southwest that is seldom mentioned. By the 1940s, almost all the farming land in the middle Rio Grande Valley was owned by

Anglo Americans who, without the government subsidies denied to Mexican Americans, might not have survived
either.[6]

SYSTEMIC LINKAGES BETWEEN EL PASO AND JUAREZ

The American sociologist Charles Loomis has developed a theoretical schemata that facilitates the analysis
of border interaction between El Paso and Juarez. He
points out that many interdependencies as well as strains
exist between the two social systems, Mexico and the
United States. To Loomis, a social system is a system
within which there is intense social interaction. Nations are types of social systems. Members of two nations or social systems interacting with each other create systemic linkages. Thus, a systemic linkage "is the
process by which the elements of at least two social systems come to be articulated so that in many ways and on
some occasions they may be viewed as a single system."
Systemic linkages do not erode away the differences between social systems. Loomis argues that processes exist
within each social system, or in this case nations, in
which the identity of each social system is preserved.
Loomis refers to these as boundary maintenance systems.[7]
The most important boundary maintenance process between El Paso and Juarez is the fact that each is part of
a separate nation state. The national leaders of each
nation reside in capitals far from the border. With in-
complete knowledge of the present economic interdependence of the Juarez-El Paso areas, they pass legislation
that attempts, usually without major success, to regulate
movement of goods and people across the border. Such
legislation or other government acts typified by the recent Mexican government decision to devalue the peso,
making American goods more expensive in terms of Mexican
pesos, sharply reduced the number of Mexicans buying
goods in El Paso stores. This act severely hurt business
on the American side of the border. The futile efforts
of the American Bureau of Immigration and Naturalization
to restrict illegal Mexican immigration into the United
States is another example.
Other boundary maintenance mechanisms include Mexican and American federal, state, and local law enforcement agencies that patrol the long international boundary. American and Mexican school systems are also boundary maintenance mechanisms. They teach national languages and cultures and attempt to indoctrinate students
with national patriotism. School texts may contain material hostile to the neighboring country. A major function of the American school system has been to Americanize or acculturate Mexican-American children into the
dominant Anglo-American culture by refusing to accept or

adjust to the existence of the Spanish language, to punish children who speak Spanish during school hours, and to exclude Mexican and Mexican-American values and cultures from the curricula.

In spite of the fact that the international boundary between the United States and Mexico separates two societies with quite separate and distinctive cultures, languages, economic systems, and life styles, processes of systemic linkages are constantly weakening boundary maintenance mechanisms.

The border population itself is a major systemic linkage. The international border between the United States and Mexico does not in reality separate two distinct populations. For much of the border region, it cuts through an area with large numbers of Spanish-speaking people residing on both sides. These people visit each other, intermarry, buy, sell, smuggle, and go back and forth across the border without permission of the governments concerned. For them the border is somewhat of an artificial line drawn across the map that may occasionally handicap their activities but never manages to quite stop them.

Not only do innumerable families in border regions have family branches living on both sides, but they acquire the citizenship of the country in which they live. One family may have both American and Mexican citizens in the same family. It is very common for Mexican women feeling birth pains to call a taxi to take them to a hospital on the American side so that their baby may be an American citizen by birth. In the same manner, poor Mexican Americans living on the American side of the border may bury a dead relative on the Mexican side where burial expenses are so much cheaper.

Many wealthy border families deliberately develop American and Mexican branches to facilitate family businesses. Thus, a Mexican rancher may send a son to an American agricultural college to major in agriculture. The son becomes an American citizen. Through him the family buys ranches on the American side and then are able to send cattle back and forth across the border as business conditions dictate. Mexican and even some Anglo-American families may also establish Mexican and American family branches to facilitate exchange of capital and goods across the border, depending on the state of the Mexican or American economy.

The enormous daily movement of Mexicans and Americans who travel across the border every day is an important systemic linkage. Every morning large numbers of Mexicans come across the border to work, visit, shop, and patronize services on the American side. The same morning many Americans cross the border to shop, visit, and patronize services on the Mexican side. This constant daily movement of people between El Paso and Juarez is of

fundamental importance to the economies of the two
cities. Any act of government that interferes with the
free flow of people through border crossing points seriously damages the economy of El Paso and Juarez.
   A lesser known but very important systemic linkage
involving large numbers of people on both sides of the
border exists between American and Mexican criminal
groups. The dramatic increase in the smuggling of drugs
and weapons and ammunition across the border during the
past ten years has reached the proportions of a major
border industry enriching large numbers of people. The
business provides employment for a significant element of
the border population, ranging from poor Mexican subsistence farmers who grow the heroin poppies to men in high
government and financial circles on both sides of the
border. The business is a violent one with many casual-
ties, but because profits are extremely high, the business seems to be expanding. Many border smugglers will
not touch weapons or drugs but will smuggle raw materials, manufactured products, and people from one side of
the border to another. Criminals living in one country
often cross into the other country to commit crime. Some
border criminal groups composed of both Americans and
Mexicans will steal cars on the American side and drive
them across the border for quick resale on the other
side. In an effort to combat, let alone control, illegal
border traffic, close linkages exist between national
American and Mexican law enforcement agencies. Relationships for many reasons are not always cordial between local police forces in Mexican and American border towns.
   It should be said that the border had had its violent aspects ever since the border came into existence.
Many people have lived by smuggling profitable illegal
goods that have a secure market on the other side, whether cattle, money, manufactured products, aliens, alcohol, drugs, or weapons and ammunition. Although the
product may change, constant smuggling is an aspect of
border life that is seldom studied by social scientists.
   The mass media is another form of systemic linkages
in the border region. Radio and television stations located in Juarez and El Paso cover very large sections of
the other side of the border. Mexican Americans living
in and around El Paso listen to Mexican radio and television programs, often the same programs dubbed in Spanish that appear on the American stations. At the same
time, American stations are listened to and watched deep
in northern Mexico.
   A distinctive part of the mass media is publishing
of Spanish-language newspapers in El Paso and Juarez that
attempt to cover all the news of northern Mexico and the
American Southwest that may be of interest to their Mexican and Mexican-American readers. Although Mexico City
papers reach Juarez, they have a very slight circulation

or sale in El Paso. On the other hand, El Paso papers are sold at newsstands deep in northern Mexico. Unfortunately, the American newspapers publish very little information about Mexico or the Mexican side of the border except crime and natural catastrophes. The Mexican papers tend to publish far more information about the United States than American papers do about Mexico.

Finally, perhaps one of the most important systemic linkages is the flow of legal and illegal Mexican immigrants to the United States through Juarez and El Paso, one of the major gateways between Mexico and the United States. This flow began in the early 1900s on a large scale and, with some reverses in the 1930s and 1950s, has continued to increase in spite of efforts by American agencies to control it. The fundamental reason for the increase is overpopulation, unemployment, and poverty in many Mexican states and the profit that many American farmers and manufacturers gain through employing low-paid illegal Mexican workers. Many industries in the American Southwest have become dependent upon illegal Mexican workers. As these workers are now moving into other sections of the country, the problem has become a national rather than a regional one and includes white-collar, skilled, and even professional workers as well as agricutural workers.

American protests about the illegal immigration have seemed rather hypocritical to Mexican ears. They note that in times of labor shortage in the United States, the border is open to every Mexican worker who wishes to cross it. They also note that the Bureau of Immigration and Naturalization often rounds up illegal workers for deportation after American crops are harvested and seldom before. Many are aware of the corruption that at times creeps into the staff of the bureau; they are very much aware of the important role that the dollars sent home have played in helping the Mexican balance of payment as well as relieving poverty and distress in many Mexican villages. As so many groups profit from the movement of illegal workers into the United States, it is very doubtful that the movement will end soon.[8]

The illegal Mexican workers moving through El Paso to other American cities have little impact on the labor market in El Paso. However, a substantial number of legal and illegal Mexican immigrants settle in El Paso for varying periods of time. Their numbers are joined by Mexicans who live in Juarez and work illegally in El Paso. The members of this group virtually dominate domestic service such as maids, unskilled construction labor, and agricultural labor. They are also found at virtually every level of blue-collar, white-collar, and professional employment in El Paso. Still a third group of Mexican-border residents possess that dreamed-of American visa that permits them to live and work in the

United States. They have the best of the border situation. They live in Mexican border towns such as Juarez
where the cost of living is lower than in the United
States and earn far more money in the United States than
they could ever earn in Mexico.[9]
The impact of these workers upon local resident Mexican Americans is severe. Unable to provide their families with an acceptable modest living, large numbers of
Mexican-American El Pasoans migrate to California and
other states in search of better-paying employment.
Thus, a constant process of population replacement goes
on in Mexican-American low-income neighborhoods of El
Paso. Mexican families constantly come in from Juarez.
They find housing in one of the low-income Mexican-American neighborhoods. Later, they or their children migrate
to other sections of the United States or to higher-
income Mexican-American neighborhoods in El Paso. The
Mexican-American population of El Paso never seems to
diminish as the constant flow of new residents from Mexico replaces those who leave.
The majority of Mexican immigrants coming into the
United States bring very little knowledge of the intellectual and artistic culture of Mexico. Rather, theirs
is the world of the rural village, the mining or smelting
town, or the urban neighborhood of a Mexican community.
They often bring with them a rich heritage of folk music
and folk stories that have seldom been collected in El
Paso *barrios*. One can still find old men and women who
fought in the armies of the Mexican Revolution and are
still filled with memories of their experiences. A student of folklore would find a rich treasury in El Paso's
Mexican-American neighborhoods and Mexican *colonias* or
proletarian slums that encircle Juarez.
The desire of the middle-class Mexicans of Juarez to
give their children the best education available creates
another interesting systemic linkage. As so many of them
believe the El Paso schools are better than those of
Juarez and want their children to learn English, they enroll them illegally in American schools. At registration
time children and parents give false addresses to the
school officials or parents may rent addresses in the
Mexican-American slums of El Paso. Without much success,
school officials are constantly trying to uncover these
children and to collect the tuition paid by higher-income
Mexican parents who also send their children to El Paso
public schools.
A substantial number of students from Juarez also
enroll at the University of Texas at El Paso. They tend
to associate with each other and seldom are involved in
Chicano movements. Upon graduation they may go to the
University of Mexico or to another American university.
A few, but an increasing number, Mexican-American students from El Paso are beginning to attend Mexican

universities and colleges to discover their roots, perfect their Spanish, and then return to the United States. However, an unknown number of Mexican Americans born in El Paso return permanently to Mexico, but no one has paid any attention to this population movement. It should be mentioned that some Anglo-American students from El Paso, unable to gain admittance to American medical or veterinary schools, attend similar schools in Mexico.

Although economic forces are integrating the economies of the Juarez and El Paso oasis into a single economic system, forces of boundary maintenance are still quite strong in areas of political and cultural institutions; inhabitants of Chihuahua and Texas are quite nationalistic. It is not for nothing that Chihuahua is known as the shield of Mexico interposed between the interior of the country and the United States. Nationalism runs strong in Texas, a border state that had prolonged border conflicts with Mexico the last half of the nineteenth and first fifteen years of the twentieth centuries. It is also significant that very few Anglo Americans in El Paso have any knowledge of or interest in the history, art, literature, or other cultural achievements of Mexico. Almost no El Pasoans patronize cultural events in Juarez except dog and horse racing and bullfights. Some antagonism exists among certain intellectual and student centers in Juarez who have forgotten little about the past history of the borderlands and tend to believe that the United States is responsible for the ills of Mexico.[10]

DEMOGRAPHIC/SOCIAL CHARACTERISTICS OF THE EL PASO MEXICAN AMERICAN POPULATION

El Paso has become a major industrial, commercial, military, import, export, transportation, and agricultural center. The largest American city in a 400-mile area, it has become a major Southwestern regional urban center. It also casts a long economic shadow deep into northern Mexico. The city grew from 130,485 residents in 1950 to 276,687 in 1960 (112 percent increase) and to 322,261 in 1970 (14.4 percent increase). Although the population rate increase declined substantially between 1960 and 1970, El Pasoans expect growth to continue as part of the prospering Southwest. Adams, commenting on the growth of El Paso, says it has shifted from a "homogeneous southern city to a California-like hodgepodge."[11]

The problem of securing an accurate count of the Mexican-American population of American cities is one that the U.S. Bureau of Census has wrestled with since 1930 without major success.[12] At least three different totals exist for the Spanish-surname and Spanish-language population of El Paso (referred to here as Mexican

Americans).[13] As the most detailed and complete data on
census tracts for El Paso were found in the volume on El
Paso, it was decided to use this total of 187,296 Spanish surname and Spanish-language residents enumerated in
El Paso in 1970. As the number of Cubans, Latin Americans from countries south of Mexico, and Puerto Ricans
in El Paso is so small, the overwhelming majority of
Spanish-surname and Spanish-language population will be
referred to as Mexican Americans. If the total of
187,296 is reasonably accurate (and there are reasons for
thinking that the census count is an underenumeration),
the Mexican Americans make up 58.1 percent of El Paso's
total population of 322,261.[14] If the total of 148,812
for Spanish-surname population is used, they then represent only 46.2 percent of the city population.[15] At any
rate, the percentage of the city population that is Mexican American seems to have increased from the 45 percent
enumerated in 1960.[16]

Mexican Americans are living in virtually every census tract in the city. Segregation supported by custom
does not exist in El Paso. Since World War II Mexican
Americans have been able to purchase houses in any suburb
within their financial capacity. There are, however,
very heavy concentrations of Mexican Americans in segregated, low-income, substandard housing tracts located
along the northern bank of the Rio Grande River. In general, the closer to the river one travels, the higher the
concentration of Mexican Americans; the farther one travels to the northeast, the greater the concentration of
Anglo Americans. Many of these segregated Mexican-American census tracts represent historic Mexican-American
urban slums that have acquired a certain amount of prestige and fame throughout the Southwest; others represent
former rural Mexican-American hamlets that have been surrounded by advancing Anglo-American housing spread.

The three best known and best defined Mexican-American neighborhoods are South El Paso, East El Paso, and
Ysleta. Perhaps the most famous and one of the oldest,
poorest, and most notorious Mexican-American neighborhood or *barrio* in El Paso is South El Paso. Surrounded
on three sides by the Rio Grande River and on the fourth
by a major traffic artery, it possesses a definite subculture of its own. Housing in the neighborhood ranges
from a mixture of two-to-three-story aging tenements
without central heating, internal plumbing or water,
well-kep one-family dwellings, small businesses, ware-
houses, and an internal *barrio*. Chihuahuita, the original nucleus of the *barrio*, is made up of a series of small
one-story Mexican-type adobe houses. Through South El
Paso run the two major El Paso roads to Juarez.

Another Mexican-American neighborhood is East El
Paso, bounded on the southeast by the Rio Grande, on the
west by South El Paso, the north by a freeway, and on the

east by Ascarate Park. Population here ranges from 91 to 96 percent Mexican American. Containing the major housing projects in El Paso, East El Paso includes areas of dilapidated single-family housing as well as middle-class housing in a decent state of repair. East El Paso has never managed to develop either the reputation or fame of its neighbors to the west or east.

To the east extends the Lower Valley in a southeastern direction along the Rio Grande Valley. The Lower Valley is a nondescript area lying between the river on the south and the freeway on the north. Much of it was cheaply built during the housing boom of the 1950s. Rather isolated from the rest of El Paso, it was annexed into the city somewhat against the will of its inhabitants. As it grew, it absorbed several Mexican-American villages that predate the coming of the Anglo Americans, such as Ysleta. Interestingly enough, in the 1960s a Spanish-speaking Indian remnant, claimed to have descended from a group of Indian refugees that accompanied the retreating Spanish from the pueblo revolt of the 1680s in New Mexico, surfaced. Claiming to be originally from the New Mexico Pueblo of Ysleta, they have been successful in securing recognition as one of the very few Indian groups that survived in Texas. The Lower Valley population is predominantly Mexican American with percentages ranging up to 91 percent.

North of the South El Paso and East El Paso neighborhoods are a series of census tracts curving around the southern and eastern borders of the central business district that are predominantly Mexican American. The inhabitants of these tracts are economically better off than the majority of the residents of South and East El Paso. They inhabit an area undergoing transition from residential to business, with no clearly defined *barrio* personality. Just north and a little east of the central business district exists a group of tracts once inhabited by the Anglo-American middle class. As new suburban housing developed in the building boom of the 1950s, Anglo Americans began to evacuate the area leaving fairly decent housing to the incoming socially mobile Mexican Americans.

The famous old Mexican-American neighborhood of Smeltertown, located on the banks of the Rio Grande west of South El Paso, no longer exists. Inhabited by workers of the neighboring Asarco Smelter who built their homes many years ago on smelter land, the district had acquired a unique well-defined personality of its own. The smelter workers were a unified group of families that had little interaction with inhabitants of other Mexican-American neighborhoods. In the late 1960s and early 1970s, medical tests revealed dangerously high lead levels in the blood of Smeltertown children. The neighborhood was evacuated and houses torn down. Other clusters

of housing inhabited by smelter workers still exist in
folds of the northern mesa along the flood plain of the
Rio Grande. Very few Anglo Americans or even Mexican-
American inhabitants of El Paso are aware of their existence.

As the sprawl of Anglo-American housing spread over
the mesa down into the flood plain of the Rio Grande
River encroaching on some of the finest farm land of El
Paso County in the section known as the Upper Valley,
hard against the New Mexico line, a number of small Mexican-American rural villages and hamlets inhabited by former field workers who now seek urban employment were engulfed.

It should be emphasized that there are very few census tracts whose population is not at least 10 percent or
more Mexican American. El Paso contains a wide variety
of Mexican-American neighborhoods most worthy of scholarly attention. There are the better known neighborhoods
of South El Paso, East El Paso, and Ysleta whose inhabitants have developed patterns of life that are neither
Mexican-American nor Anglo-American but a mixture of the
two with some interesting local cultural variations.
These neighborhoods are culturally isolated from modern
Anglo America. There are third- to fifth-generation Mexican-American families who do not use English in neighborhoods whose populations are bilingual and partially
acculturated into the Anglo-American society. Socially
mobile acculturating Mexican Americans move from these
neighborhoods into predominantly Anglo-American middle-
and upper middle-class suburbs. Thus, the scholar has
at his disposal Mexican-American neighborhoods ranging
from first and second generation *barrios*, historic Mexican-American communities, and Mexican-American groupings
distributed from those who have just entered El Paso from
Mexico to those who have lived in the city for several
generations or more. It is thus possible to study the
various processes of accommodation, acculturation, cultural conflicts, a diverse Mexican-American class structure, and quite distinct Mexican-American subgroupings.

Besides information on the distribution of the population, the 1970 census contained a wealth of data on the
economic and social characteristics of the El Paso population. Space does not permit a presentation of the
available material on the Mexican Americans. Therefore,
information on certain specific indices of economic well-
being are presented here such as level of income, poverty
ratios, unemployment, occupational distribution, and
achieved educational levels.

Income

Median income for the average family in the United
States in 1970 was $9,569 and was substantially lower for

Texas ($8,514). El Paso, one of the poorer cities in the state, was marked by a median family income of but $7,490. The Negro population of El Paso enjoyed a slightly higher median family income ($6,845) than did the Mexican Americans ($6,619).[17]

Mexican-American inhabitants of South El Paso had the lowest median family income in 1970 ($3,279 to $3,630 in three of its tracts) and the poverty of this *barrio* is clearly evidenced. An interesting, almost unknown, collection of Mexican-American neighborhoods that range along the Rio Grande River from South El Paso to the Lower Valley and the freeway on the north to the river on the south, vary somewhat among themselves. Most of the early public housing projects are in this section, but the incidence of home ownership is high, with median incomes ranging from $3,784 to $8,060.

The median income in Ysleta, the once independent Mexican-American community that predates El Paso, was $5,656 and $5,162. In the predominantly Mexican-American area that runs along the banks of the Rio Grande River from Ysleta to East El Paso, the median income ranged from $6,407 to $7,736. Many of these tracts were built up in the boom of the 1950s and are occupied by Mexican-American families with high rates of home ownership. In another series of tracts in the Lower Valley, from Ysleta to the freeway on the north and the Franklin Canal on the south, the median family income was higher than in the tracts analyzed so far. In this area live substantial numbers of middle-class Mexican Americans but, unfortunately, very little is known about them. Their median family income ranges from $8,525 to $13,611.

Mexican Americans living in the strongly Mexican-American census tracts that cover most of old El Paso, an area that was largely Anglo-American before World War II, were not as well off as those living in the census tracts discussed above, but they were financially better off than the inhabitants of South El Paso with median incomes ranging from around $5,000 to over $8,000.

Northeast El Paso is a newly developed area and not fully articulated into the life of El Paso, inhabited by large numbers of Anglo-American newcomers, military personnel, and acculturating Mexican Americans. Mexican-American incomes tended to be higher here than in most of the census tracts discussed except those in the western segment of the Lower Valley. Median incomes were $6,323 to $8,112. These Anglo-American neighborhoods have experienced a heavy Mexican-American invasion since the 1950s.

Turning to the newly developing neighborhoods spreading west along the mesas from the campus of the University of Texas at El Paso into what is known as the Upper Valley, we find the middle- and upper-income suburbs that are spreading across the cotton fields toward

New Mexico. They have flowed around a number of Mexican-American hamlets once inhabited by farm workers. The highest median annual income is $10,226. Predominantly Anglo-American suburbs, these census tracts contain newly developed upper-income housing areas on the southwestern slopes of the Franklin Mountains and middle-income districts on the mesas that run down from the mountains toward the flood plain of the Rio Grande. One area is an older upper- and middle-income Anglo-American suburb devouring the cotton fields in the Upper Valley. Two others are worthy of mention. One is a tract that runs from the river up toward Mesa Street on the north and from the University of Texas campus westward to the New Mexico line. It contains newly developing middle-income Anglo-American housing tracts plus a few older Mexican-American nuclei. On the other hand, the second tract contains older middle-income and a few upper-income blocks in an older section of the city, a large tract running from the university campus eastward. The median income of the Mexican-American inhabitants of these Anglo-American districts was $5,551 and $11,762.

To summarize, the lowest median annual incomes are found among the inhabitants of the oldest and poorest Mexican-American neighborhoods of South El Paso, East El Paso, and Ysleta. Higher median incomes are characteristic of the more middle-income census tracts, for the most part predominantly Mexican-American, that stretch like a half bow around the western, northern, and eastern edges of the central business district. The highest annual median incomes, above $10,000, are concentrated in three tract clusters. The first cluster, running in the Upper Valley hugs the northeastern and southwestern flanks of the Franklin mountains. The second is located on the western edge of the Lower Valley. These tracts contain relatively new housing developments that are, with one or two exceptions, predominantly Mexican-American. The third cluster is located in the Anglo-American neighborhoods of Northeast El Paso. One tract, a high-income tract, is uniquely different from the others as it is located close to low-income Mexican-American neighborhoods but there are enough high-income Mexican-American residents clustered in certain neighborhoods close to the university to pull it into a high, median-income category.

Occupational Distribution

Data on the occupational and professional composition of the labor force of the United States are among the most important population data provided by the U.S. Census Bureau. A person's occupation and the derived income are among the most important determiners of his life style, his social status and social class, and reveal significant information on discrimination, acculturation, and social mobility. In Table 6.1, data on the occupational work force of El Paso has been tabulated by numbers and percentages of workers in major occupational categories. The total columns include both Mexican-American and Negro workers. For the El Paso labor force as a whole, 16.0 was classified as professional compared to 22.3 percent for Negroes and 8.6 percent for Mexican Americans. It seems as though both the Anglo Americans contained in the total number and the Negroes have a higher percentage of professionals among their ranks. As political and community leadership tends to come from the professional stratum more than from others, the paucity of professionals among Mexican Americans may explain their slowness to organize politically in El Paso. One suspects that many Negro professionals have migrated to El Paso to work for the many government and military agencies in the city.

The reverse was true in the category of managers and administrators. Here the Mexican Americans were better represented than the Negroes as compared to the total column. Although these statistics tell us nothing about the importance or income of the positions of managers and administrators, one may infer that few Mexican Americans in El Paso occupy the higher positions among corporations or as government officials, while they are well represented as owners and managers of small businesses.

The importance of Mexican Americans as mediators in business between Anglo-American owners and managers and Spanish-speaking clients was evidenced by the percentage of Mexican Americans employed as sales workers compared to Negroes and total work force. The fact that so many businesses in El Paso are dependent upon Spanish-speaking clients would advantage the Mexican American and disadvantage the Negroes. The same factor would help to explain the percentage of Mexican Americans employed as clerical and kindred workers in comparison to that of the Negroes and total labor force. One might suspect that discrimination might play a role here.

The one occupational category in which a significantly large percentage of the Mexican-American labor force was employed in 1970 was that of craftsmen and foremen, etc., where more Mexican Americans than even Anglo Americans were employed. One reason may be the large number of Spanish-speaking workers to be supervised. The percentages of the Mexican-American labor force, of the Negroes, and of the total seem to indicate that in the operatives except transport category, far more Mexican Americans than either Negroes or Anglo Americans were employed as industrial and construction workers in El Paso. It may well be that neither Anglo Americans or Negroes were willing to accept the low wages offered while Mexican Americans had few alternatives.

Table 6.1 Occupational Distribution for City of El Paso—1970

Occupation	Total	Percent	Spanish Surname	Percent	Negro	Percent
Totals	100,510		54,789		1,835	
Professionals	16,099	16.0	4,694	8.6	410	22.3
Managers and Administrators	9,155	9.1	3,103	5.7	70	3.8
Salesworkers	8,565	8.5	3,927	7.2	38	2.1
Clerical and Kindred Workers	19,024	18.9	8,855	16.2	207	11.3
Craftsmen, Foremen, etc.	13,177	13.1	8,398	15.3	114	6.2
Operatives except Trans.	11,905	11.9	9,995	18.2	199	10.9
Transport Equipment Operatives	4,274	4.3	2,974	5.4	96	5.2
Laborers except Farm	4,536	4.5	3,481	6.3	61	3.3
Farm Laborers	492	.5	316	.6	5	.3
Service Workers except Private Household	11,750	11.7	7,651	14.0	587	32.0
Private Household Workers	1,533	1.5	1,395	2.5	48	2.6

SOURCE: U.S. Bureau of the Census, Census of Population and Housing; 1970 CENSUS TRACTS, Final Report (1)-62, El Paso, Texas, SMSA, U.S. Government Printing Office, Washington, D.C., 1972, pp. 11, 22, 28.

Higher percentages of Mexican Americans and Negroes worked as transport equipment operators than did Anglo Americans. The statistics for the farm workers may be somewhat misleading; less than 1 percent of either Mexican Americans, Negroes, or workers in the total labor force of El Paso were counted as farm workers. The truth seems to be that large numbers of rural Mexican Americans in El Paso County will accept work as farm workers and that urban unskilled workers with agricultural experience might do the same. Agricultural labor has low prestige among Mexican Americans, and many may be reluctant to define themselves as farm workers. This category may include more workers than the figures indicate.

Service workers excluding private household was one category in which a far higher percentage of Negroes worked than did Mexican Americans or Anglo Americans. Slightly less Mexican Americans than Negroes and Anglo Americans found employment as private household workers. The statistics for this category are rather inaccurate as they may not include the extremely large numbers of illegal Mexican women who work as domestic household and service workers in El Paso.

In summary, the Mexican Americans were poorly represented in the professional category, somewhat better represented among managers and administrators, well represented as sales workers and clerical and kindred workers, produced far more craftsmen and foremen than either Anglo Americans or Negroes, supplied the majority of industrial and construction workers in El Paso, about the same number of transport equipment operators as Negroes, and slightly more laborers except farm and farm workers. In the category of service workers not in private households, the Negroes had a far greater percentage employed than either Anglo Americans or Mexican Americans, while as private household workers, Anglo Americans were less well represented than either the Mexican Americans or Negroes. Of course, these data are somewhat artificial as they do not include the illegal border crossers and the green carders who find ready employment in the El Paso labor market. It seems feasible to assume that if these were counted, the percentage and numbers of Mexican Americans employed as craftsmen, foremen and related occupations, operatives except transport, laborers, farm laborers, service workers, and private household workers would be sharply increased.

Public Assistance

In 1970, the percentage of families receiving public assistance in El Paso was 9.5 percent for Negroes and 11.2 percent for Mexican Americans. As one looks at the low percentage of Mexican-American families that received public assistance in that census, it is obvious that the

majority of poor Mexican-American families who receive
public assistance tend to conceal the fact from neighbors
and relatives. Public welfare is the court of last re-
sort when all other resources have been exhausted.
If the census data is correct, the highest percentage on welfare was found in northeast El Paso. The reason for this high percentage in a northeast census tract
is not known. The next highest percentage was in South
El Paso, the eastside, and Ysleta, all in the poorest
sections in El Paso.

Our data showed that the amount of poverty in a census tract is not a sure indicator of the number of people
receiving public assistance, in which case the highest
percentages receiving public assistance would be in the
South and East El Paso tracts. Poverty is not the only
variable recorded here. As the majority of Mexican-American inhabitants of South El Paso were born in the United
States, Mexican citizenship that might not qualify a person for public assistance is not the answer either. This
is but another aspect of Mexican-American life in El Paso
that requires research.

Poverty Ratios

The U.S. Bureau of the Census adopted the figure of
$3,743 as income for a family of four as the poverty
threshold for the completed year 1969. Although the
material by now is well out of date, no better data is
available by census tract. It should be kept in mind
that inflation and unemployment have sharply increased
poverty among the Mexican Americans since 1969. The 1980
census will be eagerly awaited to ascertain whether the
United States has gained or lost ground in the war
against poverty.

For the city of El Paso, 16.8 percent of all families resident in 1969 received less than $3.743; for
Texas it was 14.6 percent and for the United States, 10.7
percent.[18] The percentage of Negro families who received
less than $3,743 was 25.3 and for Mexican-American fami-
lies it was 24.7. The worst conditions of poverty were
found in the Mexican-American neighborhoods of South and
East El Paso with 40 to 59.9 percent of all families
dwelling in poverty. One can imagine the difficult economic struggles that the inhabitants of South El Paso
have to survive. Conditions were no better in the East
El Paso census tracts bordering on South El Paso.

Extremely high percentages of families living in
poverty were also tabulated for Ysleta (35-49.9 percent).
Next in severity of poverty came two East El Paso tracts
with 30-39.9 percent of all families defined as being
below the poverty threshold.

The more prosperous families with less than the El
Paso average for families classified as living below the

poverty threshold of 16.8 percent resided in several clusters of census tracts. Those who lived in the predominantly middle-class Mexican-American neighborhoods declined to 10 to 14.9 percent. In the predominantly older Mexican-American neighborhoods in the east central district of the city, in the Lower Valley, and in three tracts in Northeast El Paso, percentages were 15 to 19.9. These are diverse tracts with different numbers of Mexican Americans living within them.

In the solidly Mexican-American middle-class neighborhoods, the percentages of Mexican Americans living below the poverty level fell in the 10 to 14.9 category. To them were added two Upper Valley tracts, three Northeast tracts, and three prospering Lower Valley tracts. This category masks a number of very interesting and diverse Mexican-American neighborhoods.

The lowest percentages of Mexican-American families living in poverty are found in the predominantly Anglo-American neighborhoods in which the Mexican Americans are a distinct minority. In the tract that runs from the western flanks of the Franklin Mountains down to about Mesa Street, the percentage was below 4.9. In the same mountain foothill type tract on the eastern slope of the mountains, the percentage was slightly higher, from 5 to 9.9 percent. The same difference is seen in three neighboring tracts in Northeast El Paso (4.9-9.9 percent) and similarly in three tracts in the western series of tracts above the freeway in the Lower Valley; the percentages were below 5 percent. Finally, in a tract on the west central part of Northeast El Paso, and in another that borders the central business district on the east, the campus of the University of Texas at El Paso on the west, and runs from the Rio Grande River on the south to the El Paso Electric Company distribution line on the north, we find from 5-9.9 percent of Mexican-American families living in poverty.

Unfortunately, space does not permit a more complex analysis. Many types of Mexican-American settlements with subtle cultural differences between them are masked by these variations in the percentages of Mexican-American families living in poverty. These neighborhoods certainly warrant far more study than they have received. Minority residence in Anglo-American neighborhoods does not always confer lack of poverty upon Mexican-American families. Except for very wealthy Anglo-American areas, one finds tracts in which the Mexican Americans are a majority with fairly low rates of poverty, and tracts in which they are a minority with equally low rates of poverty. Thus, the ethnic factor is not the single primary variable involved in the poverty of Mexican Americans in El Paso.

150

Median Number of School Years Completed

In order to function successfully in the complex in-
dustrialized and urbanized economic system of the United
States, mere literacy and knowledge of English, although
essential, are not enough. Individuals who have not at
least a high school education will undoubtedly encounter
even more serious problems in finding more than temporary
unskilled employment. The median number of school years
completed by members of a minority group is an important
measurement of the group's ability to avoid poverty, to
secure employment, and to climb the socioeconomic ladder.
Education is becoming one of the more important channels
of social mobility in the United States.
    In 1970, the population of Texas had reached median
school years of 11.6 and for the United States, 12.1.[19]
The median school years completed for inhabitants of El
Paso for 1970 was 12.1 also. Within the city, the
Negroes had achieved a much higher median of school
years finished (12.2) than had the Mexican Americans
(8.6). However, the situation among the Mexican Americans is not as severe as it seems. The continuous stream
of poorly educated Mexican immigrants into the El Paso
area tends to mask the much higher educational achievements of Mexican Americans educated in El Paso. Once can
therefore expect that Mexican-American first-generation
neighborhoods will have lower educational attainments
than second- and third-generation areas.
    This is evidenced by the fact that Mexican Americans
living in high-income predominantly Anglo-American tracts
have completed the highest median number of school years
(13-14.9). Mexican Americans resident in six northeast
El Paso tracts, in the higher-income Mexican-American
tracts in the western edge of the Lower Valley, in one
Upper Valley tract, one west central tract, and one central city tract, have completed from 12 to 12.9 years.
    Mexican Americans in two northeast tracts and one
central city tract have completed from 11 to 11.9 years.
In the central city middle-class neighborhoods once inhabited by Anglo Americans but now largely taken over by
Mexican Americans, the median school year achieved, 9 to
9.9, was characteristic of the Mexican Americans living
in one northeast tract, one central tract, and three
Lower Valley tracts.
    Mexican-American residents of five central city
tracts and four east tracts had completed only from 8 to
8.9 years. These are all predominantly Mexican-American
tracts that include not only some middle-class Mexican
Americans but also many low-income residents as well as
recent Mexican immigrants. In one Lower Valley tract
and one on the eastern edge of the Upper Valley, with
many relic Mexican-American hamlets and neighborhoods,
the Mexican-American inhabitants were less well educated,

having achieved but 7 to 7.9 median school years.
Lower median school years achieved were found among
the Mexican Americans resident in two East El Paso
tracts, one central city tract, and one Ysleta tract.
Here the median ranged from 6 to 6.9 years. The lowest
medians, 5 to 5.9, were found among the inahbitants of
the Smelter tract, one South El Paso tract, two East El
Paso tracts, one Lower Valley tract, and one Ysleta
tract. The southside residents of three tracts had
finished only from 4 to 4.9 years, and those living in
another South El Paso tract, from 3 to 3.9 years.
Thus, in general, the inhabitants of the low-income,
first-generation segregated settlements of South and East
El Paso had the lowest educational attainments, and those
living in high-income, integrated, predominantly Anglo-
American neighborhoods had achieved the highest median
school years.

NOTES

1. Among the representative studies of the border-
lands are the following: John F. Bannon, The Spanish
Borderlands Frontier, 1513-1821 (New York: Holt, Rinehart and Winston, 1970); Herbert E. Bolton, The Spanish
Borderlands: A Chronicle of Old Florida and the Southwest
(1921); Abraham P. Nasatir, "The Shifting Borderlands,"
Pacific Historical Review 34 (February 1965): 1-20; Burl
Noggle, "Anglo Observers of the Southwest Borderland,
1825-1890: The Rise of a Concept," Arizona and the West 1
(Summer 1959): 105-131: Richard L. Nostrand, "The Hispa-
ic Borderland: Delimitation of an American Culture Region," Annals, Association of American Geographers 60
(1970): 638-661.
2. Studies of the rural Mexican villages and migrant farm workers of the Upper Rio Grande Valley and
Southwestern Texas include the following: Hugh C.
Calkins, Tewa Basin Study, II: The Spanish American Villages (Albuquerque: Southwest Region, Soil Conservation,
U.S. Department of Agriculture, 1935); Nancie L.
Gonzalez, The Spanish Americans of New Mexico (Albuquerque: University of New Mexico Press, 1967); Clark Knowlton, "Culture Conflict and Natural Resources," Social
Behavior, Natural Resources and the Environment (New
York: Harper and Row, 1972), pp. 109-145; George I. San-
chez, The Forgotten People (Albuquerque: Calvin Horn,
1967); Frances L. Swadesh, Los Primeros Pobladores
(Notre Dame: University of Notre Dame Press, 1974).
3. See particularly: Leo Grebler, Joan W. Moore,
and Ralph C. Guzman, The Mexican-American People (New
York: The Free Press, 1970); Chris E. Garcia, ed., La
Causa Politica: A Chicano Politics Reader (Notre Dame:

University of Notre Dame Press, 1974); Arthur J. Rubel,
Across the Tracks: Mexican Americans in a Texas City,
published for the Hogg Foundation for Mental Health
(Austin: University of Texas Press, 1966); Gus Tyler,
ed., Mexican Americans Tomorrow (Albuquerque: University
of New Mexico Press, 1975); Ralph Gomez, ed., The Changing Mexican American (El Paso: Texas Western Press,
1972); Rodolfo Acuna, Occupied America (New York: Canfield Press, 1972).
     4. C. Daniel Dillman, "Urban Growth Along Mexico's
Northern Border and the Mexican-American Border Program,"
The Journal of Developing Areas 4 (July 1970): 487-507.
     5. Mark Reisler, "Passing Through Our Egypt: Mexi-
can American Labor in the United States" (Dissertation,
Cornell University, 1973), pp. 1-121.
     6. Sigurd A. Johansen, "Rural Social Organization
in a Spanish-American Culture Area" (Ph.d. dissertation,
University of Wisconsin, 1941).
     7. Charles P. Loomis, Zona K. Loomis, and Jeanne B.
Gullahorn, Linkages of Mexico and the United States.
Research Bulletin 14, Agricultural Experimental Station,
Michigan State University, 1966, pp. 4-7.
     8. Nelson G. Copp, "Wetbacks and Braceros: Mexican
Migrant Laborers and American Immigration Policy, 1930-
1960" (Dissertation, St. Mary's University of San Anton-
io, Texas, 1963); Peter N. Kirstein, "Anglo over Bracero:
A History of the Mexican Worker in the United States from
Roosevelt to Nixon" (Dissertation, St. Louis University,
1973).
     9. Dillman, "Urban Growth."
     10. A good history of the Mexican State of Chihua-
hua, across the river from El Paso, is Florence C. Lister
and Robert H. Lister, Chihuahua House of Storms (Albuquerque: University of New Mexico Press, 1966).
     11. Mark Adams, A Report on Politics in El Paso
(Cambridge, Mass.: Joint Center for Urban Studies, MIT
and Harvard University, 1963), pp. 1-2.
     12. As has been pointed out, the Bureau of the Cen-
sus has tried from 1930 to 1970 (without success) to
enumerate accurately the Mexican-American population of
the United States. Even though the Bureau of the Census
tried to improve its concepts and methodology for the
1970 census, its enumerations do not seem to have been
any more accurate than those of preceding census years.
As the U.S. Civil Rights Commission stated in 1974: "The
Bureau's techniques for measuring the number of persons
of Spanish-speaking background in 1970 was a compromise
and not the result of its customary careful scientific
planning. It is no wonder that the 1970 census, more
than any previous census, was criticized for its measure
of this group." For the 1970 census, the Bureau of the
Census used the terms Spanish Surname, Spanish Heritage,
and Spanish Language to refer to all the varied groups

that might be defined by these terms. Some of the reasons why the Bureau has such difficulties are as follows:
(1) the existence of a very large number of illegal Mexican immigrants, significant enough to influence census
findings in some states, who are most reluctant to be
counted; (2) many families and individuals, especially
adult males, are quite mobile and hard to count; (3)
large numbers of rural Mexican-American migrant workers
who reside in the Southwest during the winter and travel
in diverse western and midwestern states during the rest
of the year may be hard to find; (4) the failure of the
Bureau to use terms with which Mexican Americans may
identify, such as Mexican American; and (5) the lack of
any term acceptable to the vast majority of people of
Mexican-American origin, such as Mexican American, Spanish American, Latin American, or Chicano. All of these
terms are rejected by substantial groups of Mexican
Americans.

13. At least three separate counts of the Spanish
Surname and Spanish Language groups exist for El Paso in
three separate census publications. As there are very
few Latin Americans, other than Mexicans, Cubans, or
Puerto Ricans, the overwhelming number of El Pasoan residents defined as Spanish Surname or Spanish Language
groups are Mexican Americans. This term will be used to
refer to the Spanish Surname or Spanish Language group in
this chapter. A count of 187,296 is found in a census
report, PHC(1)-62, on the El Paso Standard Metropolitan
Statistical Area. A second count of 148,286 is contained
in a Supplementary Report, PC(SI)-62, and the third,
148,286, in PC(2)-ID, Persons of Spanish Surname. It
should be noted that two samples adjusted to represent
the total population of Spanish Surname and Spanish Language population were used in the 1970 census, a 15 percent sample, and a 5 percent sample. The difference in
numbers may reflect the difference in samples to some
degree. The El Paso volume includes all persons of Spanish surname and those who reported the Spanish language
as their mother tongue or were living in families where
head or wife reported Spanish as a mother tongue. The
other two census publications used only those identified
as having a Spanish surname. It should be kept in mind
that in New Mexico and southern Colorado, significant
numbers of Mexican Americans may have other than Spanish
surnames.

14. U.S. Bureau of the Census, Census of Population
and Housing, 1970, Census Tracts, FINAL REPORT, PHC(I)-
62, El Paso, Texas SMSA (Washington, D.C.: U.S. Government Printing Office, 1972).

15. U.S. Bureau of the Census, Census of Population
and Housing, 1970, Supplementary Report PC(SI)-61, SMSA's
Characteristics of the Spanish Surname Population by Census Tracts (Washington, D.C.: U.S. Government Printing

154

Office, 1974).

    16.   Adams, <u>A Report</u>.

    17.   U.S. Bureau of the Census, <u>Census Population</u>, <u>1970</u>, Vol. 1, Characteristics of the <u>Population, Part 1</u>, <u>U.S. Summary, Section 1</u> (Washington, D.C.: U.S. Government Printing Office).

    18.   Ibid., p. 469.

    19.   Ibid., p. 468.

7
Pluralism in El Paso, Texas

David B. Eyde

INTRODUCTION

One often hears reference to the American Southwest as a plural society. The purpose of the following pages is to apply a model of cultural and social pluralism to relations between Anglo Americans and Mexican Americans in El Paso, Texas, in order to gain some clarification of the sense in which El Paso, and by extension some other areas of the Southwest, may be described as pluralistic. The model used is derived with modifications from those suggested by Despres and Smith.[1] In applying the model to El Paso, an attempt is made to arrive at a preliminary conceptualization of a complex social system. What follows is not a description of new substantive findings. The gross generalizations offered are based upon some familiarity with the community and its inhabitants, and with the relevant literature, but they do not reflect intensive field work or other research. Important references are D'Antonio and Form and Stoddard.[2]

Following Despres,[3] a distinction can be made between those societies which are ethnically homogeneous and those which are ethnically heterogeneous. Among the latter, a distinction can be made between those in which ethnic heterogeneity is reflected in a pluralistic integration into society-wide institutions and those in which it is not. The result is a threefold classification of human societies: homogeneous, heterogeneous, and plural. Still following Despres,[4] local institutions, "those which serve to structure activities and express cultural values within the context of the local community," will be regarded here as providing an index of ethnic heterogeneity, while broker institutions, those which integrate the local community into the wider society, will be regarded as indicative of the degree and kind of plural integration of the society as a whole. Local institutions and broker institutions will be discussed in turn.

In reading the following, the reader should be aware that the discussion of Mexican and Mexican-American

institutions have reference to institutions found in, or
closely tied to, the predominantly Spanish-speaking
barrios of El Paso. Some people of Mexican ancestry in El
Paso do not participate in these institutions. They are,
overwhelmingly, middle-class people who have made the
firm decision to assimilate to Anglo-American society, or
whose parents made that decision. Such people must be
distinguished from those who, though they are middle
class, continue to participate in Mexican-American institutions in the *barrios*. There are two Spanish-surnamed
middle classes in El Paso: those who continue to participate in--indeed, are often leaders in--*barrio* activities,
and those who have cut themselves off from such activities. The relationship between these two Mexican-
American middle classes is reminiscent of the situation
decribed for *campesinos* (Indians) in the Bolivian Nor
Yngas by Leons.[5] She notes that in recent years there
have been two trends within this group. First, there has
been increasing social mobility of some *campesinos* across
ethnic boundaries. Second, there has been increasing
social differentiation and stratification within the
campesino group. The two trends are occurring simulta-
neously but are not unrelated. The children of *campesinos* who have risen within that group have the possibility of acquiring an education which can lead to their
entrance into the dominant ethnic group.

Two further complicating factors should be mentioned: bilingualism and biculturalism. In El Paso, the
local institutional activities of the vast majority of
Mexicans and Mexican Americans are carried out in Spanish. This means, whatever other differences there may
be, these institutions are linguistically inaccessible to
most Anglo Americans. At the same time, many Mexicans
and Mexican Americans are monolingual, or are uncomfor-
table with English; for them, Anglo local institutions
are relatively closed. But the situation is not symmet-
ric. Most Mexican Americans are bilingual, many fluently
so. Anglo local institutions are relatively more acces-
sible linguistically to Mexican Americans than are Mexican and Mexican-American institutions to Anglos. Many
other factors are involved, but it certainly seems probable that, in general, Mexican Americans understand Anglos better than Anglos understand Mexican Americans. An
investigation of this linguistic asymmetry as it affects
economic transactions, patterns of marriage, socioeconomic mobility, and so forth, would be extremely interesting. This subject will be touched upon again when
broker institutions in El Paso are discussed.

Many Mexican Americans are not only bilingual but
are also genuinely bicultural. By their ability to shift
from one set of institutional assumptions and structures
to another, according to social context, they give an
appearance of cultural convergence of assimilation.

Often, however, what appears to be assimilation is really "behaving like a Roman when in Rome," or acting like an Anglo American in an Anglo context while retaining complete ability to act like a Mexican American in a Mexican-American context. This is not to say there has been no acculturation or that Mexican-American culture is identical to that of Mexico. Obviously there have been modifications and innovations, but, as will be indicated by what follows, Mexican-American culture still constitues an independent system of values and assumptions embedded in institutional structures different from those of Anglo Americans.

LOCAL INSTITUTIONS

Family and Kinship Networks

The traditional Mexican extended family system and the associated kinship solidarity are in a state of disarray among Mexican Americans and immigrant Mexicans. Urban conditions and high geographical mobility account for this. Nevertheless, as a model of family relations, the extended family persists as a conscious ideal, sometimes achieved, among most Mexicans and Mexican Americans. They repeatedly emphasize the solidarity of the extended family as one of the outstanding, valued differences between their culture and that of Anglo Americans. They do not positively value the independent nuclear family as do Anglo Americans. So long as the valued familial models of the two groups differ, it would appear fair to conclude that with regard to the family and kinship networks there is an institutional difference between the two groups.

Economic Activities

El Paso has an urban economy. Its principal productive activities are not an aspect of local institutions but, rather, of broker institutions, to be considered later. Consumption activities, on the other hand, are carried out at the local level, and in such activities there are differences between Mexicans and Mexican Americans on one hand and Anglo Americans on the other. Mexicans and Mexican Americans expend relatively large amounts of money on church-related activities, rites of passage, and large-scale parties for kin and neighborhood. Often all three of these are combined, as in a baptism or wedding concluding with a large party. Anglo Americans, including Anglo Catholics, tend to consume conspicuously by purchasing expensive goods and entertaining particular people who are significant in their lives.

For Anglo Americans, the institutional structures, in terms of which conspicuous consumption is carried out, are provided by the class structure of the society as a whole and, perhaps, primarily for the middle class, the structure of the place of employment. For most Mexicans and Mexican Americans, it is the network provided by kin and neighborhood that provides the structure for conspicuous consumption. Taking consumption as the crucial aspect of local economic activities, we may conclude that there is an institutional difference between the two groups.

Religious Activities

The neighborhood church is a primarily local institution while the hierarchies which integrate most neighborhood churches into wider groupings are broker institutions. Only the former will be considered here.

Mexicans and Mexican Americans are in general Roman Catholics. Anglos are in general Protestants. Of course, a significant number of Anglo Americans are Catholics, but the differing languages of most Anglo-American Catholic and Mexican-American Catholic services effectively serve to segregate the two groups. Moreover, English-speaking priests tend to be Anglo Americans (often Irish Americans) while Spanish-speaking priests are frequently Spaniards or, in any case, not Anglo Americans. The linguistic and cultural differentiation of priests may well reinforce value differences between Anglo congregations on the one hand and Mexican and Mexican-American ones on the other, even among Roman Catholics. When the broader contrast between typical Anglo-American Protestantism and typical Mexican-American Catholicism is considered, it appears reasonable to judge there is an institutional difference between the two groups with regard to local religious activities.

Educational Activities

Despite recent efforts in the area of bilingual and bicultural education, it is still the case that schools in El Paso are dominated by Anglo Americans and by anglicized Mexican Americans. The instruction communicates Anglo-American values. While Mexicans and Mexican Americans participate in the schools, they find them a source of stress because of value incompatibilities. This is a situation of differential incorporation[6] in which the superordinate Anglo group controls the institution and its formal values, rules, activities, and social relationships. Acculturative pressure is exerted upon the subordinate Mexican and Mexican-American group which resists, attempting to express its own cultural ideas and values within the imposed institutional structure.

Associational Activities

The contrast here is quite sharp. Anglo Americans participate widely in a variety of special purpose organizations. Mexicans and Mexican Americans join few voluntary organizations. Those they do join tend to be church-related organizations. (It will be recalled we are dealing here only with organizations that operate at the local level. Organizations which are city- or regionwide are dealt with below.) There is an institutional difference between the two groups with regard to associational activities.

Social and Recreational Activities

It has already been noted that Mexican and Mexican-American entertainment is likely to be related to rites of passage and/or church-related, and that the invitation is likely to be a general one to kin and neighborhood. Anglo-American entertainment, on the other hand, tends to be purely social and to be directed toward particular others significant in place of employment or other special purpose group. It should be added that the Mexican and Mexican-American bar acts much more as a neighborhood men's club than does a comparable Anglo-American establishment. There is an institutional difference between the two groups with regard to social and recreational activities.

Local Government Activities

We are interested here in orientation toward authority and its relationship to local government authorities. Mexican and Mexican-American political leadership at the neighborhood level is particularistic in that a leader's position depends upon his maintenance of personal ties with a network of kin and neighbors. His power is based partially on granting of favors and partially on personal charisma. Political power at the local level for the Anglo American is far more a matter of applying universalistic criteria within the context of formal association. Though the offices may be the same, they articulate with the organization of the neighborhood in different ways. Particularly for the Mexican and Mexican-American leader himself, there may be considerable stress in that the values of the community which he leads do not correspond to those embodied in the institutional structure of which he is a part. Local government activities are carried out in a context of differential incorporation into an institutional structure.

A MODEL OF ETHNIC HETEROGENEITY IN EL PASO

Ethnic heterogeneity is very high in El Paso. In none of the areas of day-to-day life carried out at the level of neighborhood or *barrio* are there institutional structures uniformly valid for all. In five areas there are institutional differences, and in two the situation is one of differential incorporation with subordination of Mexicans and Mexican Americans. The neighborhoods of El Paso show a strong pattern of ethnic heterogeneity. It follows that El Paso can be discussed in terms of minimal cultural sections,[7] culturally differentiated groups functioning within the context of the local community, in this case the *barrios* and neighborhoods of El Paso.

BROKER INSTITUTIONS IN EL PASO

To what extent do broker institutions in El Paso integrate the minimal culture sections into the ethnically defined societywide blocks which Despres calls "maximal cultural sections"?[8]

Educational Institutions

With the exception of one outlying area recently incorporated into the city, El Paso has a unified school system. This system was, until 1970, devoted to cultural assimilation of Mexicans and Mexican Americans. This policy was imposed on neighborhood schools by the district as a whole. It was regarded as undesirable by most Mexican Americans insofar as it threatened complete extinction of their culture. Mexican Americans believed they were discriminated against within the school system. The system was thus an institution of differential incorporation in that acculturative pressures were being exerted on a subordinate group by a dominant one. The University of Texas at El Paso, until 1971 the only institution of higher education in the city, was similarly a broker institution which involved differential incorporation of Mexican Americans into an essentially Anglo-American educational system.

Recent developments in bilingual, bicultural education at the grade school level indicate the situation described has changed to some degree. More striking is the rise since 1970 of self-consciously Chicano classes being offered at youth centers in association with various community action programs and at the University. They are important new developments. Moreover, it is clear that in the eyes of many administrators, faculty, and students, El Paso Community College, established in 1971 with federal funds, is, or ought to be, a politically active Chicano institution.

Communication Media

In El Paso, until recently, there has not been a single newspaper, television station, or radio station owned by Mexican Americans or expressing a Mexican-American viewpoint. All, with the exception of one Mexican-owned newspaper, were owned and operated by Anglo Americans, and all, to make a sweeping but fair generalization, expressed a generally conservative Anglo-American businessman's world view. Even programming or newspaper articles directed toward the Mexican-American community were notable for their rarity. The absence of Mexican-American media was, to a degree, compensated for by three Spanish-language newspapers, two Spanish-language television stations, and a large number of Spanish-language radio stations available to an audience in El Paso, but all of these were disseminated from Ciudad Juarez, Mexico, across the Rio Grande from El Paso. In general, they paid remarkably little attention to Mexicans or Mexican Americans in El Paso. The media in El Paso, until recently, constituted institutions of differential incorporation in that acculturative pressures were exerted on a subordinate group by a dominant one.

The foregoing paragraph, though written in the past tense, describes the current situation quite well. Nevertheless, since 1970 there have been some interesting new developments. A self-consciously Chicano radio station has been established. All three television stations, under pressure from political activists within the Mexican-American community, have introduced similarly self-consciously Chicano programs. There also has been a spate of short-lived, small-scale Chicano publications.

Commercial and Industrial Organizations

In El Paso there are few, if any, large-scale corporations with personnel recruited exclusively from one ethnic group. Within the corporations, employers will insist position is determined by ability and ethnicity is irrelevant. Many Mexicans and Mexican Americans, however, are convinced that ethnic factors do operate in job allocation. It can, in any case, be pointed out that there are not very many unskilled or semiskilled civilian Anglo-American workers in El Paso; few stay because employment opportunities are much better elsewhere. The result is that such jobs are held overwhelmingly by Mexicans and Mexican Americans, tied to the city by the linguistic and cultural difficulties encountered outside the border region.

With regard to skilled and white-collar positions, El Paso is quite complex. Both Anglo Americans and Mexican Americans work at these levels. Of particular interest is the fact that many Mexican Americans have a competitive advantage over most Anglo Americans or Mexicans with regard to those jobs that require dealing with the public or mediating between management and labor. The frequency of monolingual Spanish speakers in the consuming public and in the labor force is such that in these positions bilingual employees are preferred by many employers. It is interesting to note that positions for which bilinguals are preferred do not reward full assimilation of Mexican Americans to the English language and Anglo-American culture. Instead, rewards lie precisely in being bilingual and bicultural.

The bulk of Mexicans and Mexican Americans in El Paso clearly do not occupy positions equivalent to those of Anglos within the corporate structure. Therefore, we can conclude that commercial and industrial organizations are institutions of differential incorporation of the ethnic groups.

Markets and Economic Transactions

While consumption goals of Mexicans and Mexican Americans and Anglo Americans differ to a degree, there is essentially no difference in the way individuals are integrated into the market economy. There is geographical differentiation between the stores partronized by Mexicans and Mexican Americans, and those of the predominantly Anglo-American suburbs, but these are ultimately integrated by a single supply-demand market. Given the subordinate position of Mexicans and Mexican Americans within the economy and the extent to which advertising exerts pressure toward acculturation in consumption, it seems fairest to classify the supply-demand market as another institution of differential incorporation.

Trade Unions and Labor Organizations

Until recently, there has been very little union activity in El Paso. Unions were for the most part for craftsmen and skilled laborers. Except for the Railway Brotherhoods, they were generally Mexican and Mexican-American, but the great majority of blue-collar workers were not unionized and, indeed, still are not. Unions, until recently, were not significant enough to be relevant to a discussion of pluralism in El Paso. It is interesting to note, however, that the locals of the Amalgamated Garment Workers of America, which succeeded in unionizing workers in 1974 at the Farah Manufacturing Company, El Paso's largest single private employer, are very much self-consciously Chicano in identity.

Governmental Agencies

At the level of municipal and county government, El Paso has, and has had for a long time, administrative agencies with many Mexican Americans among ther personnel. In large part, this follows from what has already been said with regard to preference for bilinguals in positions dealing with the public. Though there is a tendency for higher echelons of government to be Anglo-American, administrative positions throughout the system are occupied by Mexican Americans. Nevertheless, those Mexican Americans who occupy higher positions tend to be very anglicized, and most Mexicans and Mexican Americans perceive municipal and county agencies as agents of the Anglo-American elite and place little trust in them. They are institutions of differential incorporation.

Until recently, the matter could have been left there, but note should be taken of the federally funded agencies, operating at the city level, which have resulted from the "war on poverty" and its successors. These agencies, such as Project Bravo, MACHO, etc., with their emphasis on community participation, have the potential of becoming broker institutions integrating Mexican Americans into a separate maximal culture section at the level of the city as a whole.

Religious and Ethnic Associations

It has already been noted that Mexicans and Mexican Americans join few voluntary associations. Those they do join tend to be church-oriented. The Roman Catholic church is itself a broker institution. In general, the church hierarchy in this region is Anglo-American and assimilationist in outlook. This has resulted in alienation from the church on the part of many young Mexican Americans. In addition to the church itself, there are a number of church organizations which are citywide broker institutions: the Knights of Columbus and women's and youth organizations. These also have tended to be dominated by Anglo Americans and assimilationist in outlook.

The principal established ethnic association of Mexican Americans is the League of United Latin American Citizens, founded in the 1920s. Membership in this organization is limited to those of Mexican or other Latin-American ancestry. But the membership has been composed largely of anglicized members of the middle class, and the organization, at least until recently, was mainly assimilationist in outlook. It seems fair to say that, until recently, religious and ethnic associations in El Paso have involved differential incorporation of minimal cultural sections rather than integration into maximal cultural sections.

Political Parties

Is there a system of differential incorporation into the polity in El Paso? At first glance, the answer appears to be "no." El Paso is, after all, organized politically as a democracy in which all citizens have an equal vote. But Smith notes that

> . . . where there are systematic structural differences between constitutional forms of incorporation and the substantive forms of social life, as, for example, in the American incorporation of Negro citizens, then as Weber said, "it is the actual state of affairs which is decisive for sociological purposes (Weber, 1947:137)." In short, despite constitutional provisions, differential incorporation may be institutionalized within a universalistic order, and not merely sub rosa. If so, it is seriously misleading to analyze the system solely or primarily in terms of its formal ideology and its inoperative or ineffective laws. Where form and substance diverge, structurally, the appropriate evidence for sociological analysis of pluralism or any other condition consists surely in the operational regularities and conditions of social life.[9]

It is quite impossible to sketch here even the outlines of the political process in El Paso. It has been extensively discussed by Adams and Adams and D'Antonio and Form.[10] The following points are significant for this discussion, however. First, very many residents of, or workers in, El Paso are not citizens of the United States but of Mexico. They cannot take part in the political processes of El Paso but are subject to them. No great effort is made on the part of local federal officials or other agents of the wider society to encourage these people to become citizens. Second, there have been few expressions of lower class ethnically Mexican-American interests in El Paso politics. As Moore says of Texas politics as a whole, "Political organization has been middle class, highly oriented toward traditional expressions of 'Americanism' and accommodationist."[11] A few candidates for mayor or alderman who expressed lower class interests have run, but have been defeated by a generally conservative electorate. (Even candidates for alderman have run at large.) Third, Mexican Americans have not exercised much political influence, but what influence there has been has been channeled through local political leaders who deliver votes in return for prestige, political position, or economic advantage within an Anglo-dominated society. Fourth, Davidson makes the point that one-party systems often "institutionalize elite or ethnic domination."[12] In El Paso, the only

significant political party, the Democratic party, is
dominated by an Anglo-American business elite. In that
party, Mexican Americans have sometimes held prominent
postions, but they have been, with few exceptions, precisely those Mexican Americans who were most anglicized.
Control of the party has remained securely in the hands
of the Anglo-American business community. So has control
of the ostensibly nonpartisan city and county governments. In order for Mexican Americans to rise to prominence, they must almost invariably be political brokers
of the middle class, oriented toward "Americanization"
and accommodation, and acceptable to at least the more
liberal wing of the Anglo-American business and political
community. The Democratic party is an institution of
differential incorporation.

Since 1970, a new political party, La Raza Unida,
has begun to be active in El Paso, as elsewhere in the
Southwest. Self-consciously Chicano, its appeal is to
Mexican Americans to form a power block to exert political pressure in Mexican-American interests in the political process. Its explicit aim is to develop into a broker institution integrating Mexican Americans into a
maximal cultural section.

A MODEL OF BROKER INSTITUTIONS IN EL PASO

It will be noted that until recently there were no
broker institutions in El Paso which integrated the
barrio minimal cultural sections into a citywide Mexican-
American cultural section. Broker institutions, in all
cases, involved differential incorporation in that they
have been dominated by Anglo Americans while Mexicans and
Mexican Americans have occupied subordinate positions and
have undergone strong acculturative pressures to modify
traditional values. El Paso is, in Despres' classification, a heterogeneous society. It is not now a plural
society in Despres' sense of possessing maximal cultural
sections. At least until very recently, such maximal
cultural sections did not exist at all.

It is striking that the last six or seven years have
seen the development of "incipient" broker institutions
which are conscious attempts to integrate all Mexican-
American minimal cultural sections into a Mexican-American maximal cultural section. The various courses in
Chicano culture, El Paso Community College insofar as it
is a Chicano institution, the Chicano radio station, Chicano television programming, the short-lived Chicano
newspapers, the Chicano locals of the Amalgamated Clothing Workers, new ethnic associations, and La Raza Unida
party are, from the point of view of this discussion,
attempts to create a maximal cultural section where one
has not existed. El Paso today more nearly approximates
Despres' model of a plural society than it did five years

ago, though the nascent broker institutions have, as yet, had little real impact on the structure of the municipality. If developments already underway continue unimpeded, the result might be something like a plural society. Writing early in 1977, it does not appear likely that El Paso will in fact develop further in this way. There is an atmosphere of fatigue about the militant Chicano movement. Federal funding, essential to a number of the incipient Chicano broker institutions, has been reduced or cut off entirely. Under pressure from the Chicano movement, Anglo-American dominated broker institutions have in some cases, as in the bilingual education program in the public schools, changed their policies with regard to Mexican Americans and Mexican-American culture. Through exhaustion, accommodation, and continued assimilation, the future structure of El Paso society will probably continue to involve differential incorporation of Mexican Americans into Anglo-American-dominated broker institutions.

NOTES

1. Leo A. Despres, Cultural Pluralism and Nationalist Politics in British Guiana (Chicago: Rand McNally and Company, 1967) and "Differential Adaptations and Micro-Cultural Evolution in Guyana," Southwestern Journal of Anthropology 25 (1969): 14-44; M. G. Smith: "Social and Cultural Pluralism," Annals of the New York Academy of Science 83 (1960); Stratification in Grenada (Berkeley and Los Angeles: University of California Press, 1965); "Institutional and Political Conditions of Pluralism," in L. Kuper and M. G. Smith, eds., Pluralism in Africa (Berkeley and Los Angeles: University of California Press, 1969); "Pluralism in Precolonial African Societies," in Kuper and Smith, Pluralism in Africa; "Some Developments in the Analytic Framework of Pluralism," in Kuper and Smith, Pluralism in Africa.
2. William V. D'Antonio and William H. Form, Influentials in Two Border Cities (Notre Dame: University of Notre Dame Press, 1965); Ellwyn R. Stoddard, Mexican Americans (New York: Random House, 1973).
3. Despres, Cultural Pluralism, pp. 21-27.
4. Ibid., pp. 23, 121-123.
5. Madeline Barbara Leons, "Stratification and Pluralism in the Bolivian Yungas," in W. Goldschmidt and H. Hoijer, eds., The Social Anthropology of Latin America: Essays in Honor of Ralph Leon Beals (Los Angeles: Latin American Center, University of California, 1970), p. 281.
6. Smith, in Kuper and Smith, Pluralism in Africa, pp. 432-435.
7. Despres, Cultural Pluralism, p. 118.

8. Ibid., pp. 121-122.

9. Smith, "Some Developments," p. 439.

10. D'Antonio and Form, Influentials.

11. Joan W. Moore, "Colonialism: The Case of the Mexican Americans," Social Problems 17 (1970): 463-472.

12. Basil Davidson, "Pluralism in Colonial African Societies: Northern Rhodesia/Zambia," in Kuper and Smith, Pluralism in Africa.

8
Religion and Pluralism Among
the Spanish-Speaking Groups of the Southwest

Richard L. Hough

Few attempts have been made to construct a sociologically informed overview of the place of religion in the history of Mexican Americans in the southwestern United States. This essay does not pretend to perform the task in a definitive way; rather, suggestions are made as to the major directions such an undertaking might take in the context of a sociological understanding of the subjects of pluralism and assimilation.

Another caveat is that it is presumptuous to talk about the place of religion in the history of Mexican Americans in general. A more proper approach would recognize that contemporary Mexican Americans are divided into numerous regional and subcultural groups that differ radically from one another. Basically, this essay will concern itself with the place of religion in Mexican-Spanish culture of the seventeenth through nineteenth centuries, and in contemporary Hispano and Mexican-American subsocieties. Each of these Spanish-speaking groups could be further divided. Ideally, contemporary Mexican-American subsocieties vary widely depending on whether one is speaking of urban Southern California or rural south Texas. Generalizations tend to be somewhat dangerous, and a more thorough examination of religious behavior among southwestern Spanish-speaking peoples would have to deal with finer variations. However, some general guidelines to that more thorough analysis can be sketched here.

The story of religious influence among these groups is by and large one of the Catholic church, and a few remarks about the church in American society are in order to provide a setting for what follows.

Andrew Greeley[1] has characterized the history of the Catholic church in American society as one dominated by ambivalence toward the host society. He argues this has been true because the church has been so predominantly an immigrant church, receiving most of its impetus from waves of immigration during the nineteenth and early twentieth centuries. During most of this period the

169

nativist bigotry and prejudice encountered by various
groups of Catholic immigrants left basically only two
styles of response available. First, the immigrant
church could respond to the United States as a hostile
nation and seek to defend immigrants and their faith
against a hostile Protestant society with individual
Catholics encouraged to maintain their distance from the
larger society. Or, they could interpret the United
States as a society in which freedom and democracy were
bound to triumph and, therefore, a climate in which Catholics and the church could flourish with individual Catholics becoming as American as possible without sacrific-
ing Catholicism.

An uneasy balance between these two perspectives has
characterized the Catholic church. In the name of the
former, a separate school system was generated. Chari-
table organizations and a tremendous range of voluntary
organizations, from labor groups to youth groups, were
made available to Catholics, enabling them to develop interests with as little contact as possible with the larger society. Further, these organizations tended to be
ethnically enclosed. As a result, the immigrants were
subjected to strong social controls and developed an
anti-intellectual attitude, a fear of close contact with
Protestants, a tendency to be very defensive about what
they perceived to be their own rights, and a strong loyalty to Rome. The immigrants tended to accept the
church's demand for loyalty because the church and ethnic
identity were so crucial for their own sense of identity.
This is part of the reason the American working class did
not leave the church as in European society.

The other response, an acceptance of American society as a fertile climate for development, tended to be
less predominant. Church leaders who adopted this view
emphasized the need for good Catholics to be good Americans also. During the World Wars this feeling manifested
itself in tremendous pride in military service, and in
postwar periods, in terms of the superpatriotism of some
elements within the church. A more reasonable expression
of concern came through English language classes, naturalization instruction, and sponsoring such typically
American social activities as Boy Scout troops and bowl-
ing teams. Such activities made "Americanization" possible for generations of immigrants.

Greeley argues that by the 1960s the status of American Catholics had changed radically. After 1960, evidence mounted rapidly so that occupational and educational achievement of Catholics differed little from achievements of Protestants of similar geographical location.
The church, for all intents and purposes, had become middle class. Moreover, the church itself has become more
Americanized and less defensive.

This is not to say that Catholics will become Protestant in their doctrinal beliefs or will abandon
their union with the Roman pontiffs, but the organizational style and posture of American Catholicism
will become more and more like that of the Protestant churches. Popular participation in decision
making and selection of leaders, more independence
for the clergy, the committee approach to church
governance, the emergence of a scholarly clerical
elite, the evolution of a social service concept of
the ministry . . . much greater freedom for dicus-
sion and criticism, and more openness toward non-
Catholic religions--all of these seem to be an inevitable part of the future of the Roman Catholic
Church in this country as it realizes that such
styles of ecclesiastical organization are inevitable
when one is dealing with a thoroughly Americanized
population.[2]

The remarkable degree to which "Americanization" has
proceeded in the Catholic church in American society as a
whole is reflected to some extent among Catholics in the
Southwest, although the picture drawn above of the Americanized Catholic church would not be too recognizable to
anyone familiar with only the Southwest. The process of
Americanization has been slowed by a number of factors.
First is the obvious point that the church serves a
Southwestern population with strong ties and easy access
to a predominantly Catholic country, Mexico. Likelihood
of Americanization is dampened by a constant flow of new
Mexican immigrants into the country and by constant interaction and communication between American and Mexican
populations.

Further, Catholicism in the Southwest has remained
disproportionately the religion of a lower socioeconomic
population. Pressures toward Americanization emanating
from the rising materialistic status of its membership
among Catholics generally in the United States have not
been present to the same degree in this population.
There is also the fact that the Catholic population of
the Southwest, unlike the great immigrant populations
from Europe, has been very nominal in its level of commitment to the church. This nominal quality stems partially from the historical nominalism of Mexican Catholics and partially from failure of the American Catholic
church to effectively reach immigrant populations.

These factors taken together have meant that resources of the church have been less plentiful than in
the rest of the country. Even leadership has not been
developed internally but has consisted predominantly of
foreign clergy. Thus, the degree to which Catholicism in
the Southwest constitutes an exception to the rule of Americanization in the church in the larger society will

be an important focus of the following discussion.

CATHOLICISM IN THE SPANISH ERA

The history of Spanish exploration and conquest of
the Southwest is heavily laced with references to Catholic clergy. Most often the clergy served as leaders of
expeditions and settlement. Cabeza de Vaca and three
fellow survivors of the ill-fated Narvaez expedition were
the first Europeans to enter the Southwest interior in
1534. After escaping Indian captors, they made their way
northward to the edge of the great plains and from there
southward into northern Mexico. Only five years later,
the first viceroy of New Spain, Antonio de Mendoza, when
he could not enlist de Vaca for the job, sent Fray Marcos
de Niza, a Franciscan, on an exploratory expedition to
find the seven golden cities of the north. Fray Marcos
paved the way for Coronado's 1540-1542 expedition.
After the Coronado expedition did not discover the
gold and riches for which they had hoped, almost four
decades passed before the Southwest again excited interest, this time in hopes of finding a northwest passage to
the east. During several tentative explorations in the
1580s, the Franciscans established contact with some of
the Pueblo Indian groups, particularly the Zuni. In 1598
the famous expedition of Juan de Onate began the first
real attempts at settlement in the Southwest. Onate had
been awarded the contract for Spanish settlement of New
Mexico. Several Franciscans accompanied him as he established the capital city of New Spain at Capa Pueblo,
north of Santa Fe. Franciscans helped record and map
Onate's numerous expeditions to chart the potential of
the new land. For the next thirty years, Franciscans
helped push exploration and settlement northward to Taos
and westward to the Hopi. The missions they established
were generally self-supporting, though they received a
small annual income from the royal Spanish treasury.
Despite success among Pueblo groups, they met serious resistance from the Navajo and Apache.
Fergusson[3] summarizes missionary work of the seventeenth century in New Mexico. By 1625 there were some
fifty churches served by twenty-six friars, but from the
1620s on, missionary progress was retarded by a series of
feuds between Spanish governors and *comisarios* of the
church, and by stiffening resistance to the church among
the Pueblos, particularly the Zuni and Jemez. Charges of
clergy misuse of Indian labor and lands increased, and
after a series of droughts and famine during the 1670s
and a renewed campaign by Governor Trevino to suppress
all "superstitious practices" among the Indians, the
Pueblo revolt of 1680 broke out. The revolt was temporarily successful and forced Spanish settlers and the

church out of New Mexico for over a decade. The Indians attempted to destroy every trace of the church while the retreating Spanish soldiers wreaked destruction on the Pueblos.

In 1692-93, Don Diego de Vargas mounted a successful campaign to reconquer the area accompanied by settlers and missionaries. During the 1690s, missionary enterprise began in earnest with missions being established from east Texas to the West Coast as Spanish governors became more concerned about countering the developing French threat from the east and establishing trade routes to the west.

A particularly dramatic example of the missionary process is that of Father Eusebio Francisco Kino in Arizona.[4] In many ways, the story of the settlement of Arizona is the story of his missionary life. From 1691 to his death in 1711 he mapped the area, established missions, and won the respect of the Indians, particularly the Pima and Papago. He supplied them with cattle, sheep, horses, and mules, and established the beginnings of ranching in the Santa Cruz and San Pedro valleys. He introduced grains and fruits along with new farming techniques. He explored the region more thoroughly than anyone before, was the first to discover that Baja California is a peninsula, not an island, and his maps became authoritative for decades. It is estimated that he rode or walked some 75,000 miles during his twenty years of exploration and settlement.

It should be noted that Kino's followers were generally unworthy of the example he had established. The two and one-half decades immediately following his death were a retrenchment period for the Spanish Empire; only very slow expansion could be financed in east Texas to counter the French and plains Indians. In Arizona, Kino's missions were not even staffed for a number of years and then only intermittently. By 1750, eight of the missions he had established were still without resident missionaries. However, the Jesuits still had established rather thorough control over the Pima and Papago.

The 1750s and 1760s brought a series of setbacks to Catholic influence in the Southwest. In 1750 the Pima Indians revolted against the Jesuits. It was never clear whether the revolt's real cause lay in the Jesuit's cruel treatment of the Indians or in the Governor's policies, but the Jesuits never again exerted real control over the Indians. In the middle 1760s, the end of the Seven Years War in Europe resulted in transferral of control over the Louisiana Territory to the Spanish. Since the French were no longer a threat to Mexico, the Spanish could economize their support of missions. In 1767, after some conflict between Jesuits and new policies of the Spanish Empire, all Jesuits were expelled. Property was seized

by the government, and many missions were secularized by
distributing land and animals among converts and turning
buildings into parish churches as opposed to missions.
    The end of Spanish missionary enterprises still had
not come. Explorers like Father Tomas Garces still were
establishing new missions and new trade routes from the
New Mexican pueblo region to the West Coast. The impact
of Spanish missions on the whole over the 300 years of
the Spanish Empire in the Southwest cannot be overstated.
Missions had encouraged a self-supporting, pastoral economy, and settlements near the missions had produced new
merchant and artisan classes. Ranching became a prosperous enterprise with their example and encouragement.
They introduced the sheep industry to New Mexico, and the
Navajos in particular were transformed into herders and
weavers. Introduction of new irrigation techniques and
expansion greatly benefited agricultural production of
the region. New crops such as wheat, barley, other
grains, and fruits were introduced; use of animal power
for plowing was started.
    However, the influence of the Catholic church cannot
be regarded as all pervasive as the Spanish Empire drew
to a close. Indian groups, by and large, still maintained a great deal of their own cultural traditions and religious expression. Leadership and resources of the
church at the Spanish era's end and the Mexican period's
beginning were still weak in terms of their potential ab-
solute control over religious life in the Southwest.

CATHOLICISM AMONG THE HISPANOS

    During the nineteenth century, several developments
occurred which further restricted power and influence of
the Catholic church in the Southwest. Mexican movement
toward independence with resultant separation of church
and state in Mexico, a tremendous influx of American,
predominantly Protestant, settlers into the area resulting in eventual Anglo dominance, and further revolt of
various Indian groups against Catholic domination made it
certain that the Southwest would remain religiously heterogeneous.
    As early as 1821, feelings against Spanish dominance
were strong enough to cause expulsion of all *padres* who
refused an oath of independence. In 1827, as war with
Spain seemed imminent, all foreign missionaries were expelled. The 1830s saw the triumph of federalists over
centralists in a struggle for political power, and in
1834 the Mexican Congress passed a law secularizing all
remaining missions. By 1844, disposition of all mission
property had been accomplished. Missionary enterprise
had largely ceased to exist, and the formal Roman Catholic church was in a near state of collapse in the Southwest.

However, within the confines of the developing Hispano subculture, influence of a domestic, folk brand of
Catholicism was still strong. Meinig[5] describes the
Hispano subculture as the product of Indian and Spanish
contact over several centuries, a blending of culture and
blood. He describes them as usually largely Indian in
background, though increasingly Spanish in language, religion, and general culture. He estimates that of some
20,000 "Spanish" inhabiting settlements of the Rio Grande
Valley in 1800, only a few hundred were wholly Spanish in
ancestry. This indigenous New Mexican population became
dominant through the nineteenth century in a territory
extending along the Rio Grande from Socorro to Taos and
extending far into northeastern New Mexico, southern Colorado, and middle-western New Mexico. Expansion ended in
the 1860s and 1879s as they encountered Anglo cattlemen
competing for the same land, water, and grass.[6]

Lamar[7] pictures the Catholic religion of the early
part of the nineteenth century in New Mexico as permis-
sive, simplistic, and even decadent by some standards,
but still a powerful influence on its adherents. The
twenty to thirty priests who ministered to the state as
often as not dominated their communities and seriously
threatened the power of any political authority beyond
the community to influence local affairs. These priests
simplified their services, retained many medieval Catholic customs, and allowed many Indian rituals to mingle
with their practices and beliefs. The geographical im-
mensity of the area they were supposed to serve and their
own lack of formal training and supervision meant there
was a scarcity of priestly services, and common law marriage, unbaptized children, and general ignorance of
church teaching was widespread. However, geographical
isolation also made them relatively immune to outside
control, and in their insulated areas they developed
supreme authority. They assumed a great deal of power in
community affairs, from performance of the rites of
birth, marriage, and death to more temporal legal, political, and economic affairs. They often extracted fear
and labor from parishioners. Celibacy was not usually
observed.

An unusually dramatic example of the above kind of
leadership was found in Father Jose Antonio Martinez of
Taos. Trained to the priesthood in Durango, he was well
traveled and learned in comparison to his parishioners.
He became undisputed boss of the community, an owner of
several ranches, a flour mill, and the first newspaper in
New Mexico. A freethinker who denounced heavy tithes and
church fees, he evidently did not hesitate to charge high
fees for his legal and spiritual counsel.[8] In many ways,
his leadership was beneficial for the community and
state. He founded one of the region's first schools and
managed to produce a number of early political and

religious leaders. Fergusson[9] describes him as the most
important figure in early New Mexico history. He provided leadership himself in the New Mexico State Conven-
tion and was often leader of the conservative, anti-Am-
erican faction in the House and Council of the state assembly during the 1850s and 1860s.

Heavily involved in secular affairs, he evidently
renounced few pleasures and obviously spent as much time
in economic and political activity as in religious affairs. When Bishop Lamy came from Rome in 1852 to reform the religious establishment of provincial New Mexico, he found it necessary to excommunicate Father Martinez along with four other native priests he found serving
the area. Despite this, Martinez continued to preside in
his church and to express in words and action his belief
that church and state should be one. He continued to
function as a leader in resisting the growing power of ·
new American influence in Taos and the state as a whole.

Although Martinez was certainly an exceptional
leader, he exemplified religion's role in integration and
preservation of Hispano culture in small villages and
towns of northern New Mexico. McWilliams[10] describes New
Mexican Hispano culture as the most cohesive Hispanic
population in the United States. He stresses the role of
religion in establishing and preserving the culture.

> The religion of the villager has also been a factor
> making for social isolation since it has always been
> a central, unifying, cohesive force in their cul-
> ture. Jealous of their loyalties, it has deeply
> penetrated every aspect of their existence and has
> been a powerful shield against intrusive alien in-
> fluences. The color of its pageantry, the mystery
> of its rituals, and the dramatic character of its
> ceremonies have always been potent attractions to
> lonely settlers in a forgotten world. Under the
> circumstances, its value as pure entertainment has
> been, perhaps, the principal explanation of its
> survival and dominant influence.[11]

Nancie Gonzalez[12] portrays the cultural traits the
religious structure helped to preserve as a combination
of folklofe, song, baptism, wedding and funeral customs,
the *Compadrazgo, cofradia* organization, passion plays,
secular dances, courtship customs, protection and se-
clusion of unmarried women, inheritance rules, beliefs
concerning health and disease, witchcraft, extended families living in multiple family dwellings, and male
authoritarianism.

In the absence of formal religious leadership,
church sacraments were often foregone in the villages,
but rituals of life were continued and translated into a
folk system of religion. Recreation usually centered

around celebration of life crises, holy days of the Catholic calendar, and the village patron saint.

A good example of the potential power of lay organization is the Penitentes, originally transplanted from Europe as a lay group, the Third Order of St. Francis, which became known as Los Hermanos de los Penitentes between 1800 and 1850.[13] They had become a penitential and flagellant group by then, preoccupied in religious terms with pain as a means of penance and death. They rejected church supervision and were best known for reenactment of the crucifixion prior to Easter, when they would supposedly fast and beat one another with cactus whips. A more interesting Penitentes activity was their political one. They came to serve as the unofficial political party in many of the communities of the Hispano subculture and were still thriving as New Mexico prepared to enter statehood. Since then they have become more subdued and secretive about their activities but still serve as the most viable potential political organization in many of the more isolated mountain Hispano villages.

One final demonstration of the importance of religious influence in Hispano communities comes from Samora's[14] study of minority group leadership in a southern Colorado bicultural community. The community contained an extension of the Hispano subculture we have described here, and the only voluntary social organizational activity Samora found revolved around the church and its activities.

In the main, religious influence within the subculture has been a conservative, isolationist force. In terms of our overview of assimilation, it would have to be argued that Hispanos are not structurally integrated into the larger society, and that even cultural assimilation proceeds little further than acceptance of the necessity of using the English language in dealing with Anglos. In relatively isolated mountain communities, further assimilation is not likely to occur rapidly. Folk-Catholic religious influence has been an important factor in maintaining this situation.

An interesting note is that Reyes Tijerina and his Alianza de los Pueblos Libres have received their most responsive hearing within the Hispano group. Tijerina has the great dream of reclaiming some four million acres of Spanish landgrants which were swindled from their original recipients. That such a program would receive a positive response from descendants of the original grantees is not surprising, but the religious context within which Tijerina presents his message again demonstrates the powerful hold of Hispano folk religion within the subculture. Tijerina is actually thought by some to be the "messiah" of an old Hispano legend of a leader who was to help them return to their old homes and positions of dominance in the Rio Grande Valley and the immediately surrounding territory.[15]

CATHOLICISM AMONG THE MEXICAN AMERICANS

The boundary between "Hispano" and "Mexican-American" subcultures in the Southwest is impossible to draw
with any accuracy. They are better conceived as polar
types on the ends of a continuum, with "Hispano" referring to the product of Spanish and Indian interaction
over centuries of Spanish influence. "Mexican American"
would describe more recent migrants from Mexico not absorbed into the older Hispano group and whose subculture
emanates from contact with dominant Anglo influence of
the nineteenth and twentieth centuries. Fuller treatment
of the place of religion in the Mexican-American subculture would ideally distinguish between variations within
the population. For example, the Los Angeles subculture
differs greatly from that of border city areas and from
those in Albuquerque and Santa Fe. All these groups differ considerably from predominantly agricultural groups
of south Texas. However, we will concentrate on the differences in religion's role between Hispano and Mexican-
American groups without concern for variations in the
latter.

Mexican Independence in 1821 and resulting separation of church and state meant that for some thirty
years the formal Roman Catholic church of the Southwest
was virtually without physical resources or leadership.
The years of Mexican control (1821-1848) saw a tremendous
influx of American-Anglo population and influence, most
dramatically exemplified in the Texas struggle for independence, with the Republic being established in 1836.
Anglo control was confirmed in the Mexican War of 1846-
1848, following annexation of Texas to the United States
and resulting in acquisition of most of Arizona and New
Mexico.

During these years the church had reached its lowest
point. However, a turning point was reached with ap-
pointment of Bishop Lamy from Rome in 1852 to reform the
church in provincial New Mexico. He found only nine
priests in the territory and excommunicated five of them.
He proved to be a "tough fighter, realistic executive and
an excellent diplomat."[16] He opened the Sisters of
Loretto academy in Santa Fe and in general gave Catholicism a new life. He also gave religious influence a new
direction in the Southwest. In place of the rigid conservatism of the Hispano religious influence, Lamy began
to establish a more "Americanized" brand of Catholicism
which emphasized as part of its pastoral role the necessity of preparing its parishioners for participation in
American life.

From 1850-1900 many religious orders contributed
priests to the Southwest, including the Oblate Fathers of

Mary Immaculate from France, Spanish Franciscans and Cla-
retian Fathers, Immaculate Heart Mission Fathers, Vin-
centian Fathers, and Piarest Fathers. However, the
church was still notoriously weak. Moore[17] notes that by
1890 the archdiocese of Tucson had one priest for every
1052 Catholics in a geographical area over 7000 square
miles, and the combined dioceses of San Antonio, Corpus
Christi, El Paso, Santa Fe, Tucson, and Los Angeles had
only 193 parish priests. Of those, only fourteen were of
Spanish surname.

Grebler et al.[18] contrast the church's character in
the Southwest to that in the east. In the east, the
church was relatively prosperous; succeeding generations
of immigrants managed to adapt to American life and move
into middle and upper-middle classes of American society,
thereby generating significant sources of material support. The church in the Southwest has served a Mexican-
American population which has remained far more subordinate to dominant Protestant Yankees than did eastern
immigrant populations.

In the east, various immigrant groups brought with
them their own priests who were crucial to preservation
of ethnic solidarity in face of the difficulties of adaptation to American life. These clergy, particularly the
Irish Catholic leadership, brought a significant concern
for getting the church accepted in American life into the
upper levels of church leadership. This was translated
into concern for Americanization of the individual Catholic. In turn, they were able to generate acceptance for
Catholicism as a perfectly acceptable identification at
most levels of life.

In the west, the clergy were largely from other than
Mexican or American background. Most of the Spanish-
speaking clergy were of Spanish origin until recently;
Spanish surname priests have always been in the small
minority. In 1921, although 94 percent of the Corpus
Christi ciocese was Spanish in surname, only 17 percent
of the clergy fell into that category. In 1930, 68 percent of the San Antonio docese was of Mexican-American
surname but only 14 percent of the priests.[19] These
facts not only made it difficult for Catholic clergy to
appeal to Mexican-American followers, but also tended to
undergird the Anglo tendency to regard Catholicism as a
foreign church.

By and large, clerical leadership in the west tended
to be much more suspicious of American life than did
eastern leadership. They tended to be authoritarian in
such pastoral concerns as sexual morality, financial contributions, and attitude toward parochial schools. They
were suspicious of Americanization programs which might
pose any jeopardy to their parishioners' faith. When
they did try to generate an Americanization influence
among parishioners, they could not bridge the gap between

Mexican and American cultures as easily as the Irish-dom-
inated clergy of the east bridged cultural gaps for succeeding generations of immigrants.

Further, there was no firmly structured church in
the west. In the east, the highly structured, Irish-
dominated church hierarchy was able to see to building of
churches and schools and provision of foreign language
priests for the growing number of Catholics. Bishops in
the Southwest were not overseeing flocks in highly concentrated urban areas that lent themselves to structure.
They could not as easily remain aware of administrative
problems and difficulties within their jurisdiction.
Communication within the church organization structure
was often problematic and was most difficult to establish
with any sizable proportion of lay people.

Finally, there was a crucial difference between degree of commitment to the church among immigratns of the
east and west. In the east, immigrants often arrived
with fierce devotion to the church, or at least with a
positive enough identification with the church to look
upon it as a place of refuge from life's difficulties in
a new land. In the west, the Mexican immigrant tended to
be much more nominally Catholic. He came from a country
where there had been a chronic shortage of priests, particularly after the revolution. In 1917, the Mexican
Constitution had even forbidden training of native
priests in seminaries. Parochial schools had been out-
lawed, and there had been a distinct anticlerical flavor
in the public educational system.

> It appears, in fact, that in these early years the
> bishops could at best hope for survival. The later
> mass immigrations from Mexico brought the Catholic
> Church hundreds of thousands of nominal Catholics.
> The new immigrants were probably as unused to Ameri-
> can Catholicism (with its heavy and rather ascetic
> Irish influence) as was the average Protestant.
> Moreover, many immigrants, fresh from the revolu-
> tionary church-baiting of Mexico, were anti-cleri-
> cal. The immigrants appear, indeed, to have come
> from precisely that population group in Mexico among
> whom Catholic influence was weakest. They were un-
> accustomed to parochial schools, financial support
> of the church, religious instruction, and regular
> attendance at Mass, all of which are important to
> American Catholics. Even the basic doctrines of
> Catholicism were so mixed with remnants of rural
> Indian paganism that the church, in summary, saw the
> new Mexican immigrants as likely 'new converts' but
> not as true practicing Catholics.[20]

McNamara[21] notes this same situation and argues that Mexican immigrants, in contrast to European Catholic

immigrants, would not necessarily seek out the church for support in the difficult task of adapting to a new culture. Therefore, the church had to seek out the newcomer. With the meager resources of the church in the Southwest, this was a difficult, if not impossible, task. Grebler et al.[21] argue that the normal response of the church to the situation was to emphasize pastoral goals to the detriment of social action programs and interests. Settlement houses and various other charity oriented programs were started in the first half of the twentieth century but were largely in service of pastoral goals. This pastoral approach completely dominated until after World War II when the Southwestern Catholic church also began to devote resources to dramatic expansion of the Catholic school system and various programs of Americanization. The church, during these postwar years, arrived at a perception of American culture as a less threatening environment in which Catholics could live and maintain Catholicity than their predecessors had possessed. Only since the middle 1960s has the church moved toward a more aggressive social action program on behalf of its Mexican-American constituency.

The main point to stress is the relative failure of the church in achieving its pastoral goals among Mexican Americans since the popular stereotype of the Mexican American is that he is "always religious and Catholic."[22] Broom and Shevsky[23] argue that the church has been the principal agency of cultural conservatism among Mexican Americans and has successfully reinforced separation from the dominant Anglo culture. Madsen[24] finds religious influence to be pervasive in the lives of lower-class and most middle-class Mexican Americans, although religion is not orthodox and sophisticated but a compounding of Spanish-Indian beliefs and folk Catholicism imported from Mexico. Loomis and Samora[25] also contributed to the stereotype when they found their small, rather isolated community believed more strongly in God-directed destiny than in man's control of his own fate. Their level of belief was much higher than that of other, non-Catholic groups.

Stoddard[26] has noted, however, that to generalize from studies of relatively isolated and/or agricultural situations that the church is an important element in achieving and maintaining a subcultural homogeneity among Mexican Americans in larger urban areas in the United States is unwarranted. Indeed, several studies seem to demonstrate the church has largely failed in reaching large segments of those populations with their pastoral concern.

Clark[27] found the church was not the all-pervading influence among Mexican Americans in San Jose, California, as it had been in Mexican areas of origin of immigrants into San Jose. Fishman[28] found home and neighborhood were regarded as more important in determining attitudes than school or church. Of 2000 urban Mexican-American boys attending Catholic high schoools, only 12 percent mentioned a priest as a source of ccunseling on close personal problems. Various estimates have been made of the proportion of Mexican-American Catholics who practice their religion on a regular basis. Wagner[29] estimated some 80 percent of the population had no active church affiliation, 15 percent were Catholic, and 5 percent Protestant. Foy[30] estimated that 95 percent of all Spanish-speaking Americans are baptized Catholics, but only 10 percent of all Spanish-speaking immigrants since World War II are practicing Catholics by U.S. standards. Results of a survey by Grebler et al.[31] on frequency of mass attendance reveals a lower level of participation in the Southwest than in northern and national samples of Catholics.

Participation of Mexican Americans in the Roman Catholic church does not seem to indicate an opportunity for significant formal religious influence on behavior exists for the great majority. The pervasiveness and importance of that influence appears to be greatly overestimated in the stereotype of the Catholic Mexican American. This impression is further substantiated when Mexican-American support for parochial schools is examined. If the church is to serve as an important tool of subcultural differentiation or assimilation, the parochial school would obviously be a significant socialization agent. However, Mexican-American support for parochial schools has never been strong. Simpson and Yinger[32] argue that few have attended the parochial schools because they can't afford it and they have learned what formal Catholic doctrine they pick up from catechism classes before their first communion and confirmation. Even there, due to lack of Spanish-speaking priests and European orientation of the church, instruction has often been in English and not tailored for this particular population. All the while, the Mexican American youth is learning folk interpretations and attitudes toward religious life at home and from his peers. Moore[33] notes that compared to the east, the Southwestern parochial school system has been notoriously weak. For example, by 1930 the combined San Diego and Los Angeles archdioces had 302,000 parishioners with 79 schools, Baltimore had 179 schools for the same number of church members, El Paso had only 12 schools for 120,000, and Corpus Christi, 27 schools for 248,000.

Immediately after World War II, a dramatic surge in concern for building Southwestern parochial schools emerged. Grebler et al.[34] summarize the reasons for the new interest:

The school building program, then, was an important

manifestation of a twofold strategy adopted by the Latin American Church leadership and to some extent by other church officials in the Southwest: 1) to preserve and defend the Catholic faith of the Mexican American and his offspring against Protestant influence and, later, against communism, moral 'liberalism' and 'secularism'; 2) to exhibit the Church to the larger society as an institution instilling American ideals into its laity of Mexican background, i.e., only under Catholic auspices and supervision could Mexicans be made into good, loyal Americans.

This new policy met with resistance from those concerned with Mexican and Mexican-American subcultures; despite determined efforts to broaden the parochial school constituency, in 1966-1967 only 15 percent of Spanish-surnamed children, grades 1-6, in high density Mexican-American areas of Los Angeles were in parochial schools.

Lack of Catholic parochial school influence is reflected by the propensity of Mexican-American laymen to disagree with teachings of the church on such topics as birth control. Attitudes on such important topics are generally strongly influenced by parochial education. Grebler et al.[35] found that 68 percent of a national sample who had completed Catholic schooling agreed with the church's teaching, but only 52 percent of those with some Catholic schooling and 44 percent of those without any Catholic schooling did so. Schooling, therefore, appears to be an important mechanism in maintaining subcultural values and attitudes in particularly salient substantive areas.

Thus, failure of the Catholic church to reach Southwestern Mexican Americans in either direct pastoral activities or through its parochial school system is well documented. Active Mexican Americans in either institution are, at best, a significant minority of their subcultural group.

Further, the direction of influence, whether toward more or less assimilation, has not been thoroughly explored. For example, the relationship of Mexican-American church or parochial school participation to assimilation has not been explored by careful social scientific research methods. There have been no careful comparisons of degree of cultural or structural assimilation of active Mexican-American Catholics as opposed to nonactive Mexican-American Catholics, Anglo Catholics, or various Mexican-American and Anglo Protestant groups in the Southwest. However, studies have generated a great deal of information concerning relative assimilation of Mexican Americans and of Catholics. We now turn to a brief summary of that literature.

Structural Assimilation

Occupation and Income. Several significant studies
have indicated that Catholics in the U.S. population as
a whole have come close to obtaining parity with Protestants.[36] However, Mexican Americans who are predominantly Catholic have been demonstrated to show considerably
below average achievement levels on these dimensions.[37]

Education. Solid research indicates that on a national basis Catholics are generally assimilated to the
point that they achieve as much or more formal education
as Protestant counterparts. Further, parochial education
has not been productive of less than average "achievement
motivation" or higher educational achievement.[38] However, the heavily Catholic Mexican-American population
has been an exception. Grebler[39] and Carter[40] provide
overviews of literature and data indicating significant
below-average achievement of Mexican Americans in education. Sanchez[41] argues that the educational institution's inability to reach and effectively educate the
Mexican-American population is only symptomatic of the
United States' general failure to provide an effective
program for acculturation and assimilation of this steadily increasing group during the 130 years since annexation of Texas and settling of the rest of the Southwest.
This may be a particularly crucial problem if, as
Featherman[42] contends, the main effects of Catholic Mexican-American background are on educational achievement
rather than occupational or income achievement or cultural attitudes toward achievement.

Intermarriage. Structural assimilation on this level has been progressing more rapidly than might have been
predicted ten or more years ago. Mittelbach and Moore[43]
and Grebler et al.[44] report a study of marital endogamy
of Mexican Americans in Los Angeles in 1963. The overall
exogamy rate for marriages involving Mexican Americans
was 40 percent with 25 percent of Mexican-American individuals marrying outside their ethnic group. This was
considerably higher exogamy than observed in earlier
studies and seems to indicate an assimilative potential
greater than has been commonly assumed. This conclusion
is buttressed by the fact that exogamy rates were even
higher in marriages involving younger Mexican Americans.
Bean and Bradshaw[45] reached a similar conclusion in an
analysis of intermarriage rates in 1850 as compared to
1960 for Mexican Americans in San Antonio. In 1850, 10
percent of all marriages involving persons of Spanish
surname were with non-Spanish surname spouses; in 1960
the percentage was twenty. In 1850, one in twenty married persons of Spanish surname were married to a non-
Spanish surname spouse while the number jumped to one in

ten in 1960.

Mittelbach and Moore[46] also give some evidence on the influence of Catholicism on intermarriage rates. They noted that Catholicism in Los Angeles was evidently not a segregating factor and that less than one-half of the marriages considered were validated by a Catholic ceremony. On this crucial structural level of assimilation, then, it would have to be argued that at least the church is not a pervasive inhibiting influence on intermarriage. However, as with other areas of structural assimilation, it must be noted that influence of the religious factor is not directly revealed in studies reported here.

Cultural Assimilation

Language. "An extensive study of 'language loyalty' among ethnic groups in the United States shows conclusively that Spanish is the most persistent of all foreign languages, and the one with the greatest prospects of survival."[47] Grebler et al.[48] found that over one-half of their respondents were bilingual with 84 percent of the Los Angeles sample and 91 percent of the San Antonio sample able to get along comfortably in Spanish. Only 71 percent of the Los Angeles sample and 57 percent of the San Antonio sample were able to get along comfortably in English.

Persistence of native language among Mexican Americans thus contradicts dramatically the experience of Italians, Poles, Germans, and other immigrant groups. Explanations for the contrast are to be found in several areas. Sanchez[49] emphasizes recurring waves of Mexican migration into the United States and a tendency for American educational institutions to be unable to cope with teaching English to Spanish-speaking students. There is also the fact that mass media utilizing Spanish, particularly radio and television stations, are common in the Southwest.[50] Finally, existence of Mexican-American enclaves in both rural and urban Southwestern areas have made it possible for a person to survive at work, play, and in most commercial activity while speaking only Spanish. Unfortunately, no evidence is available concerning the relationship of religious activity and assimilation on this cultural level.

Normative assimilation. Both popular stereotypes and social scientific investigation have often assumed Mexican-American cultural orientations and norms have inhibited the ability to be successful "achievers" in American society, but lately that kind of viewpoint is being questioned. Stoddard[51] argues that the picture of the Mexican American as passive, somnolent, irresponsible, present-oriented, etc. is to be questioned. Grebler et al.[52] found that Mexican-American samples did not appear to possess "distinctively traditional values of the kind frequently attributed to them."

Like other Americans, and probably like other urbanites in industrial countries, most want to get ahead in their work; they want work that gives them intrinsic satisfactions; many hope for job security and higher income. On the whole, Mexican Americans are not notably more passive nor do they value integration with relatives more than most other populations on which data were available.[53]

Featherman[54] provides an interesting perspective on this question. He compared male Jewish, Anglo-Saxon Protestant, Other Protestant, Roman Catholic excluding Italian and Mexican, Italian and Mexican Roman Catholic, and those with no religious identification from the Princeton Fertility Study. Sampling was done in New York, Philadelphia, Pittsburgh, Detroit, Chicago, Los Angeles, and San Francisco. His data indicate that in terms of achievement the Jewish group was highest and the Italian and Mexican Roman Catholic the lowest. He further determined that though the Italian and Mexican Roman Catholic group differed from others in terms of achievement motivation (norms and values), the motivational variables could not account for effects of social origins or education in attainment. Further, motivational variables could not account for effects of religio-ethnic background on achievement when education was taken into account. Finally, even the religio-ethnic origin variable ceased having any independent effect on achievement with education taken into consideration. His work suggests that perhaps the key element in maintaining the degree of structural separation that can be observed is due more to variations in educational achievement than to any subcultural normative orientations.

Identification. Stoddard[55] provides a very complete summary of the literature of Mexican-American identification. In terms of self-identification, he finds Mexican Americans to be very ambivalent as to what titles or designations they prefer. There were great variations in self-identification between geographical regions, length of residence in the United States, social classes, age, and whether the title user was Anglo or Mexican American. On the whole, however, a very strong impression emerges that Mexican Americans are in the process of establishing a self-identity that does not imply complete assimilation into the larger American population.

On the whole, Southwestern Mexican Americans present an interesting set of contrasts on various levels of assimilation. In structural terms they appear to be gaining slowly in educational, occupational and income

parity with Anglos. However, evidence also establishes
significant below-average achievement on their part in
these three areas. Intermarriage rates with Anglos, on
the other hand, appear surprisingly high given relatively
low levels of assimilation on other structural levels.
In terms of cultural assimilation, similar contra-
dictions emerge. Mexican Americans evidently do not hold
cultural norms and values which generate a distinctively
different orientation toward achievement than persons in
the larger society. However, they do tend to be distinctive in terms of preservation of native language and preferring not to identify completely with the society in
which they live.
Very unfortunately, and this is perhaps the key
finding of this review of the literature, there is minis-
cule evidence on the role of Catholicism in assimilation
of Mexican Americans. We know little more than when the
literature search was begun concerning whether active
Mexican-American Roman Catholics are more or less assimilated on various levels of the assimilation process than
are less active or non-Catholic Mexican Americans.
Three developments in the religious behavior of
Southwestern Catholics must be noted briefly because of
likely linkages to assimilation. First, increasing
clergy involvement in social action programs may lead to
the structural level even while they promote pluralism at
the cultural level. Second, the *cursillo* movement appears likely to develop pluralistic tendencies at the
cultural level and increased assimilation at the structural level. Finally, conversion of Mexican Americans to
Protestant religious bodies would logically seem to have
assimilative potential even though the small amount of
research that exists indicates this is not the case in
fact.

The "Social Action Priests." The tendency for Roman
Catholic priests to become involved in programs seeking
alleviation of prejudice and discrimination toward Mexican Americans in American society, and more generally in
secularized concerns about poverty in that population,
has increased dramatically in the last ten years. Grebler et al.[56] review the history of clergy social action
on behalf of Mexican Americans and emphasize that social
action as a goal for its own sake began only after World
War II. Prior to that, social action was generally undertaken within the context of more pastoral concerns.
Failure of the Catholic church to reach Mexican Americans with pastoral concern has been noted above. Stoddard[57] correctly argues that priests are caught in a
double bind when they try to serve lower class Mexican
Americans. On one hand, the parishioners are very suspicious of priests who become involved in political

activities.[58] On the other, they also tend to be alienated from priests who are noninvolved in secular affairs
and in trying to alleviate the more trying conditions under which their parishioners live.

McNamara[59] analyzed the roles priests have played in
social action programs and establishes a basic dinstinc-
tion between the priest who becomes involved in programs
such as the war on poverty efforts and "field worker
priests" who participated in Mexican-American agricultural workers' strikes in Delano, California, and the lower
Rio Grande Valley in Texas. He argues that the former
involvement is likely to be most often observed since it
involves a much less naked confrontation with political
and economic power structures than does the latter. The
church as a formal organization can more easily support
the antipoverty program activist in the face of criticism
by parishioners than it can for the field worker priest.

As to results of such priestly involvement, it would
have to be speculated that the more pirests become involved in such activities, the more likely they are to
become direct agents of structural assimilation for their
parishioners. However, in order for them to be effective
representatives of parisioners, they may well have to
adopt ideologies and normative orientations of the "Chicano Power" sort of advocate, thereby increasing resistance to cultural assimilation at identificational levels.

One qualification to likely effects on assimilation
by social action priests is that they are likely to remain in the small minority among Catholic clergy. Grebler et al.[60] found that among Los Angeles priests serving
Mexican Americans, the great majority did not preach
about social issues directly or with any regularity, they
took little part in state, civic, or neighborhood organizations and showed a definite preference for traditional
pastoral roles and organizations. One would suspect this
is the norm among priests. However, in San Antonio they
found that where the church hierarchy is more favorable
to social action involvement, the majority of pastors did
become involved in various secular organizations and tended to be aware of and involved with social teachings of
the church, though the majority did not often preach about
them. Even in San Antonio, however, priests showed a definite preference for traditional pastoral roles.

The *Cursillo*. According to Wagner,[61] the first Cursillo de Cristiandad was held in Majorca in 1949 in the
St. Honoratus monastery. First introduced to Texas in
1957, it has since gained diocesan approval in nearly all
of the Southwest. Essentially, the *cursillo* is a religious retreat centering on a "little course" in Christian-
ity. The retreat setting creates strong potential for
personal involvement and development of a sense of

community. Emphasis is on developing abilities among laymen to experience the power that comes with the Holy Spirit in a religious community and to use that power in living a Christian life. There has been a strong emphasis on social action as a necessary extension of religious doctrine, with problems of race and poverty often being discussed.[62]

Popularity of the *cursillo* appears to be increasing in the Southwest. Its effects in terms of assimilation have not been empirically explored, but it is interesting to speculate that it may have the same effect of social action programs in the church in general. That is, it may produce abilities to cope more effectively with problems of achieving structural assimilation at economic and occupational levels and at the same time produce more ethnic consciousness among the Mexican Americans to whom it primarily appeals.

THE PROTESTANT CHURCHES AND THE MEXICAN AMERICAN

Although not a great deal is known concerning the extent and characteristics of the small proportion of Mexican Americans who are Protestant, a few investigations give some indication of how important these groups might be. The dominant impression is that less than 5 percent of Mexican Americans are to be found in Protestant churches. Grebler et al.[63] estimated that of nearly 10 million Protestants in five Southwestern states in 1960, only approximately 1 percent of 100,000 are Mexican American. If their estimate of total Mexican-American population in the Southwest in 1960 as 3.5 million is accurate, then some 2.5 percent of that population is affiliated with Protestant churches. However, they undoubtedly underestimate this Protestant population since they include only members of "Spanish" churches in 13 denominations. They also reported that in Los Angeles and San Antonio, they found 5 percent to be Protestant. If that percentage can be extended to the entire Southwestern Mexican-American population, there may be better than 200,000 Protestants.

Something of the extent of Protestant work among Mexican Americans is indicated by data in Table 8.1. Of the top six Protestant groups in total number of Mexican-American members, two are sectarian groups, two are conservative Protestant, and two are more liberal Protestant. On the whole, sectarian religions attract a disproportionate share of Mexican Americans as compared to Anglos. This would become even more obvious had the survey included Jehovah's Witnesses, who are very active in recruiting Mexican Americans. Mormons have also don a significant amount of work among Mexican Americans for years and are doubtless well represented. Grebler et

Table 8.1 Distribution of Protestant Religious Efforts Among the "Spanish," by Denomination, 1960[a]

	Total Mem-[b]bers	Total U.S. "Spanish" Churches	% "Spanish" Churches, West & SW	Nat'l Budget 1960[d]	Denom. Inst. Serving "Spanish"[e]
Assemblies of God	29,054	392	77	[f]	3
Methodist Church	28,000[g]	221	82	$782,000	18
Southern Baptist Convention	28,000[g]	559	95	602,000	3
American Baptist Church	7,950[g]	106	55	46,000	6
United Presbyterian, U.S.A.	6,604	94	75	691,000	30
Seventh Day Adventists	5,000	68	65	n.a.	8
Presbyterian Church in the U.S.	2,842	38	100	65,000	1
Disciples of Christ	1,851	18	50	53,000	2
Lutheran Church, Missouri Synod	1,245	7	100	60,000	2
Evangelical United Brethren	972	14	70	237,000	10
United Lutheran Church	604	4	0	15,000	n.a.
Congregational Christian Church	543	7	71	9,000	n.a.
Church of God (Anderson, Ind.)	465	7	100	16,000	n.a.
Total	113,130	1,535	81	$2,600,000	84

[a]Grebler et al., 1970:488. Derived from Glen W. Trimble, "Responses to the Brief Survey of Church Related Spanish American Work in the Continental United States," National Council of Churches.

[b]Includes only those in "Spanish-American" congregations.

[c]Includes 1,225 churches in five states with sizable Mexican-American populations and twenty-four churches in western and southwestern states where "Spanish" probably means Mexican-American, i.e., Washington, Oregon, Idaho, Montana, Oklahoma, Utah, and Wyoming.

[d]National budget refers to amount spent for work among Mexican Americans by the denomination.

[e]E.g., hospitals, schools, community centers.

[f]Entirely indigenous.

[g]Estimated by denomination official.

al. accept the Mormon Church estimate of 15,000 Mexican-
American adherents.[64]
    Some debate has taken place over assimilative re-
sults of Protestant activity among Mexican Americans.
Penalosa and McDonagh[65] found that in Southern California, upwardly mobile Mexican Americans were retaining
their Catholic designation. Conversion to Protestantism
appeared to be a substitute for, rather than a means to,
accomplish mobility and structural assimilation.
    Weigert et al.[66] surveyed a purposive sample of min-
isters of Mexican-American congregations in El Paso. The
likely assimilative influence of the congregations varied
with type. Ecclesiastical congregations (Congregational,
Episcopalian, Lutheran, and Presbyterian) had ministers
who were better educated and committed to social action
goals; these ministers probably appeal most to the upwardly mobile. Evangelist and Fundamentalist ministers
(Methodist, Baptist, Church of Christ, Church of the
Nazarene, and Mormon) appeared to be primarily concerned
with individual salvation, and adherence to a strict personal ethical code as necessary for proper religious
life was not as full-hearted as the Pentecostals. They
tended to reflect increasing accommodation to dominant
norms of the society. Paradoxically, however, despite
willingness to accept normative integration of members
into the larger society, their relaxation of strict personal moral prescriptions might well mean they will not
generate much structural assimilation on the part of
their parishioners. Pentecostals (Assembly of God, Independent Methodist, Apostolic Ascension) espoused a much
more aggressive and demanding ethic; they also shared a
strong emphasis on literal interpretation of the Bible,
the value of speaking in tongues, and an interest in
divine healing. Paradoxically, again, though Pentecostal
groups may encourage separation from dominant forms of
religious expression in society around them, they may
also be generating an ability to gain structural access
to the larger society by insisting on personal codes of
thrift, honesty, hard work, etc. Johnson[67] raised the
same question in more general terms in, "Do Holiness
Sects Socialize in Dominant Values?" It appears that
Pentecostal sects may do just that.
    Weigert et al.[68] note other characteristics of min-
isters that may help them serve as agents of mobilization
and transition for parishioners. They tend to be upwardly mobile themselves, are bilingual, and are personally
committed to a Protestant ethic perspective on achievement in this world. However, the structural situation in
the churches themselves do not tend to promote assimilation in that they tend to be very segregated.[69] They are
largely run by Mexican Americans and do not provide any
direct opportunity for members to move into an integrated
religious structure. Further, the groups often resist

192

integration even when it is proposed, for fear the ethnic
minority might lose what power it has in the context of
the larger religious body.
Therefore, there is a complex mixture of assimilative and nonassimilative potential in the Mexican-American Protestant church. Unfortunately, no significant research has been undertaken to demonstrate which of these
potentials are being fulfilled along which dimensions of
assimilation by what kinds of groups. Further, no one
knows with any degree of accuracy how many Mexican-Americans are to be found in non-Spanish-speaking Protestant
churches and what effects such membership has on assimilation beyond the church context. There is a great deal
of speculation and a crying need for accurate data on the
influence of Protestantism on assimilation of Mexican
Americans in the Southwest.

NOTES

1. Andrew M. Greeley, The Denominational Society
(Glenview, Ill.: Scott Foresman and Co., 1972), pp. 176-
193.
2. Ibid., pp. 194-95.
3. Edna Fergusson, Our Southwest (New York: Alfred
A. Knopf, 1952).
4. Odie B. Faulk: Land of Many Frontiers: A History
of the American Southwest (New York: Oxford University
Press, 1968), pp. 40-42; Arizona: A Short History (Norman: University of Oklahoma Press, 1971), pp. 19-23.
5. Donald William Meinig, Southwest: Three Peoples
in Geographical Change, 1600-1970 (New York: Oxford University Press, 1971), pp. 12-14.
6. Ibid., pp. 27-35.
7. Howard Roberts Lamar, The Far Southwest, 1846-
1912: A Territorial History (New Haven: Yale University
Press, 1966).
8. Carey McWilliams, North From Mexico: The Spanish-Speaking People of the United States (New York:
Greenwood Press, 1968), p. 118.
9. Fergusson, Our Southwest.
10. McWilliams, North From Mexico.
11. Ibid., p. 64.
12. Nancie L. Gonzalez, The Spanish Americans of New
Mexico: A Heritage of Pride (Albuquerque: University of
New Mexico Press, 1967), p. 29.
13. Lamar, Far Southwest, p. 29.
14. Julian Samora, ed., La Raza: Forgotten Americans
(Notre Dame: University of Notre Dame Press, 1966).
15. Gonzalez, The Spanish Americans.
16. Lamar, Far Southwest, p. 102.
17. Joan W. Moore with Alfredo Cuellar, Mexican
Americans (Englewood Cliffs, N.J.: Prentice Hall, 1970).

18. Leo Grebler, Joan W. Moore, and Ralph C. Guzman, The Mexican-American People: The Nation's Second Largest Minority (New York: The Free Press, 1970), pp. 451, 452.
19. Ibid., pp. 667-668.
20. Moore, Mexican Americans, p. 86.
21. Grebler, Moore, and Guzman, Mexican-American People, pp. 449-486.
22. Ellwyn P. Stoddard, Mexican Americans: In Search of a New Identity (El Paso, Tx.: Texas Western Press, 1970).
23. Leonard Broom and Eshref Shevky, "Mexicans in the United States: A Problem in Social Differentiation," Sociology and Social Research 35 (January-February 1952): 150-158.
24. William Madsen, Mexican Americans of South Texas (New York: Holt, Rinehart and Winston, 1964).
25. Charles P. Loomis and Julian Samora, "Prejudice and Religious Activity in Mexico and the United States: A Note," Sociological Analyis 26 (Winter 1965): 212-216.
26. Stoddard, Mexican Americans, p. 83.
27. Clark, 1959: 96-97.
28. Joshua A. Fishman, "Childhood Indoctrination for Minority Group Membership," in Milton L. Barron, ed., Minorities in a Changing World (New York: Alfred Knopf, 1961), pp. 177-196.
29. John A. Wagner, "The Role of the Christian Church," in Samora, La Raza, pp. 27-45.
30. Feliciana Foy, National Catholic Almanac (St. Anthony's Guild, 1962).
31. Grebler, Moore, and Guzman, Mexican-American People.
32. George E. Simpson and J. Milton Yinger, Racial and Cultural Minorities: An Analysis of Prejudice and Discrimination, 4th ed. (New York: Harper and Row, 1972).
33. Moore, Mexican Americans, pp. 86-87.
34. Grebler, Moore, and Guzman, Mexican-American People, p. 459.
35. Ibid., pp. 474-475.
36. Norval D. Glenn and Ruth Hyland, "Religious Preferences and Worldly Success: Some Evidence from National Surveys," American Sociological Review 32 (1967): 73-85; Andrew M. Greeley and Peter H. Rossi, The Education of American Catholics (Chicago: Aldine, 1966).
37. Grebler, Moore, and Guzman, Mexican-American People, pp. 101-290; David L. Featherman, "The Socioeconomic Achievement of White Religion-Ethnic Subgroups: Social and Psychological Explanations," American Sociological Review 36 (April 1971): 207-222.
38. Greeley and Rossi, Education.
39. Grebler, Moore, and Guzman, Mexican-American People, pp. 142-179.
40. Thomas P. Carter, Mexican Americans in School:

A History of Educational Neglect (New York: College Entrance Examination Board, 1970).

41. George I. Sanchez, "History, Culture and Education," in Samora, La Raza, pp. 1-26.

42. Featherman, "Socioeconomic Achievement."

43. Frank G. Mittelbach and Joan W. Moore, "Ethnic Endogamy: The Case of the Mexican Americans," American Journal of Sociology 74 (July 1968): 50-62.

44. Grebler, Moore, and Guzman, Mexican-American People, pp. 405-418.

45. Frank D. Bean and Benjamin S. Bradshaw, "Intermarriage Between Persons of Spanish and Non-Spanish Surname: Changes from the Mid-Nineteenth to the Mid-Twentieth Century," Social Science Quarterly 51 (September 1970): 389-395.

46. Mittelbach and Moore, "Ethnic Endogamy."

47. Grebler, Moore, and Guzman, Mexican-American People, p. 423, citing Joshua A. Fishman and John E. Hofman, "Mother Tongue and Nativity in the American Population," in Joshua A. Fishman, ed., Language Loyalty in the United States (The Hague, London and Paris: Mouton and Co., 1966), p. 37.

48. Grebler, Moore, and Guzman, Mexican-American People, pp. 428-431.

49. Sanchez, "History, Culture."

50. Grebler, Moore, and Guzman, Mexican-American People, p. 197.

51. Stoddard, Mexican Americans, pp. 54-56.

52. Brebler, Moore, and Guzman, Mexican-American People, pp. 432-439.

53. Ibid., pp. 438-439.

54. Featherman, "Socioeconomic Achievement."

55. Stoddard, Mexican Americans, pp. 47-74.

56. Grebler, Moore, and Guzman, Mexican-American People, pp. 460-467.

57. Stoddard, Mexican Americans, p. 85.

58. Clark S. Knowlton and Sal Ramirez, "A Comparison of Spanish-American Leadership Systems of Northern New Mexico and El Paso" (Paper presented at Texas Academy of Science, 1965), pp. 21-22.

59. Patrick H. McNamara: "Social Action Priests in the Mexican-American Community," Sociological Analysis 29 (Winter 1968): 177-185; "Priests, Protests, and Poverty Intervention," in Louis A. Zurcher, Jr. and Charles M. Bonjean, eds., Planned Social Intervention: An Interdisciplinary Anthology (Scranton: Chandler Publishing Co., 1969), pp. 369-376.

60. Grebler, Moore, and Guzman, Mexican-American People.

61. Wagner, "Role of the Christian Church."

62. For further discussion, see Sigmund Dragostin, "The Cursillos as a Social Movement," in William T. Liu and Nathaniel J. Pallone, eds., Catholics/U.S.A.:

Perspectives on Social Change (New York: John Wiley &
Sons, Inc., 1970); Grebler, Moore, and Guzman, Mexican-
American People; and Dianne T. Fairbank and Richard L.
Hough, "Religiosity and Prejudice: A Tale of Two Cities"
(Paper presented at the Pacific Sociological Association
Meetings, Scottsdale, Arizona, Spring 1973).

    63. Grebler, Moore, and Guzman, Mexican-American
People, pp. 486-512.
    64. Ibid., p. 506.
    65. Fernando Penalosa and Edward C. McDonagh,
"Social Mobility in a Mexican-American Community," Social
Forces 44 (June 1966): 495-505.
    66. Andrew J. Weigert, William D'Antonio, and
Arthur J. Rubel, "Protestantism and Assimilation Among
Mexican Americans: An Exploratory Study of Ministers'
Reports," Journal for Scientific Study of Religion 10
(Fall 1971): 219-232.
    67. Benton Johnson, "Do Holiness Sects Socialize in
Dominant Values?" Social Forces 39 (1961): 309-316.
    68. Weigert, D'Antonio, and Rubel, "Protestantism."
    69. Grebler, Moore, and Guzman, Mexican-American
People.

9
Correlating Bilingualism/Biculturalism and Socio-Educational Factors in a Survey of Mexican-American Students at a Southwestern University

Jacob Ornstein-Galicia
Paul W. Goodman

INTRODUCTORY REMARKS

The University of Texas at El Paso apparently has the largest percentage of Mexican-American student enrollment of any senior institution in our fifty states, and is unquestionably the most highly bilingual/bicultural. The investigation to be described represents an attempt to supply much needed data on the comparative characteristics of young adult Chicanos (to be used interchangeably with Mexican-Americans) and their Anglo peers (any non-Chicano). It is not always realized that Mexican Americans, some seven-to-nine million in all, constitute the nation's second largest minority after the blacks and, like the latter, are most likely to belong to lower socioeconomic classes.

A search of the literature reveals extremely few research projects concerned with the behavior and attitudes of Mexican-American college students; the bulk of the research is concerned with public school youngsters, mostly of earlier ages. Nevertheless, the need remains great, given the importance of higher education in the vocational and social welfare of minority groups.

Accordingly, the Cross-Cultural Southwest Ethnic Study Center (SWESC) has, ever since its creation under a Spencer Foundation grant, attempted to remedy the above lack to the extent of its abilities and resources. It is being sought to build up a "data bank" in a number of disciplines cognate to the educational process. Among these are linguistics and related communication fields. Our essay is based mostly on the work of the project on Sociolinguistic Studies on Southwest Bilingualism (SSSB), initiated in 1968.

It needs further to be noted that our survey has been taking place in El Paso, the largest metropolitan city on the United States-Mexico border, with a U.S. population in 1971 of some 370,000 persons. Approximately 50 percent of this population is Spanish surnamed, and the enrollment of such students at our university in the

197

year our investigation was intiated amounted to 30.1 percent.

Many investigators feel that the bilingual/bicultural context of our study lends itself to comparisons with the situation in emergent nations of the Third World. A point in support of this is that a number of the more militant ethnic movements, black, American Indian, as well as Chicano, in their thinking and declarations disassociate themselves from the "superpowers," preferring to align themselves with Third World forces, and indeed do participate actively in their symposia and conferences. In a volume written at this university and titled Chicanos and Native Americans: Territorial Minorities,[1] some of these issues are touched upon:

> The pattern of political behavior of Chicanos and Native Americans within the U.S. political system has characteristics peculiar to those two minorities that set them apart from other American ethnic groups. They are the only minority societies that came into the U.S. nation-state as a result of expansion and territorial conquest . . . Chicanos and Native Americans, unlike any American immigrant minority or even the Blacks (who were carried or induced away from their land, property and sociopolitical institutions), have characteristics of a territorial minority. That concept is generally alien to the American political experience, but very familiar in the European, Asian, and African political scene of shifting borders, expanding politics, and consequent change in sovereignty over conquered territories and people.

In the case of Mexican Americans, many of them, particularly activists, often express themselves against "domination" by the Anglo language, culture, and power structure. Only since World War II, and especially the past fifteen years, have they begun to challenge such "dominance" actively. Nowhere has the struggle been fiercer than in the educational sector. Recent history records that a few years ago Chicanos revised dominance patterns with an election of all Chicano civic administration as well as school board in Crystal City, Texas. In the El Paso area, the Ysleta Independent School District has reflected constant turmoil since the suspension in the fall of 1973 of a group of Chicano activists (some later reinstated). Among their demands were increased recognition of Mexican-American language and culture, as well as culture-fair tests which would not discriminate against them. Charles A. Ferguson and Anwar Dil observe:[2]

In some nations of Europe and the Americas new
forces of ethnicity and new demands of linguistically identified groups are posing severe problems,
not only in countries such as Belgium, Canada, and
Yugoslavia where the tensions have long been recognized, but also in nations such as Great Britain,
Spain and the United States where questions were
generally assumed to be very minor.

Since Spanish speakers constitute the largest for-
eign-language or bilingual minority in the United
States, it would thus seem that our intention to under-
take a systematic study of how socioeducational factors
may correlate with bilingual/bicultural status of Mexican
Americans is overdue. However, analogies with emergent
nations may be more rewarding than apparent at first
blush. Suffice it to say that certain extremist factions of Chicano (as well as black and native American)
movements even envision breaking off from the United
States of America--much as the Parti Independent Quebec-
ois is committed to an independent Quebec in Canada.
Unfortunately, sociolinguistic research on Spanish-
English bilinguals/biculturals has focused almost exclusively on young children because of the concentration of
government funds in this area.
One great disparity between dominant, or "mainstream," and subordinate, or minority "non-mainstream,"
groups is precisely in the realm of socioeconomic status
(SES). It is only one step from that to state that nowhere better than in the differentiated markers of language is the distance between groups manifested, hence
the advantage of studying such problems from a bidimen-
sional sociolinguistic viewpoint.
It is a truism that minority groups, in line with
the Orwellian "less equal" concept, tend to fall into
the lower SES, while dominant ones, be they numerically
superior or not, correspond to the upper ones. A concomitant or correlate of such status is a low-prestige
or badly stigmatized language variety, such as black
English of the ghettoes or the Southwest dialect of
Spanish, often referred to pejoratively as "Tex-Mex,"
"Border Long," and even less flattering terms.

SOCIAL CHARACTERISTICS OF THE SAMPLE

The procedure followed aimed at securing a stratified random sample of all full-time, unmarried students
from our undergraduate school population. A sample of
301 subjects was obtained, consisting of 148 Anglo and
153 Mexican-American student respondents, constituting
about 5 percent of the population described. The categories used for stratification were Mexican American vs.
Anglo, sex, academic class (first year, etc.), and school

of enrollment (Liberal Arts, Education, etc.), comprising some sixteen in all. Students were selected randomly within each of the categories and contacted by telephone by bilingual peers employed by our project. To all of these our Sociolinguistic Background Questionnaire[3] was administered, as well as a College and University Environment Scales (CUES) test,[4] aimed at probing their attitudes toward this particular institution. Results from the latter instrument are discussed elsewhere[5] and will be excluded from consideration here. In addition, a 10 percent subsample was taken of the overall sample, limited to Chicanos, who were then subjected to extensive linguistic elicitation. The purpose of this was to ascertain their fluency in Spanish and English respectively, and, with the help of answers from the Questionnaire, to probe their attitude regarding regional language varieties, particularly their own.

In this study, we are dealing with a population also differentiated by the fact that both through their Spanish and English they are immediately recognizable as Mexican Americans, utilizing as they do a highly interferential variety of Spanish and of English. To a large extent they are speakers of "bilingual" of "contactual" dialects.[6] Our essay can only begin to touch upon the intricate web of relations existing between language, culture, and social factors.

SES was sought in our study both as a correlate of language use and as a possible indicator of the extent to which young Mexican Americans are utilizing the university as a means of achieving upward social mobility. Our procedure was to derive the SES of each student from his father's occupation and education.

An eight-point occupational scale was devised, based on Duncan's Socio-Economic Index Scores for occupation. This scale score was added to an eight-point revised, reverse Hollingshead and Redlich educational attainment scale. The two scale scores were added together and from this a student's socioeconomic class was determined. Goodman explains his methodology in full elsewhere.[7]

One may see from our data that the university is serving as an instrument for social mobility that is part of this country's dream. Sixty-two percent of our students come from families of the lower-middle class, upper-lower class, or lower-lower class. However, whereas only 51 percent of the Anglos came from these three classes, 89 percent of Chicanos were part of these three lower-class groups. SES difference between these two groups was significant at the .001 level of confidence. Actually, although providing chances for upward social mobility for both Anglos and Chicanos, more of the latter are using the university for this purpose. Here again there may be a good analogy as regards the function of school in upward vocational and social mobility by both bilingual minorities in older sovereign states and by lower status groups in ex-colonial emergent lands.

A very high proportion of students attending our university are employed, and it was discovered that on the whole the Anglo students receive better hourly wages than do their Mexican-American peers. Whether this is due to skill differences, discrimination, or other factors is yet to be determined. Nevertheless, since it is hard to imagine that university undergraduate students possess substantial differences in skills or ability, the most likely explanation seems to be based on ethnic prejudice or SES disadvantage. Along with this, there is no question that Anglo students have superior social contacts which are less likely to be possessed by Chicanos and which would yield access to better job opportunities in the community.

LANGUAGE DIMENSIONS

Our discussion thus far has centered upon some differences between Anglo and Chicano students, mostly attributable to SES distinctions. Now it is time to focus upon linguistic factors. At this point we have a subsample of thirty, whose language performance in both English and Spanish was measured. Next we surveyed the entire bilingual group (N=151) of the overall sample in order to ascertain how language usage and loyalty were related to social class. In addition to that, the entire sample (N=301) was canvassed for a comparison of language attitudes of Chicano and Anglo students.

Our subsample of thirty was selected at random from the overall sample, similarly stratified, making up 10 percent of these or 20 percent of the Mexican-American student sample. These bilinguals were subjected to our complete battery, including Sociolinguistic Background Questionnaire, the CUES test, and our optional part B of the Questionnaire. The latter consists of three sets of topics in Spanish and English respectively (with bilingual instructions) from which students were asked to choose identical themes in both languages to write compositions. They were thus induced to function at the highest level of their performance level. In addition, the same three sets of identical questions, or similar ones, were used by peer interviewers in an open-ended interview in both languages, lasting from thirty minutes to an entire hour. A panel of three independent judges, themselves bilingual, were asked to rate the oral and written output of each student.

It should not surprise linguists to note that Spanish performance was in general appreciably lower than was the case in English. Nevertheless, scores in both languages were clustered at well above the intermediate level and between 3.0 and 3.9 on a five-point scale. In

the Southwest, and in most multilingual areas, there is
a complementary distribution of Spanish vs. English of
the respective language pair in the various domains of
living, with English generally reserved for the formal
ones. Obviously this does not make for "balanced bilingualism" but sociolinguistic facts remain what they are.
The poorer overall performance in Spanish of our subsample may be because the majority of the students had the
lion's share of their schooling in English as the language of instruction (bilingual schooling is only now
beginning to make many inroads). In the formal domains
of living, their experience had been in English, not
Spanish. Another noteworthy factor beyond this is that
the three-member panel of independent judges may have
leaned in the direction of severity in their Spanish
ratings.

We were interested in discovering how language performance ratings correlated with other kinds of scholas-
tic performance and found the only correlations significant at the .05 level of confidence were English performance and Spanish performance, and English performance and
grade point average (GPA). SAT verbal was not correlated
with any of our other variables. This is possibly because the English language performance may well be a result of college English education, which is linked to GPA
and Spanish language performance.

One of the most important dimensions of language in
a complex national state is language loyalty and language
usage. This has been especially true in the United
States where the use of English and the abandonment of a
foreign language were almost the required passport to
middle-class American respectability. Americans may ad-
mire people who are multilingual, but the general attitude has been that one of these languages must be English
and a native-speaking quality of English at that. As the
social commentator Will Herberg said:[8]

> As the second generation prospered economically and
> culturally, and moved upward in the social scale,
> assimilation was speeded; the speeding of assimila-
> tion stimulated and quickened the upward movement.
> First to go was the foreign language with the mani-
> fest symbol of foreigners and a great impediment to
> advancement.

The most comprehensive and up-to-date material on
this question may be seen in Joshua Fishman's monumental
Language Loyalty in the United States[9] and other writings
by this scholar.

A section of our questionnaire dealt with this question of language loyalty and usage. We asked students to
indicate how much English and/or Spanish they used in
various settings: home, school, recreation, work, and in

the environment, i.e., shopping, writing letters, etc.
We hypothesized that for Mexican-American students the
higher the social class, the more use of English there
would be in any of these settings. Only two of our correlations, home and environment, were significant. The
correlations of use of English and social class during
recreation and at work were almost zero. The correlations we did obtain were not overwhelming and one can interpret this from data that Spanish in El Paso is not
disappearing with assimilation, if assimilation means
entry into the upper social classes. Our data clearly
show that in three life settings out of five there was
little social class difference in the use of language by
our Mexican-American students. In other words, Mexican-
American students tended to use equal amounts of Spanish
or English in certain life settings regardless of social
class. In general, we can conclude that if upper class
status represents assimilation, it does not represent
nonuse of Spanish language in our community. However, in
this regard undoubtedly the closeness of the border is a
factor in strengthening language maintenance.

Perhaps another reason for the wide use of Spanish
by all social classes in our sample is because social
class is not related to number of generations in the
United States. We had hypothesized that most upper-class
Mexican-American students would have fathers who were
born in the United States while lower-class members of
this classification would have fathers who were born in
Mexico. Our data indicate this is not so. While higher
percentages of upper-class Mexican-American student fathers were born in the United States, the differences were
not statistically significant. Thus neither upper SES
nor usage of a foreign language appears to be closely related to birth in the United States.

How do social class differences among Mexican-American students affect loyalty to Spanish language, loyalty
to Mexican-American customs, and acknowledged degree of
assimilation problems? We had hypothesized that all of
these would show significant negative correlations. That
is, with upper social classes there would be less loyalty
to Spanish language and Spanish customs and fewer assimilation problems. This hypothesis did not hold up. Loyalty to Spanish customs showed no social class differences nor did loyalty to Spanish language. Quite to our
surprise, we found a positive significant correlation indicating that the higher the social class, the higher the
degree of assimilation problems. Perhaps a new ethnic
pride instilled by the recent Chicano movement may help
explain that there is no social class difference in loyalty to Chicano language or customs. Upper-class students had more assimilation problems than lower-class
peers, perhaps because they were in more direct competition with Anglo folkways and mores. The lack of social

class correlation with loyalty to Spanish language and
Spanish customs seems to strengthen our proposition that
language usage is not connected strongly to social class
and/or assimilation in this geographical area.

There is an increasingly recognized area of interest
in sociolinguistic study concerning attitudinal components of language study. We were tremendously interested
in our subjects' perceptions of Spanish and English
skills and of regional language varieties.

It has been found in the literature that self-rating
of language tends to correlate highly with reality. An
analysis by Goodman and Brooks[10] on the overall sample of
Chicano students finds them to be more "language conscious" than their Anglo peers in regard to both Spanish
and English. These workers found in their analysis that
52 percent of Mexican Americans, or a majority, indicated
having made special efforts to improve English as compared with only 39 percent of the Anglos.

In view of the fact that Chicanos had rated themselves lower than their performance, at least in the language sample, it is obvious that they feel less confident
in their English language skills than their monolingual
peers. This would appear to provide an additional incen-
tive for taking action to upgrade proficiency. Nevertheless, a corollary would also seem to be unfortunate feelings of inadequacy regarding their ability to communicate. This has, of course, been compounded by deeply in-
grained feelings of subservience and humility (as por-
trayed in movie and literary stereotypes). Obviously
this must also play a role when Mexican-American youths
are found to secure poorer paying jobs in comparison with
Anglo peers.

When it came to Spanish skills, a similar picture
emerged, with 75 percent of Mexican Americans reporting
efforts to improve in this language, and only 32 percent
of Anglos so reporting. Obviously, Spanish for most Anglos does not carry with it the same motivation as does
English for Mexican Americans.

The apparent concern with communication skills in
our Chicano subjects is well worth further research along
attitudinal lines throughout the Southwest. It would be
particularly relevant to ascertain to what extent English
language skills are regarded as a function of success in
formal education. English-language knowledge in our subsample correlated significantly with successful grades;
to what extent this correlation is true for the entire
sample and school remains to be discovered.

Endeavoring to ascertain our subjects' perception of
the language varieties used in this area, we included
several items in the questionnaire for this purpose and
found the students believed that all four varieties are
available in the Southwest. A mere 5 percent of the Chicanos believed that the Spanish heard here was "Formal,

Educated Style," while no Anglos thought so. The most frequent response was "Border Slang" (41 percent) since 51 percent of the Anglos chose this designation and 31 percent of the Mexican-American students agreed with them. The second most popular choice was "Informal, Everyday" chosen by 37 percent of the whole sample. For this category, Chicanos registered a higher percentage (40 percent) than did Anglos (32 percent). The remaining students chose "Southwest Dialect" and again this was favored by more Mexican-American students (24 percent) than Anglo students (17 percent). Again we found a statistically significant difference between our two groups at the .001 level of confidence.

One may note that the entire subject of Spanish language in the Southwest has suffered terribly from all sorts of oversimplification as well as downright distortion. Pejorative attitudes have prevailed among Mexican Americans and Anglos alike, in large part because of the relatively high degree of English interference. Parallels here with the status of Canadian French and such stigmatized varieties as *Joual* are obviously striking.

Since even 31 percent of the Mexican Americans rated Southwest Spanish as "Border Slang," there appears to be a great need for "reeducation" of both Chicanos and Anglos as regards language attitudes. By contrast, the 35 percent terming it "Southwest Dialect" and the 40 percent "Informal, Everyday" variety were quite realistic. By and large, the attitudes reflected by both groups, particularly the Anglos with 51 percent typifying it as "Border Slang," would deter rather than facilitate programs and texts intended to utilize Southwest Spanish as a basis for approaching Standard Educated English, as well as to examine it as a legitimate informal language variety.

In this connection certain sectors of Mexican-American militant movements go so far as to clamor for the recognition of a "Chicano language" which would in linguistic terms equate with the Southwest Spanish dialect or variety (a quip among linguistic scholars is that a language is a dialect with an army!).

In the liberalized pro-ethnic atmosphere of today, when "social dialects" and low-prestige language varieties are acquiring unprecedented prestige, there is a movement to define the nature and role of Southwest Spanish (highly stigmatized until now) in constructive and favorable terms. Thus viewed, it can emerge as fulfilling significant functions in the communication network, with a large percentage of the estimated seven million Chicanos employing it in informal domains. In addition, it is being realized among educators that Southwest Spanish (formerly often forbidden on school premises) can serve as a valuable point of departure for acquiring another code in the individual's linguistic repertoire of

standard educated or literary Latin American (Mexican)
Spanish. An informed and sympathetic view by an internationally known linguist may be found in J. Donald
Bowen.[11] Here again, in Third World terms, Southwest
Spanish, despite the existence of a literary language,
approaches the status of a vernacular because it is predominantly employed in informal, oral domains.
   We also attempted to determine the student's own
self-evaluation of the varieties of Spanish and English
controlled by them. Although most students felt they
used formal, educated style English, more Chicanos than
Anglos felt their proficiency was of the informal, everyday style. This was despite the fact that test proficiency of the subsample in English was quite high.
   Turning now to self-evaluation of the bilingual, 87
(more than half) claimed "Informal, Everyday" language
and 14 (somewhat more than 10 percent) "Southwest Dialect." A surprising 48 (about a third) felt that they
could handle "Formal, Educated Style." The latter sta-
tistic is all the more surprising since so few had characterized the general variety of regional Spanish so
highly, while the tiny number of three respondents claiming only "Border Slang" is more reassuring than anything.
Only one Spanish-surnamed individual disclaimed ability
to handle any variety! An important implication here is
that lower self-evaluation of both their own lingual
skills and the lower status or prestige of the language
varieties controlled by them obviously puts the Mexican
Americans at an appreciable disadvantage as contrasted
with their Anglo counterparts. This must account in part
in the latters' poor representation in the fields of science, technology, engineering, medicine, and business administration as well as such social sciences as sociology, psychology, political science, and linguistics. Here
again the analogy to Third World youth seems striking, as
long as entrance into the professions remains a key indicator of progress made by a group with "minorities"
struggling to achieve white-collar status.
   In addition, our findings require a great deal more
interdisciplinary attention than we have been able to accord them thus far, as well as replication elsewhere.
One of the implications that needs more consideration is
the relationship of the features of our particular sample
to both the language situation and to "language policy"
in the Southwest, as well as in the United States in general. As suggested in the citation from Ferguson and
Dil, although such issues have been taken for granted in
the technologically developed Western nation, recent
militancy has demonstrated the error of this attitude.
   One needs to reexamine the literature of the subject, largely dealing with the "emergent" nations, for
legitimate parallels, including such earlier sources as
Rice.[12] Of more recent date is Fishman, Ferguson, and

Das Gupta.[13] In their introduction, they comment tellingly:

> At a time when the major part of the human race is entrapped by such problems, most American linguists continue to be only marginally interested in language development . . . and most sociologists and political scientists are just becoming aware of language as an aspect of societal and national functioning. At the same time sociolinguistics is still a very fragile flower, cultivated only at a handful of universities and focused primarily on microphenomena at the level of the speech act in face-to-face interaction.

Pedantic though this procedure may seem, it is illuminating to make a few additional comments on the above volume. In his essay, "Sociolinguistics and the Language Problems of the Developing Countries," Fishman observes:[14]

> In general, the problems of disadvantaged population might hopefully be seen in broader perspective if they were considered against the background of co-territorial languages differences more generally and of planned language shift in particular. The long experience of other countries in coping with home-school dialect differences of a major sort (e.g., in England, Germany, Italy) may be illuminating . . .

Also germane are the essays by Dankwart A. Rustow,[15] Heinz Kloss,[16] who should be read bearing in mind William A. Stewart's seminal essay,[17] and Jiri V. Neustupny,[18] who urges the need to develop a general theory of "language" problems and "language" policy, which would attempt systematically to describe the communication patterns of given countries in terms of their effectiveness.

It would definitely be interesting to apply notions like Neustupny's to our Southwestern bilingual communication network. Certainly, in view of the recurrent clamor for better representation of Spanish in the school and other domains, and in the light of some of our own findings, it would seem that there are definitely some areas of ineffectiveness despite the complementary distribution of the roles of Spanish and English. (One should mention here also the Language Science and National Development Series being published by Stanford University Press.)

Other aspects of language and culture in the Southwest, as they are reflected in our Sociolinguistic Studies on Southwest Bilingualism, are discussed by "team" members Brooks, Goodman, and Renner in the studies mentioned and by Ornstein.[19]

A CORRELATION MODEL: USES AND APPLICATIONS

To cope with such a wealth of varying data, we have attempted to develop a correlational pattern described in Ornstein.[20] In its aspirations for a broader framework in which to view the complex of factors involved in the bilingual status, our "relational" or "correlational" model attempts to relate bilingualism (and its analog, biculturalism) within the social contexts in which the individual exists and functions. Evaluations of a bilingual's performance in the language pair and/or varieties controlled by him, no less than his attitudes and loyalties toward the respective languages and cultures, as well as his distributive use of languages are regarded as constants, in the light of which one may examine selected societal factors relevant to his existence.

Accordingly, our central concern is the question of how the bilingual/bicultural person fares as compared with the monolingual/monocultural, both within the "small groups" and the macrosociety in which he has membership, or aspires to membership. These are the basic issues which seem to us the most worthwhile to explore at this juncture in history, rather than to focus on microscopic aspects of bilingualism with the inevitable futility which is thus occasioned. At the same time, this hardly implies that narrow-gauge analytic studies should not be encouraged along both linguistic and social dimensions. Our model, then, is avowedly a "societal" one intended to serve interdisciplinary purposes.

At the same time, we have, because of the urgency of the needed information, attempted to focus on socioeducational relationships. Obviously, however, if the model has anything to offer, it could also be applied to such areas as sociopolitics where an individual's welfare and progress may vary according to differentiated ethnolinguistic or political affiliation. Therefore, the basic reference point tends to be a monolingual/monocultural (monodialected/monocultural) individual belonging to some dominant or elite group compared to a bilingual/bicultural minority group. Such an approach, it would seem, would make it possible for a linguist to join hands with the social scientist in a more dynamic and practical way than has been the case up to now.

In our opinion, it is in particular the educational dimension of bilingualism/biculturalism where our type of approach might legitimately have the greatest application at present. As matters now stand, there exists a large body of research literature on linguistic aspects of bilingualism, another on educational aspects of minority groups and school performance, while psychologists, sociologists, and political scientists contribute their own studies on some particular characteristic of an ethnic

group. There is an understandable inhibition about
treating more than one of these dimensions at one time
and in one study. Since it is the educational arena
where minority youth can go beyond the disadvantaged
status, the school sector appears to offer the best point
of interdisciplinary convergence.

In view of current dissatisfaction with middle-class
norms, it may not be too absurd to suggest that scholars
might begin to take into consideration the possibility
of differentiated norms of dimensions for ethnic groups
outside the mainstream. This would perhaps mean that in
the school sector there would be recourse to a dimension
which would evaluate a given ethnic group not against
mainstream standards but in the light of their own common
cultural experience. Hence our comparison of Chicanos
with Anglos might still be carried out, but another dimension would be needed: the comparison of Chicanos with
one another. Yet in recent U.S. experience, open college
admissions and quotas which favor underprivileged minorities have aroused controversy as devices for obtaining
equality. At the time of this writing, the case of Marco
de Funis is before the Supreme Court because of his rejection, although an honor student, to the University of
Washington Law School despite acceptance of "minorities"
with poorer records.

Socioeducational correlates of bilingualism/bicultu-
ralism then have a vast possible number of implications.
The need for more ethnic field research for coping with
much of the turmoil in American education is highlighted
by a group of Mexican-American educators. In a recent
manifesto, Dr. Simon Gonzales asserts:[21]

> An educational philosophy for the instruction of
> Mexican Americans requires concerted attention to
> the area of research. The paucity of data regard-
> ing our ethnic group requires that we increase our
> demands that institutions of higher learning address
> themselves to this need and also provide opportuni-
> ties for Chicano graduate students to gain vitally
> needed experience by participating as research as-
> sistants.

Whether or not this is a function of poorer self-
image and imagined or real inferior communication skills,
the fact is that blacks, Mexican Americans, and particularly Indians represent an unduly small proportion of
students in our professional schools and workers in middle-class, white-collar fields. At our own university,
where the situation is relatively favorable, most Mexican
Americans are enrolled in the School of Education; to become public school teachers is the traditional first step
upward of the minority. Many in Liberal Arts also follow

mainly a teaching track.

It is hoped that further studies will address themselves to this vital problem of poor minority representation in American higher education in general. Pepe Barron and Alfredo de los Santos, Jr.[22] point out that 95 percent of all Spanish-speaking students who enter college drop out before completing their fourth year. They urge that each institution devise some means to counteract this, adding:

> In order to fulfill the potential of every student in a cultural democracy and preserve the right of every American to remain identified with his or her own ethnic group while learning the necessary skills to compete in the economic life of our society, engineering schools must give immediate attention to the special needs of Chicanos, Boricuas and others who are linguistically and culturally distinct.

It might be added that one could substitute almost any other professional field, except for public school teaching and nursing, and the above would still hold all too true.

Beyond these points we cannot go except to reaffirm our conviction that increasing attention to the macrophenomena of bilingualism/biculturalism, whether through a correlational approach or otherwise, appears promising.

As far as studies like the present are concerned, the current clamor for special educational norms for disadvantaged minority groups might, therefore, raise serious doubts and objections to attempted correlations between Mexican Americans and Anglos. This issue is too broad for us to decide, but it is felt that this hardly invalidates our approach, given the vast spectrum of differences present in any minority group, not excluding the Chicanos.

SOME CONCLUSIONS AND IMPLICATIONS

Probably the greatest value of the study has been the explicit attempt to probe interrelations of language skills and social factors in a broader frame of reference than has usually been the case for sociolinguistic studies.

Two parameters of issues emerge from the research being done by our "team" on Mexican-American bilinguals. One of these, again reminiscent of youth in emergent lands, is the matter of relative position of prestige of minority dialect speakers, part of whose alienation from the mainstream is due to the stigmatized nature of their language varieties, and their exclusion from higher paying jobs because of inability to communicate in the standard educated model of mainstream groups, in our

case, English. We have seen that our subsample rated
their English capabilities significantly lower than Anglos, even when some of their performance scores would
justify a higher self-image. Their evaluation of the
kind of Spanish used in this locality, as well as their
evaluation of the Spanish they personally use, is also
indicative of a poorer self-image, although this may be
compounded by feelings of inferiority brought about by
lower SES position and poorer hourly wages paid them.

These same students, however, reflect a high degree
of loyalty to Spanish language and Chicano customs as
well as abundant use of Spanish language and Chicano customs in all but formal domains. Contrary to the findings
of Grebler, Moore, and Guzman,[23] the extent of use of
Spanish and loyalty to it is not, in our overall sample,
associated with SES. On the contrary, Chicanos of all
SES generally reported an abundant use of Spanish
usage, although it is true that higher SES Mexican Americans did indicate an extremely great amount of English
use at home and in the "environment."

We therefore seem to be in the presence of a sort of
inconsistency or ambivalence that might well contribute
to personality conflicts. While on one hand there is a
high degree of loyalty to Spanish language and Mexican-
American culture, on the other hand, Chicano culture on
the inferior ratings are accorded regional Spanish. This
problem needs to be explored much further and deeper than
has been possible for us to do here. It would be particularly desirable for scholars, especially Mexican-American ones, to probe these ethnolinguistic conflicts and
the roles played by them in the formation of attitudes of
hostility to mainstream America among Chicano militant
and separatist movements. Much like youth in newly
emergent Third World nations, Chicanos do not fail to re-
act by comparing their material and financial situation
unfavorably with their mainstream counterparts, in this
case more privileged or elite Anglos. Our data have attempted to demonstrate such divergences statistically
since so many allegations about minorities are based on
rhetoric alone. Although not downgrading local Spanish
varieties as much as their Anglo peers, their general
tendency was to rate their own lingual skills (in both
languages) lower than performances merited.

So many implications appear to emerge in this study
that we can do little more than comment on just one in
conclusion. What, for example, are the psychological and
sociological results of the SES differences encountered
in the investigation, along with the concomitant lower
wages earned by Chicano students? In addition to the
lower self-evaluation of language abilities, what other
manifestations of poorer self-image may stem among the
Chicanos from social class divergences? How do Mexican-
American students such as ours, interested in upward

mobility, really compare with Third World peers, of whatever ethnic stock, as long as they are similarly outside the mainstream?

Our subjects, as members of America's largest foreign language minority, require study in which special constructs are involved to relate not only the socioeducational but also sociopolitical and ecological correlates of the bilingual/bicultural status of this "territorial" minority.

Finally, we can conclude by saying a great deal of further research is mandatory before the findings in this study can be satisfactorily confirmed. Not only are replicative studies needed which might yield similar results but also our investigations which might corroborate or reject our individual assumptions and conclusions. Our conviction is that the area treated still offers a number of challenging and significant research tasks. Hopefully, both our study and future related ones can bring greater knowledge of the intricate web of interethnic relationships and better understanding among humans of one another.

NOTES

1. Rudolph O. de la Garza, Z. Anthony Kruszewski, and Tomas Arciniega, Chicanos and Native Americans: The Territorial Minorities (Englewood Cliffs, N.J.:Prentice-Hall, 1973).

2. Charles A. Ferguson and Anwar S. Dil, "Language Universals of National Development" (Paper presented to the Conference on Cultural Transmission, IX International Congress of Anthropological Sciences, Oshkosh, Wisconsin, August, 1973).

3. Bonnie S. Brooks, Gary D. Brooks, Paul W. Goodman, and Jacob Ornstein, Sociolinguistic Background Questionnaire: A Measurement Instrument for the Study of Bilingualism, rev. (El Paso: Cross-Cultural Southwest Ethnic Study Center, University of Texas at El Paso, 1972).

4. C. Robert Pace et al., College and University Environment Scales (CUES, Form X-2) (Princeton, N.J.: Educational Testing Service, 1969).

5. Wayne Murray: "Research in Progress," Bulletin of the Cross Cultural Southwest Ethnic Study Center 1 (March 1972): 3; "Ethnic and Sex Differences as Related to Perceptions of a University Environment" (Diss., New Mexico State University, 1972); "Mexican-American and Anglo Perceptions of a University Environment" (Paper presented at the Rocky Mountain Association for Educational Research, New Mexico State University, Las Cruces, New Mexico, November 1972).

6. Einar Haugen, The Norwegian Language in America: A Study in Bilingual Behavior, 2nd ed. (Bloomington: Indiana University Press, 1969).

7. Paul W. Goodman, "A Comparison of Spanish-Surnamed and Anglo College Students" (Paper presented at the Rocky Mountain Social Science Association Annual Meeting, Boulder, Colorado, 1970).

8. Will Herberg, Catholic, Protestant and Jew (New York: Vantage Press, 1960), p. 20.

9. Joshua A. Fishman, Language Loyalty in the United States (The Hague: Mouton, 1966).

10. Paul W. Goodman and Bonnie S. Brooks, "A Comparison of Anglo and Mexican-American Students Attending the Same University" (Paper prepared for the Cross-Cultural Southwest Ethnic Study Center, University of Texas at El Paso, 1973).

11. J. Donald Bowen, "Local Standards and Spanish in the Southwest," in Ralph W. Ewton, Jr. and Jacob Ornstein, eds., Studies in Language and Linguistics, 1972-1973 (El Paso: Texas Western Press, 1973).

12. Frank A. Rice, Study of the Role of Second Languages in Asia, Africa and Latin America (Washington, D.C.: Center for Applied Linguistics, 1962).

13. Joshua A. Fishman, Charles A. Ferguson, and Jyotirindra Das Gupta, eds., Language Problems of the Developing Countries (New York: John Wiley and Sons, 1968), p. 10.

14. Joshua A. Fishman, "Sociolinguistics and the Language Problems of the Developing Countries," in Fishman, Ferguson, and Das Gupta, Language Problems, p. 12.

15. Dankwart A. Rustow, "Language Modernization and Nationhood--An Attempt at Typology," in Fishman, Ferguson and Das Gupta, Language Problems, pp. 187-206.

16. Heinz Kloss, "Notes Concerning a Language-Nation Typology," in Fishman, Ferguson, and Das Gupta, Language Problems, pp. 69-86.

17. William E. Stewart, "A Sociolinguistic Typology for Describing National Multilingualism," in Joshua A. Fishman, ed., A Reader on the Sociology of Language (The Hague: Mouton, 1968).

18. Jiri V. Neustupny, "Aspects of 'Language' Problems and Policy in Developing Societies," in Fishman, Ferguson, and Das Gupta, Language Problems.

19. Jacob Ornstein: "Sociolinguistics and New Perspectives in the Study of Southwest Spanish," in Ewton and Ornstein, Studies in Language; "Language Varieties Along the U.S.-Mexican Border," in G. E. Perren and J. E. M. Trim, eds., Applications of Linguistics in Selected Papers of the Second International Congress of Applied Linguistics (Cambridge, England: Cambride University Press, 1971); "Sociolinguistics Investigation of Language Diversity in the U.S. Southwest and Its Educational Implications," Modern Language Journal 55 (April 1971): 224-229; "Mexican-American Sociolinguistics: A Well-Kept Scholarly and Public Secret" (Paper presented at the Fourth Triennial Conference on Symbolic Processes,

214

Washington, D.C., April 27-28, 1972). Appears in Bates Hoffer and Jacob Ornstein, eds., Sociolinguistics in the Southwest: A Symposium (San Antonio: Department of English, Trinity University, 1974); "Sociolinguistics Changes Viewed Within a Tagmemic Framework" (Paper presented at the 11th International Congress of Linguists, Bologna, Italy, August 28-September 2, 1972. To appear in Luigi Heilman, ed., Proceedings of the 11th International Congress of Linguists.); "Applying Sociolinguistic Research in the Educational Needs of Mexican-American Bilinguals/Biculturals in the U.S. Southwest" (Paper presented in Copenhagen, Denmark, August 22-27, 1972); "Toward an Inventory of Interdisciplinary Tasks in Research on U.S. Southwest Bilingualism/Biculturalism," in Paul R. Turner, ed., Bilingualism in the Southwest (Tucson: University of Arizona Press, 1973); "Toward a Classification of Southwest Spanish Non-Standard Variants," Linguistics 93 (December 1973): 70-87; "Relational Bilingualism--A Socio-Educational Approach to Studying Multilingualism Among Mexican Americans" (Paper presented at the X International Congress of Anthropological and Ethnological Sciences, Chicago, Illinois, September 1973. To appear in William McCormack, ed., Language in Many Ways (The Hague: Mouton)).

20. Ornstein, "Toward a Classification.

21. Simon Gonzalez in Manuel Reyes Mazon, Adelante: An Emerging Design for Mexican American Education (Albuquerque: University of New Mexico, Institute for Cultural Pluralism, 1972).

22. Pepe Barron and Alfredo de los Santos, Jr., "Are Chicanos Attending Universities?" Institute of Electronics Engineers Transactions on Education E-17 (February 1974): 10-12.

23. Leo Grebler, Joan Moore, and Ralph Guzman, The Mexican-American People: The Nation's Second Largest Minority (New York: Free Press, 1970).

10
Patterns of Accommodation of Mexican Americans in El Paso, Texas: An Analysis of a Barrio

Clark S. Knowlton

CHANGING PATTERNS OF ACCOMMODATION

The social and economic position of Mexican Americans in El Paso has been deeply influenced by location of the city on the American-Mexican and Texas-New Mexico borders. Distant from major centers of population and of economic and political power in Texas, El Paso has never been fully articulated into the economic and cultural life of the state. Closer to metropolitan centers of New Mexico, El Paso social systems and patterns of ethnic and racial interaction tend to resemble more the flexible pragmatic discrimination patterns of New Mexico than the harsher, more rigid patterns of most of Texas. Racial and ethnic relations in El Paso have been deeply influenced by two significant factors: the minority position of Anglo Americans in the El Paso region and dependence of the city upon trade with Mexico.

Although Anglo Americans became the numerical majority in the adult population of El Paso in the late 1950s, they are still a numerical minority in the El Paso-Las Cruces-Juarez oasis, and many feel quite threatened by their minority position. They believe themselves to be in danger of being overwhelmed by Mexican and Mexican-American numbers, the Spanish language, and Mexican and Mexican-American culture. Therefore, they are most reluctant to accept such innovations as bilingual education, cultural maintenance of Mexican-American culture, and incorporation of Mexican culture and history into the general educational curriculum. They regard themselves as a beleaguered outpost of Anglo-American civilization that must be preserved and strengthened through acculturation of Mexican Americans.

As the dominant political and economic elite of El Paso has always been economically dependent upon trade with Mexico and politically dependent to a degree upon Mexican-American voters, they have been most reluctant to antagonize their customers, clients, and voters by permitting overt expressions of prejudice and

discrimination. Furthermore, from time to time wealthy
Mexican Americans and Mexican leaders have developed to
where they were in a position to retaliate effectively
against such tendencies.

The system of discrimination that developed in El
Paso was flexible and pragmatic. Unsupported by legal
codes or well-articulated ideologies, its major function
was to protect Anglo-American political, economic, and
cultural dominance by controlling social and economic
mobility among Mexican Americans. Light-skinned Mexican
Americans who spoke good English, lived in the proper
neighborhoods, were well educated, had achieved positions
of influence and wealth through their own abilities, and
had adopted Anglo-American cultural values, were socially
recognized and permitted to function fully in the economic, professional, and political life of the city. Un-
acculturated Mexican Americans who were darker skinned,
spoke English badly, lacked a good education, or seemed
to threaten Anglo-American dominance, found the doors of
social and economic mobility closed to them. Violence,
lynchings, vulgar public expression of prejudice, and
open demonstrations of discrimination were not tolerated
nor were potential threats to Anglo-American dominance.

Successful Mexican Americans interested in political
or public life were granted positions on boards of directors of public agencies such as school boards or harmless
positions on political tickets. Thus, Mexican Americans
usually served on the city council but for the most part
were given the department of buildings and grounds rather
than police or finance. These were positions that placed
the Mexican American in the public eye, permitted him to
build up a political following, and even to make money,
but that denied him the substance of real political
power. This Anglo-American system of dominance was not
successfully challenged until the 1960s.

The most important historical events that slowly
eroded the system of dominance were: the Mexican Revolution, continued flow of Mexican immigrants, World War II
and the G.I. Bill, the Kennedys, the War Against Poverty,
and Mexican-American civil rights movements of the late
1960s and early 1970s. At present, the system of Anglo-
American dominance is in disarray although not over-
turned.

As revolutionary violence during the Mexican Revolution of the late 1910s swirled through northern Mexico,
entire Mexican populations fled from Juarez and other
neighboring Mexican communities to safety on the American
side. Many never returned. Among them were members of
the Mexican middle and upper classes. Defeat of federal
Mexican forces set recurrent waves of refugees into El
Paso. As one revolutionary general or another suffered
defeat, his troops and followers also fled to El Paso,
and the Mexican population increased very substantially.

Although the majority did return to Mexico when the violence ended, substantial numbers did not. Many wealthy
as well as middle-class and poor Mexicans remained. The
Mexican population of El Paso increased sharply. Furthermore, the habit among Mexican border businessmen of
purchasing El Paso real estate and investing funds in El
Paso banks and businesses as a hedge against revolution
or inflation continued long after the revolution. The
rather thin Mexican-American middle and upper classes
were reinforced, and a Mexican and Mexican-American society came into existence that created its own social
clubs, patterns of recreation, and often private schools.
Many Mexican-American business and political leaders were
influential and powerful enough to secure economic, social, and political recognition among Anglo-American businessmen and political leaders.

Continued flow of legal and illegal Mexican immigration through El Paso has played an important role in the
economic life of the city. It should be recognized that
the American Southwest has never been defined as foreign
territory to inhabitants of Mexico. From the very beginning of the economic development of the Southwest, American entrepreneurs had to depend upon Mexican and Mexican-
American labor. Railroads, agricultural interests, and
mining and smelter interests have constantly recruited
Mexican and Mexican-American labor in El Paso and Juarez
since the 1900s. The vast illegal flow of Mexican workers continues today because it is profitable to Anglo-
American business and economic interests and to Mexico.
If it ceased to be profitable, it would terminate. Efforts to control the movement have been at best sporadic
and ineffectual.

The movement of Mexican workers into the El Paso
area depresses wages to at or below subsistence levels.
Illegal Mexican workers tend to monopolize low-wage low-
skilled jobs in El Paso. The result is that migration
of unskilled and semiskilled Anglo Americans and blacks
into the El Paso area is inhibited. Large numbers of
unskilled Mexican Americans and Mexicans who live on the
American side, unable to progress economically, migrate
from border regions to more interior American states and
cities. This is a movement from El Paso to industrial
and metropolitan centers of the West, although some Mexicans and Mexican Americans do enter the migrant labor
stream in agriculture. Thus the flow of illegal and legal Mexican workers through El Paso depresses the local
wage structure for unskilled and semiskilled labor.
Large numbers of local Mexican-American families are
displaced who then migrate to other western cities. This
is a process that has existed since World War I.

At the same time, the existence of a large poorly
educated Spanish-speaking population opened channels of
social, political, and economic mobility for bilingual

Mexican Americans who mediated between Anglo Americans and Spanish-speaking groups. Mexican Americans found ready employment as sales personnel, white-collar workers, law enforcement and government employees, insurance salesmen, small businessmen, and professionals. Anglo Americans, not speaking Spanish and unfamiliar with Mexican and Mexican-American populations, were forced to rely upon Mexican-American intermediaries in politics, the professions, and business.

Many unscrupulous Mexican Americans were able to play this ignorance of the Anglo Americans and the ignorance of the local Spanish-speaking population about the Anglo-American workers against each other for their own enrichment and political and economic influence. That is, Anglo Americans were led to believe that certain Mexican Americans could deliver the vote of Mexican-American neighborhoods or could secure the business of Mexican-American clients. Mexicans and Mexican-Americans were led to believe the influence of the same leaders could secure employment, protection and assistance with the police, immigration bureau, or other Anglo-American government agencies. This process can still be observed in El Paso.

Mexican Americans have always had a flair for small business. Mexican-American urban slums and working-class neighborhoods are filled with peddlers and skilled workers operating small businesses in the street or in their apartments. Most of these are not registered with the city government nor have licenses. By operating long hours, utilizing family labor, keeping costs down, and carefully regulating credit, they are able to compete quite well with Anglo-American establishments. Although the failure rate is high, many of these small entrepreneurs, through careful husbanding of funds, are able to open small grocery stores, garages, construction companies, bars, repair shops, and other businesses. In time, a few graduate into wholesaling. Most of these small businessmen try to invest some of their profits into real estate. The enormous increase in El Paso land values since World War II created a few wealthy Mexican-American families.

World War II and the G.I. Bill of Rights were an important watershed in Mexican-American history.[1] Military experience created both a sense of ethnic identity and an American identity forged in military camps and on the field of battle, which accelerated the process of acculturation, awakened aspirations, and destroyed cultural isolation. War veterans returned home with marketable skills and opened small businesses of their own or secured better paying jobs as skilled workers. They were joined by the large number of Mexican-American veterans who, securing vocational and on-the-job training, were able to find placement in the business world. Many of

those trained as electricians, plumbers, carpenters, etc.
went into business for themselves, and a goodly number
prospered as small contractors, builders, and craftsmen.
   A smaller number of veterans entered the universities; as a result, a significant number of Mexican-American professionals came into existence. Majoring in law,
medicine, business management, social work, education,
and accounting, the veterans were able to find employment
after World War II. By this time, the Mexican-American
community was prosperous enough to provide a living for
Mexican-American lawyers, accountants, and other professionals. Educational and professional success of Mexican-American professionals awakened the educational aspirations among their relatives, friends, and neighbors.
More and more Mexican Americans found their way into the
colleges and universities. Taking advantage of G.I. Bill
housing provisions, Mexican-American veterans bought
homes in traditional Anglo-American neighborhoods, now
being evacuated by Anglo Americans, in newly developing
Anglo-American housing tracts in northeast El Paso, in
western El Paso stretching from the older neighborhoods
into the Upper Valley, or in segregated middle-class
Mexican-American neighborhoods.
   The veterans returned home anxious to move into the
mainstream of American society that they had observed in
other sections of the United States. Securing an education, they abandoned the Spanish language, spoke English,
and insisted upon their children learning English. With
their encouragement, the school system began to punish
Mexican-American children who spoke Spanish on the play-
grounds. Important segments of the Mexican-American veterans, the first generation of Mexican Americans to do
so, abandoned Spanish and deliberately acculturated into
Anglo-American society. Some of them anglicized their
names.
   The Mexican-American community began to differenti-
age into an urban and rural poor who preserved Mexican-
American values and the Spanish language and an urban
middle class who abandoned Spanish and Mexican-American
cultural values insofar as they were consciously able.
The latter tended to denigrate the former. Perhaps one
of the worst aspects of the situation was loss to the
Mexican-American community of many potential professionals, intellectuals, and prospective leaders. It is true
that this process did not evolve as far in El Paso as
elsewhere because ability to speak both Spanish and English conferred financial advantages upon bilingual Mexican Americans, many of whom had relatives in Juarez.
   Thus, effects of World War II and the G.I. Bill accelerated the process of acculturation and social differentiation among Mexican Americans, created a strong professional and white collar stratum as well as increased
the numbers of skilled workers and small businessmen. A

large, vigorous middle class and skilled working class
came into existence, able to compete economically and
professionally with Anglo Americans. Once Mexican-American veterans had cleared away the underbrush in Texas of
the more obvious practices of discrimination and segregation, their militancy and challenge to the Anglo-American
political and economic system gradually muted and diminished. Prosperity, employment, economic and social mobility, and the cooptation of professionals and successful Mexican Americans into the Anglo-American system contained the veteran challenge quite successfully. Discon-
tented Mexican Americans migrated to California or other
areas rather than fight Anglo-American dominance.

A serious political challenge was not mounted until
the 1960s against this dominance in political positions.
In the late 1960s, the Kennedy people, partially blocked
in Texas by hostile conservative Democrats, had to turn
to groups partially excluded from the political process
such as Mexican Americans, labor, blacks, and the liberals. Viva Kennedy clubs were organized, composed of ambitious young Mexican-American political hopefuls and
professionals. A remarkable process of mutual affection
developed between the Kennedys and the Mexican Americans.
No Anglo-American political leader had ever secured such
an affectionate response and deep loyalty as did John and
Robert Kennedy. The Mexican-American community supported
them, and many Mexican Americans received a thorough political training through their experience in the Kennedy
movement. Several Mexican-American political organizations such as PASO were organized to screen candidates
and work for those favorable to Mexican-American objectives. It was a middle-class Mexican-American movement,
but it did awaken Mexican Americans to their political
potential. When Johnson ran for president, Viva Johnson
clubs were organized that also provided political opportunities for ambitious Mexican-American professionals.
Mexican-American names began to appear on both Republican
and Democratic party tickets, usually matched against
each other.

The next important event was the War Against Poverty. It came into El Paso rather quietly but within a few
years had penetrated into every Mexican-American neighborhood in the city. Job opportunities were provided to
hundreds of Mexican Americans who staffed the programs.
These people received a thorough training in organizing,
drafting, and implementing programs, as well as an excellent knowledge of the power structures of their communities. Many were able to move from one position to another until they had entered federal, state, or local
government agencies.

The programs broke through the apathy of poor Mexican-American neighborhoods and involved large numbers as

clients and staff. Many *barrio* people served on boards
of directors. Not only did they earn more money, they
also acquired skills. And *barrio* Mexican Americans--for
the first time--began to mount serious and systematic political and economic challenges to Anglo-American political and economic dominance in El Paso.

The involvement of federal government was beyond the
control of local business and political elites. As Mexican Americans began to move into positions of responsibility in the ranks of federal agencies, Anglo Americans
had to deal with them as clients. Many more Mexican Americans found employment this time in more responsible
local political, business, and professional circles as a
response to federal programs and federal pressures.

One offshoot of antipoverty programs was the emergence of Mexican Americans from the lower strata of the
Mexican-American neighborhoods. Children of poor parents
began to find their way into universities and colleges.
Many of them had received jobs and training as street or-
ganizers and program managers. They were angry and deeply stirred by the Negro civil rights movement and by the
violence of the late 1960s and early 1970s. Militant
Mexican-American movements proliferated among students
and young people. Much of their anger was directed
against existing Mexican-American middle-class, professional, business, and community leaders who were accused
of accepting the political, cultural, and social status
quo. These young people from the *barrios* had lost en-
thusiasm for acculturation and English monolingualism.
Spanish moved from the despised lower class language to
an "in" language. Young Mexican Americans who did not
speak Spanish had little prestige in Mexican-American
circles. College students were less interested in acculturation than in fighting for an idealized Mexican-American culture and socioeconomic system. Under the impact
of all this, the Anglo-American political and economic
system began to weaken.

Election of Mexican Americans to political office in
El Paso is complicated by the nonpartisan free-for-all
nature of El Paso's political system. No effective political machine exists in the city through which Mexican
Americans might seek political representation or assistance in mobilizing Mexican-American voters. Candidates
are usually representatives of special interests in the
city. Tickets for mayor and city council are put together. Today most of these tickets contain one Mexican-
American name. The candidates then run their own campaign and solicit their own financing. Special interests
and the press, as a result, have considerable power in
the El Paso political process.

Raymond Telles, a charismatic Mexican-American politician active in county affairs where the first major
Mexican-American legislative breakthroughs took place

through the mobilization of the Mexican-American vote, was elected the first Mexican-American mayor in 1957. He did not create an effective political machine nor train Mexican-American political leaders to take his place. Upon being coopted as a diplomatic representative to a Latin American country, he left no one to take his place. Telles never returned to El Paso, but he did serve as a role model, and more and more Mexican Americans are now running for political office. They frequently lose, but more and more are being elected, especially to the state legislature. It is now customary to have Mexican-American representation upon almost every slate of county and city candidates. Elected Mexican Americans are not controlled by any strong political organization and thus are free to support whatever issues they desire.

A strong, sporadic but effective onslaught has been directed against the El Paso school system. Before World War II, very few Mexican-American teachers could be found. After the war, increasing shortage of teachers forced the El Paso school system to hire increasing numbers of Mexican Americans. For the most part, they were assigned to Mexican-American neighborhood schools. Those found in Anglo-American neighborhood schools taught Spanish. When the school administrators were queried about the absence of Mexican-American teachers in Anglo-American neighborhood schools, the answer was that school administrators were afraid Mexican-American accents might contaminate accents of Anglo-American children.

As late as 1966, there were few Mexican-American counselors and principals in El Paso's school system. Gradually, as attacks against the system mounted in the 1960s, qualified Mexican Americans were hired and assigned to various positions in school administration. As various bilingual and other programs designed to improve educational opportunities of Mexican-American children became available in the 1960s, the number of Mexican-American employees increased. However, it was not until the end of the 1960s that the school system abandoned the barbarous custom of punishing Mexican-American children for speaking Spanish during school hours. At the present time, Mexican-American teachers, counselors, and principals are found distributed throughout the school system but not in proportion to the number of Mexican-American schoolchildren. In recent court cases, the school system has been ordered to take measures to end segregated Mexican-American schools. Such measures do not always have full support of local Mexican-American parents who prefer local neighborhood schools nor of Mexican-American children who have strong neighborhood loyalties toward specific schools that are traditionally Mexican-American.

In summary, Anglo-American dominance still exists in El Paso. The system is in the process of reformulation.

Mexican-American professionals, businessmen, government
employees, and political leaders are steadily increasing.
They are not as concerned about Anglo-American acceptance
as before. Middle-class Mexican Americans are freely
admitted to civic clubs and professional organizations.
They also have developed their own clubs and associations
such as the G.I. Forum, composed of Mexican-American veterans, and the League of United Latin American Clubs.
From their ranks come many independent Mexican-American
politicians with whom Anglo Americans are forced to nego-
tiate. Mexican Americans have penetrated throughout the
school system. They are found in executive positions in
local federal, state, county, and municipal offices. Although Anglo Americans can no longer maintain a monopoly
of political power or of the professions, they still retain control of the economic system of the city. Anglo
Americans have by no means retired from political activity in the city, but the system of discrimination and of
race and ethnic relationships is slowly coming to resemble that of some eastern cities in which old Anglo-
American groupings, although retreating from local political systems, still retain economic control.

SOUTH EL PASO

     Of the first-generation Mexican-American urban *bar-
rios* and slums in the Southwest, South El Paso is one of
the most densely populated, oldest, poorest, and more
prestigious. Immigrants from South El Paso have carried
its fame to most of the Mexican-American neighborhoods
in southern New Mexico, Arizona, and California. Many of
the fads that mark *barrio* life, especially on the West
Coast, may have had their inception in South El Paso.
Although the *barrio* of South El Paso is densely inhabited, accurate data is still lacking on total number of
residents. In 1970, the Department of Planning, Research
and Development of the City of El Paso reported that
South El Paso contained 20,000 inhabitants--19,500 Mexican Americans, 400 Anglo Americans, and 100 Negroes.[2]
As the Bureau of the Census has consistently underenumer-
ated urban Mexican Americans, the estimate may have been
too low. Since then, population has declined until in
1977 it may be around 14,000 people living in about one
square mile or so. Located between the central El Paso
business district and the city of Juarez, Mexico, land
values in South El Paso have increased significantly during the past few years. Its location makes it quite desirable for the establishment of light industry and ware-
houses. The three highways and one railroad that cross
South El Paso to connect El Paso with Juarez enhance the
desirability of South El Paso for such commercial and
industrial activities.

Land owners have exerted considerable pressure upon city governments to change zoning from residential and light industrial. Local inhabitants have been able to slow down but not stop zoning changes. Property owners endeavoring to accelerate the shift from residential to industrial have demolished considerable numbers of tenements to force the inhabitants to leave. Many Southsiders, unable to pay higher rents demanded outside South El Paso, resist by rent strikes and refusing to leave tenements marked for demolition. The result is a steady increase in vacant lots available for many illegal activities.

The history of South El Paso is relatively unknown. Like many other significant rural and urban Mexican-American communities, South El Paso has drawn little attention from Southwestern social scientists. The oldest section of the *barrio* seems to be a small cluster of one-story adobe houses located along several narrow streets in western South El Paso. This section is still called Chihuahuita among inhabitants of the area. Use of this name indicates the complex may have come into existence as a Mexican-American settlement well before the turn of the century. Chihuahuita or Little Chihuahua was the name given from about the 1880s to the 1920s to segregated, low-income Mexican-American urban neighborhoods in much of the Southwest. The coming of the railroads to El Paso in the early 1880s isolated much of the section from the rest of the city.[3]

The presence of Mexican immigrants in the area is reported by an El Paso Times reporter describing an early morning walk on April 14, 1883:[4]

> He thought an hour might be profitably spent seeing what kind of people lived dog-like in hovels and perished dog-like in them. Fighting his way through a pack of mangy curs, he entered a hole dug in the earth into a single room roofed over with the tin from old oyster cans and a few loose boards. Terrible stench in interior. No windows, no ventilation, no furniture, nothing save squalid misery and dirt. Every hovel visited was the counterpart of the other; some were over the ground and some nearly under it . . . The water supply came from a shallow hole dug near the tracks of the Atchison, Topeka and Santa Fe Railroad. Why are such hovels permitted to exist?

In spite of the reporter's condescension, his description bears witness to the presence of Mexican immigrants residing in what is now South El Paso. Evidently they were impoverished squatters erecting temporary homes

out of any material available as hundreds of thousands of
rural Mexican immigrants have done in the outlying suburbs of modern cities. The process can be seen today in
the ever-increasing sprawl of similar squatter settlements around Juarez, Mexico.
    Mexicans were not the only settlers in the area.
Railroads brought in numbers of Chinese workers in the
late nineteenth century. Most seemed to have settled in
a Chinatown located in the eastern part of South El Paso.
As hundreds of Chinese sought refuge in El Paso, escaping
from the violence of the Mexican Revolution, the city's
Chinatown expanded. However, after World War I, the
Chinese gradually moved away, and Chinatown was settled
by Mexican Americans and gradually forgotten. An end-of-
the-century red-light district also existed in South El
Paso and gradually diminished in the first decade or so
of the twentieth century. The old bordellos, far better
built than the majority of existing tenements, now house
Mexican Americans.
    As the Mexican-American population of South El Paso
expanded, it gradually diversified in social class and
occupations. A Spanish immigrant, Olivas Villaneuva Aoy,
established a private free school for Mexican-American
children in South El Paso in 1885. The school, now bearing the name Aoy, grew into a public school, one of two
large elementary schools in South El Paso, located within
blocks of each other.[5]
    As evidence of growing numbers and stability of the
Mexican-American population and its occupational and social class differentiation around the turn of the century
were the growing number of churches established at this
time. The First Mexican Baptist Church opened in the
summer of 1890, the Mexican Congregational Church in
1892, the El Mesias Methodist Church and Mexican Community Center sometime before 1901, the Sacred Heart Church
in 1892, and St. Ignatius Church in 1905. St. Ignatius
and Sacred Heart are the two Roman Catholic parish
churches in South El Paso. The founding of such a wide
variety of churches is not only evidence of the zeal and
outside support of Protestant missionary activities among
the expanding Mexican-American population, but also of
increasing numbers of Mexican-American families able to
support such religious activities. Unfortunately, few
studies have been made of the socioeconomic characteristics of Mexican Americans who join various Protestant denominations. A tentative hypothesis may be that in this
period Mexican Americans joined such denominations as
part of their process of acculturation into Anglo-American society. The presence of a substantial Mexican-American population in South El Paso around the turn of the
century is proven by a newspaper report of an El Paso
flood in 1897: "All of El Paso south of Fifth Street and
East of Santa Fe was a sea of water and hundreds of

Mexican homes and the homes of quite a number of Americans were washed away . . ."[6]

The violence of the Mexican Revolution in the 1900s brought about a considerable increase in the Mexican-American population of South El Paso. Tom Lea, mayor of El Paso (1917-1919), is reported as saying: "As Juarez bulged with soldiers, the civilian population began to migrate en masse to El Paso to stay with friends and relatives."[7] Although large numbers of these temporary refugess returned to Juarez as fighting ebbed from the city, their place was more than taken by groups of refugees from the civilian population of Northern Mexico escaping the violence and economic dislocations of the revolution from diverse social classes and brought into the streets of South El Paso the political and emotional turbulence of revolutionary Mexico.[8]

The unfortunate socioeconomic conditions of South El Paso are revealed in a series of army reports during this period. As the violence of the Mexican Revolution approached the American border, marked by increased raids across the border, the American army established a military post in South El Paso on the edge of the Rio Grande River, facing Juarez. Army commanders were apparently quite apprehensive about the impact of poor sanitary and health conditions in the neighborhoods on the health of their troops and requested many times that South El Paso be cleaned up. Thus, a newspaper editorial comments:

> No false pride should influence the city administration in decline or hold lightly the suggestion from General Pershing that modern sanitary methods might be introduced into Chihuahuita with definite profit to the entire community. The City has not only neglected the elementary welfare of half its population but it has tolerated conditions in that section that have constituted a terrible menace to all the rest of the city.[9]

An El Paso housing survey indicts South El Paso conditions a year later:

> Probably in no place in the United States could such crude, beastly, primitive conditions be found as exist in Chihuahuita. The condition of this section is largely an economic one and the treatment should be radical.[10]

And radical that treatment was. The same paper reports in December of 1915 that 325 shacks were down and their inhabitants presumably moved to Juarez. Apparently, the shacks were replaced by a standard two-to-three story, U-shaped, red brick tenement without heating, toilet, or bathing facilities, containing standard two-room apartments of small size. Thus, authors of the detailed Kessler Report of 1925, a comprehensive analysis of the city issued by the El Paso City Planning Commission, stated:

> Between the business center of El Paso and the Rio Grande lies an area of three-fourths of a square mile constituting the most densely populated area in the city. A few of its main streets are lined closely with small but busy retail shops; some industrial establishments are in the area, and railroads occupy some parts of it. But for the most part it is covered with one-story or two-story tenement houses crowded with human beings.[11]

Conditions did not improve between the 1920s and 1930s. In an application for federal housing funds in 1937, Walter Stockwell, editor of the report, wrote:

> The present housing in substandard districts consists mostly of two-room apartments without private toilets or bathing facilities and without sinks or water supply inside the apartments. The only heat is from the cook stove and large families use these apartments . . . It is the conclusion of the local Authority that indecent, unsafe, and unsanitary conditions in the housing of the City as a whole are confined almost entirely to the substandard areas of the South Side.[12] (Note that the area is referred to as "the South Side" rather than as Chihuahuita.)

Except for establishment of three small housing projects in South El Paso before World War II, conditions did not improve very much during the 1940s. Before then, undoubtedly, streets were paved, water mains installed, and lighting added as part of city improvement, but conditions in the tenements did not change. Thus, a 1948 city survey found that there were 345 substandard tenements in South El Paso. At that time population was estimated at around 23,000. The number of families having a shower was 5 percent; a bathtub, 3 percent; and a private toilet, 3 percent. Average number of families per toilet was 7.06. Only 19.07 percent of the total city population resided in South El Paso, but the area accounted for the following: all city welfare cases (71.09 percent), all fire calls (31.03 percent), all police calls (26.04 percent), all adult crime (51 percent), all delinquent juvenile cases (88.20 percent), and all infant mortality (66.07 percent). There were 12,438 substandard dwelling units in the neighborhood.[13]

The same conditions were found to exist without change by the El Paso City Planning Department in 1962.

The authors of this study found, in three South El Paso census tracts, a total of 631 tenement structures. Of these, only 115 were in good repair and 515 (69.9 percent needed repairs. Poor and inadequate electrical installations were found in 94.8 percent of all tenements with 597 needing electrical repairs and major plumbing repairs needed in 86 percent of the tenements. Out of 531 tenements studied, 444 had no bathing facilities and 568 (90 percent) had no heating appliances but were heated by natural gas cooking ranges. The report states: "We are of the opinion that many persons would be asphyxiated each winter, if it were not for the loose windows and doors and cracks in the floors and walls allowing enough fresh air to enter the rooms to supply oxygen to the occupants."[14]

Council members found the major causes for existence of such conditions in South El Paso were: (1) disinterested absentee ownership; (2) apathy of absentee owners about human rights and feelings, and a definite lack of public interest; (3) economic inabilities of people residing in the area; (4) the continued existence of tenement structures to be inhabited; (5) sentimental attachment to the *barrio* of people residing within this area; (6) continued influx of immigrants; (7) it is the oldest part of town; (8) zoning regulations and land use restrictions; and (9) reluctance of apartment owners outside of South El Paso to rent reasonable apartments to tenants with large families.

Thus, evidence tends to demonstrate existence of first generation Mexican-American neighborhoods in South El Paso since the early 1880s. From the very beginning of settlement down to the present, deplorable socioeconomic conditions have continued to exist. Although report after report commented on these conditions, very little has ever been done by municipal agencies except for establishment of a small number of public housing units in the 1930s and early 1940s. During the late 1960s and early 1970s, additional public housing units were built in other neighborhoods but not in South El Paso. One suspects that the city fathers feel that perhaps if nothing is done to improve conditions, the population might be induced to move, making the land available for other more profitable uses.

Even though the supply of tenement housing in South El Paso steadily diminishes, it still continues its major functions as "half-way house" for legal and illegal Mexican immigration into the United States. Physically intermediate between Juarez and El Paso, the neighborhood is both physically and culturally isolated from other sections of El Paso and from Anglo-American culture. Almost the only Anglos seen in South El Paso are school personnel, social workers, police officers, and firemen. Very few young people in South El Paso have

any permanent contacts with Anglo Americans except
through television and the schoolroom.

Spanish is the language of South El Paso and very
little English is ever spoken. An inability or unwill-
ingness to speak Spanish in South El Paso would be taken
as "cultural treason," subject to severe sanctions. Adults speak the Spanish of their native Mexican communities but children and teenagers speak the tough, vigorous, rapidly changing oral street Spanish heavily infiltrated with English. Called *lengua de los tirilones* or
"language of the street people or street fighters," it
resists all efforts to replace it with English or border
Spanish. Although Coltharp calls it a "criminal argot,"
it is not only the language of street gangs but of all
neighborhood children and young people, delinquent and
nondelinquent alike.[16] Changing rapidly in vocabulary
from generation to generation, it is but one of a number
of Spanish dialects existing in and around El Paso that
remains to be studied. The dialect seems to be primarily
confined to South El Paso and neighborhoods into which
South El Paso families have moved. From South El Paso it
has spread to other urban *barrios* in California and elsewhere.

As the majority of the population is barely literate
in either Spanish or English, in part due to a school
system that has attempted to replace Spanish by English,
creating generations of Mexican Americans functionally
illiterate in both written Spanish and English, newspapers are not commonly found in South El Paso. Those
that circulate most tend to be Spanish-language border
newspapers, such as El Fronterizo, that circulate on both
sides of the border. Local people prefer Spanish-language radio stations but Anglo-American television programs. As more and more American television programs are
translated into Spanish and carried on Mexican border
stations, the preference tends to change. Inhabitants of
South El Paso have very little knowledge of the so-called
"high culture" of either Mexico or the United States.

South El Paso's population is not as isolated from
Juarez as it is from Anglo-American El Paso. South El
Pasoans do some of their shopping in Juarez and tend to
have many relatives living in Juarez or other communities
in northern Mexico. Constant social interaction between
relatives living on each side of the border retards acculturation in South El Paso and introduces some selected
Anglo-American concepts into Juarez and other Mexican
communities. In many ways, a unique border culture among
Mexican and Mexican-American inhabitants of the border
region is coming into existence in the American Southwest
and northern Mexico with regional cultural variation.
This border culture, absorbing cultural traits and com-
plexes from both Anglo-American and Mexican cultures, is
confined to Mexican and Mexican-American populations of

the border regions with little impact on urban Anglo Americans. Quite often it is this evolving and changing border culture that so many young Mexican Americans have in mind when they analyze their own *barrio* culture.

Before the current rash of demolitions, South El Paso was physically divided into a mosaic of small neighborhoods separated from each other by heavily traveled streets, vacant lots, or changes in housing types. These neighborhoods were not as meaningful to adults who tended to identify more with South El Paso than with the more immediate neighborhood, but they were meaningful to children and teenagers. These neighborhoods were often confined to a cluster of neighboring tenements, to a side of a city street, or at times to a larger grouping such as a block. Each neighborhood had a name, usually drawn from nearby streets, by which it was known to other teenage and children groups. In the past, young adults of each neighborhood called themselves and were known by a traditional name inherited by one generation after another. In times of gang activities, the names became gang names. During periods of gang inactivity, they were the names used to identify social groupings of older children and young adults in specific neighborhoods.

Coltharp gives the impression that South El Paso has always been characterized by extremely high rates of criminal and delinquent gang behavior.[17] This is simply not true. Cycles of gang activity exist, marked by periods of active and inactive gang behavior. These cycles tend to follow each other. The 1950s and early 1960s were periods of peace in the streets. Now gang activities are increasing again in South El Paso.

One interesting aspect of gang activity in South El Paso is that southside gangs have usually confined their activities to South El Paso. Rarely have gang members from this neighborhood engaged in fighting with gangs from other neighborhoods. Little contact has existed with Juarez teenage groups, just across the river, except for an occasional shower of rocks, nor have South El Paso gangs engaged in fighting with Anglo-American gangs.

The traditional gang is loosely structured. At the core is a group of *tirilones* or "street fighters" who spend their days and evenings together engaged in a varied range of activities to secure money and spend it pleasurably. Around the core are grouped young adult males who may engage in delinquent activity or not at their own discretion; very little pressure except teasing will be exerted upon them. If the neighborhood is invaded by another gang, all teenagers and young men will rally to defend their neighborhood. The gangs engage in very little planned activity. As professional crime is absent from the area, delinquent activities are confined to street fighting, shoplifting, armed robbery, breaking into railroad cars, and blackmailing local businessmen.

Those who escape being sent to prison or detention homes, or specialize in petty crime, tend with adulthood to fade into the general working-class Mexican-American population.

Gang leadership tends to be exercised by young men with charisma, money, cars, or access to goods and services (such as drugs) not always available to others, and by those who have "heart" and a reputation for courage and aggressiveness. Boys upon marriage, securing a permanent job, or attending college, are expected to drop out of gang activities. Girls usually refrain from joining gangs, but in each neighborhood there will be found a group of girls from disorganized families who form female gang auxiliaries and, wearing gang jackets, consort with male gang members in a dependent status position. A rather interesting age segregation exists among boys. Boys below the age of thirteen or fourteen seldom join in gang activities, although they may be used as scouts or spies. Every boy in the *barrio*, young or old, who has suffered mistreatment or abuse anywhere in El Paso can expect assistance and revenge from the boys of his own neighborhood.

Street lore grows up in times of gang activities about daring street fighters and resourceful gang leaders. Thus a legend has grown up about one boy who crawled over tenement rooftops by himself to drop down from the roof behind the gang leader of a hostile gang standing on the street corner surrounded by many of his followers. The boy, placing a knife at the throat of the gang leader, marched him from his own gang territory into the neighborhood from where the boy came. The leader was thoroughly manhandled and then allowed to escape. Much gang lore becomes embodied in the folk music of South El Paso with its cycles of prison, gang, and marijuana songs. These songs many not last more than two generations in the streets and, unfortunately, no effort has been made to collect them.

Social organization of the adult tenement population in South El Paso is quite varied by neighborhood. In many tenement areas, people are constantly moving in and out; little stability of population exists. In other tenement clusters, population is more stable; in sections marked by ownership of private homes, very little mobility exists. Speaking in general, there is one family in each tenement that represents the interests of the landlord. He keeps an eye on the tenement population in return for either free or greatly reduced rent.

Families on the first floor of two-to-three story tenement buildings have higher social status than families living on the second and third floors. Usually, in most tenements, a core of individuals and families who have lived in the tenements for a long time. They know each other well and are often ceremonial kinfolks,

comadres and *copadres*, who have sponsored each other's
children in baptismal ceremonies. A close group, they
are the heart of each neighborhood. Around them are
grouped a much larger number of families who, often more
mobile, have little contact with other families except
those that are related by family ties or come from the
same community in Mexico. South El Paso neighborhoods,
until the antipoverty programs of the 1960s, had almost
no formal social organizations except church-related associations, and large numbers of people had, by choice,
very little social interaction with other tenement
dwellers. They may not even know the names of families
that live next door.

Although income levels are extremely low, many tenement families are constantly struggling to increase income by opening small businesses. Color television sets
may be purchased on time and neighbors charged small
amounts to see programs. Other families may sell candy,
soft drinks, or baked goods from their apartments. If
they accumulate small amounts of capital, they may open a
small grocery store or bar. Chances of success are not
very good, but some families are able to expand their
businesses by hiring family members, staying open long
hours, and selling dangerously on credit. Others with
special skills operate street repair shops, sell from
tenement to tenement, or engage in a variety of trades.
A few sell illegal alcohol from the back doors. The
profitable drug traffic is always a temptation to Mexican Americans anxious to escape the poverty in which they
live. Small business is one of the most important means
to develop a small capital, to provide employment to
family members, and to improve one's social and economic
position. South El Paso is filled with small businesses,
the majority of which may never come to the attention of
licensing or taxing agencies.

It should be kept in mind that South El Paso is but
one of many first- and second-generation Mexican-American
neighborhoods in El Paso. The socioeconomic and cultural
characteristics of each of these neighborhoods is somewhat different from the others. It is extremely dangerous to generalize from one about cultural and socioeconomic characteristics of other neighborhoods in the city.
Each is a unique *barrio* fully worthy of study and research.

SUMMARY

The accelerated pace of social differentiation, urbanization, industrialization, affluence, acculturation,
and the rise of the civil rights movement have diluted
and eroded the subtle historic patterns of discrimination
in El Paso. Today Mexican Americans are found in almost
all professions, white-collar occupations, and skilled

trades, even though the majority are still unskilled or semiskilled. It is far easier to discriminate against a non-English-speaking, poorly educated Mexican-American migrant farm worker or a semiskilled industrial worker than against a well-dressed, English-speaking Mexican-American professional who lives in a good neighborhood, belongs to civic clubs, and is active in community affairs. The sharp increase in the number of professionals, white-collar workers, accountants, businessmen, executives, contractors, and skilled workers, often operating their own shops, has brought about a revision of old Anglo-American stereotypes about Mexicans and Mexican Americans. The fact that Anglo Americans today often must deal with Mexican-American heads of government bureaus who can grant or deny benefits has also affected the social position of Mexican Americans in El Paso. Finally, the substantial increase of Mexican Americans in the El Paso state legislative delegation and other county and city political positions which Anglo Americans must now relate to in the political structure is having its effect. Old stereotypes and patterns of discrimination are being modified to adjust to the new Mexican American, but the economic and cultural dominance of the Anglo American in El Paso has still not been severely weakened. Politically, Mexican Americans are beginning to encroach upon the traditional political positions and political mechanisms of the Anglo American.

Now that Mexican Americans have become more urban than rural, they are in a position to generate considerable political strength. In El Paso, political influence of Mexican Americans is still not proportional to the number of residents but this influence is steadily increasing. It is only a matter of time before Mexican Americans come to occupy ever more political positions proportionate to their population in the El Paso city and county. Politics will become an important channel of social mobility among El Pasoan Mexican Americans. Occupational, social class, and political differences are emerging among them. They are now, nor will they be in the future, a monolithic political, economic, or social bloc. The incipient class and political differences within the Mexican-American community were obscured and concealed by the need of Mexican-American leaders to present a solid front to the Anglo-American world and by Anglo-American ignorance of the Mexican-American community. As this need and this ignorance diminish, Mexican-American divergences will emerge. One may well expect growing conflict between partially acculturated Mexican Americans who are economically, educationally, and socially successful and acceptable to Anglo-American society and less acculturate groupings evolving out of low-income *barrios* and rural farm workers.

Another area of growing potential political and

economic conflict will develop between Mexican Americans
and other minority groups such as blacks and American Indians. Basic economic, cultural, and political interests
of these groups do not necessarily coincide. Illegal
Mexican immigrants are replacing blacks in some low-
skilled, low-income jobs in east Texas and California.
Black demands that tight controls be placed on illegal
Mexican migration are strongly resisted by Mexican Americans who feel such controls may have a negative impact
upon them. Employers and law enforcement officers are
not always able to differentiate between Mexican Americans and Mexican immigrants. Conflicts between minorities may provide skilled Anglo-American political and
economic leaders opportunities to play off one minority
against another.
     Culturally, the tortilla curtain still stands firmly
along the Rio Grande. Very few Mexican Americans or Anglo Americans in and around El Paso have any knowledge
about Mexican history, culture, or artistic, literary, or
scientific achievements. Very little has been done to
integrate such data into the educational curriculum from
elementary to university level. The result is that few
Mexican Americans, because of the successful crusade of
Southwestern schools against Mexican culture and history,
have any knowledge of Mexico beyond what their parents or
grandparents, usually very poor immigrants in flight from
Mexican poverty, have told them.
     An unstudied phenomenon is the small but persistent
number of Mexican Americans born in El Paso who return to
Mexico with their parents or as young adults to seek education in Mexican schools or employment as scholars,
writers, or artists in Mexico. They do exist, but little
is known about them at present.
     Educationally, the struggle for bilingual education
and integration of Mexican-American culture and historical experience into El Paso schools has gained a foothold
but little else. The Spanish language is still treated
as an inferior relation utilized to improve learning of
English as a second language but not treated seriously as
a world language important in its own right. At present,
an Anglo-American counterattack is being mounted against
bilingual education. What is now needed is a thorough
objective evaluation of the diverse types of bilingual
programs to ascertain their true worth in improving educational advancement of Mexican-American children.
     In terms of assimilation, structural assimilation
has not taken place.[18] Mexican Americans have acquired
many Anglo-American cultural values and behavior patterns
as they must to function successfully in an Anglo-American dominated society. In many ways Mexican Americans
have successfully compartmentalized Anglo-American and
Mexican-American values and ways of behavior. Among Anglo Americans they may behave as Anglo Americans. Among

Mexican Americans, they interact as Mexican Americans. The process undoubtedly creates cultural and psychological stresses and strains. It can be said that mechanisms of boundary maintenance between Mexican Americans and Anglo groupings and cultures have been strengthened by reevaluation and growing appreciation of Mexican-American culture and social systems, and a downgrading of Anglo-American values and social systems. Among Mexican Americans, the desire to assimilate, once so strong in the early 1950s, has largely vanished. In Gordon's schemata, "structural assimilation, amalgamation, and identificational assimilation" in El Paso have strongly slowed down and perhaps structural assimilation and identificational assimilation are more and more unlikely to take place.

Acculturation of Mexican Americans is seriously weakened by growing illegal migration of Mexican workers into the United States. Today most illegal migrants settle in larger metropolitan cities rather than in smaller towns and rural areas. They steadily reinforce the position of the Spanish language, boundary maintenance systems of low-income Mexican-American urban *barrios*, and Mexican cultural values, although these same values now vary from one generation of Mexicans to another.

In the El Paso area, social, economic, political, and cultural change among Mexican Americans are the predominant cultural theme. They are affected both by dramatic rate of technological, economic, educational, and social change in American society and by rate of change within the Mexican-American community. Processes of change are not necessarily either the same or proceeding at the same rate in the two societies. All one can say is that the social, economic, and political position of Mexican Americans in El Paso will be quite different in ten years, barring a major depression, than it is now.

NOTES

1. Clark Knowlton, "Culture Conflict and Natural Resources," Social Behavior, Natural Resources and the Environment (New York: Harper and Row, 1972).
2. Department of Planning, Research and Development, City of El Paso, Texas, 1970.
3. C. L. Sonnichsen, Pass of the North (El Paso: Texas Western Press, 1968), pp. 227-230.
4. El Paso Times, April 14, 1883.
5. A Short History of South El Paso (El Paso: Department of Planning, Research and Development, 1967), p. 7.
6. Ibid., p. 2.
7. M. B. DeWetter, "Revolutionary El Paso, 1910-1917," Password of the El Paso Historical Society, Part 1, Vol. 3, No. 2 (April 1958): 46-59; Part 2,

236

Vol. 3, No. 3 (July 1958): 107-119; Part 3, Vol. 3, No. 4 (October 1958): 145-158.
8. Short History, p. 12.
9. The El Paso Herald-Post, August 26, 1914.
10. The El Paso Herald-Post, September 27, 1915.
11. Short History, p. 24.
12. Ibid., pp. 26-28.
13. Ibid., p. 30.
14. Slums Council Citizens Advisory Council, City of El Paso, "Report to the Mayor and City Council," 1964.
15. Ibid., pp. 16-17, 19-21.
16. Lurline Coltharp, The Tongue of the Tirilones (University, Ala.: University of Alabama Press, 1965).
17. Ibid.
18. Milton M. Gordon, Assimilation in American Life: The Role of Race, Religion and National Origin (New York: Oxford University Press, 1964).

11
Sociopolitical Reactions to Public Policy:
Tenant Attitudes about a Relocation Program

James W. Lamare
Mary Steffey Lamare

One of the major weaknesses in the growing public
policy literature is lack of research directly measuring
the impact of governmental programs upon the sociopolitical orientations of people immediately affected by political action. There are empirical rumblings that what
emerges from the government, or at times what fails to
emerge, does indeed structure political and more general
orientations. Public opinion studies[1] suggest that government action or inaction has influenced adult views in
the last decade, especially in the policy arenas concerning Vietnam, race relations, law and order, political
protests, the operation of government, and the economy.
Even among children there are signs that the issues confronting, or policies emanating from, public officials
are serving as stimuli in political learning.[2]

While suggestive, these studies are indirect empirical probes into the relationship between public policy
and political perspective. Usually the samples contain
people not necessarily directly affected by a particular
governmental program. Respondents are, however, analyzed
with an eye toward assessment of governmental policy performance. The standard methodology is to investigate
responses to questions about policy matters or issues
over time and to trace governmental practices in these
policy arenas. If a change in opinion is detected, it is
surmised that this movement is a function of governmental
activity.

Direct assessment of policy impact upon sociopolitical orientations requires weighing reactions of people
immediately affected by a governmental program.[3] Such a
methodology is employed in our study which focuses upon
poor Mexican Americans living in El Paso, Texas, who were
uprooted from theirliving quarters when the city decided
to condemn their tenement apartments and afford the displaced the opportunity to relocate into public housing
units. Before we turn to the specific methods and the
findings, first a word about the policy and its origins.
As is the case in most larger cities in the United

States, El Paso has a long history of containing within
its midst dwellings that are inadequate, unsanitary, and
overcrowded. Most of these housing units are tenements
that serve as living quarters for the poorest Mexican
Americans. Geographically, they are located in the
southernmost section of the city in a square-mile area
resting on the border of Mexico.

Until recently, very little had been done by the
city to improve housing conditions in south El Paso. As
of 1968, the 20,000 residents in this area lived in 5,070
dwelling units, three-fourths of which were classified by
city officials as "deteriorating/dilapidated."[4] Only
fifty-eight of these units contained an inside toilet in
their two rooms. Families living in only 120 of these
tenement apartments had the luxury of a shower or a
bathtub.

The first systematic, large-scale effort to face
this deplorable housing situation came into existence in
the summer of 1973. A number of occurrences converged
that year which resulted in remedial public policy.
First, the mayor, elected in 1972, was desirous of altering the housing situation in south El Paso. During a
previous tenure as mayor (in the 1950s), he had attempted
to tackle some of these housing problems, but political
and economic obstacles prevented much action. On Easter
Sunday, 1973, the mayor was given the opportunity to
begin anew the search for change when a substandard tenement exploded because of a gas leak, killing seven persons and injuring many more. Protests from various
groups of the city provided the foundation to explore
corrective strategies. The mayor, with the consent of
the City Council, appointed a special committee to investigate the southside housing situation and to proffer
remedies. What was recommended and adopted by city officials was a plan to enforce the existing (since 1969)
housing code. The owners of tenement buildings would now
either have to meet stringent specifications or have
their structures condemned. An added component was the
decision by the Housing Authority in El Paso to give
residents displaced through condemnation top priority in
entrance into public housing units. Without this cooperation, the possibility of people made homeless through
condemnation made code enforcement politically suicidal.
The culmination of these events was the birth of the
Tenement Eradication Program of the City of El Paso.

Of interest to students of public policy, either
from the ranks of the political or academic world, are
the reactions of those relocated from condemned tenements
into public housing units. Did this policy alter views
of government? If so, in what direction, positive or
negative? Were newly formed attitudes about the government linked to evaluations of the new residential environments where the relocated were moved?

Answers to these questions come from a randomly selected sample consisting of one-half of the tenants relocated from condemned tenements into public housing units at the end of 1974. From the original sample list of 280 relocated tenants, 224 (80 percent) were successfully surveyed by trained bilingual interviewers during October and November of 1974. The interviews, pretested among thirty-six other relocated tenants, lasted an average of thirty minutes and were conducted, at the request of every person sampled, in Spanish. In nuclear families, the husband and wife of the relocated family were both questioned.

THE IMPACT OF THE PROGRAM

Our intial point of inquiry was to assess the extent to which the relocation policy influenced the respondents' view of government. The sample was asked, "Has moving into this apartment in public housing affected your opinion of the government?"[5] One-third (N=72) of the relocated tenants answered in the affirmative. Within this minority evincing a change in perspective in the aftermath of policy implementation, there is about a two-to-one ratio of relocated who are more positive about the government in comparison to their more negative counterparts. Sixty-two percent of the changers noted that their opinion is now better about the government, while the remainder felt worse about political officials.

To assess the relocated tenants' evaluation of their new environs, they were asked a series of questions affording them an opportunity to compare their new apartment, housing unit, and neighborhood as well as social services and living conditions (health, transportation, schools, job opportunities, distance from work, environment for the young, garbage collection, and police protection) with the counterpart of these items where they formerly resided.[6] The vast majority said their new apartment (over 95 percent) and the public housing unit (over 80 percent) were better than the buildings that were condemned. These sanguine feelings began to wane in comparing various aspects of their new living situation with where they lived before. A bare majority (51 percent) viewed their new "neighborhood" as better than their old *barrio*. In comparing particular services and living conditions in the current neighborhood with those in the previous one, the respondents, overall, gave negative appraisals. While garbage collection and environment for the young were considered better by around 60 percent of the relocated, less than a third felt positive about transportation (22 percent), the quality of schools (32 percent), job opportunities (11 percent), distance from work (27 percent), and the police (26 percent).

Moreover, 57 percent did not feel their health had been improved by the move into public housing. Perhaps these feelings of favorable ratings of the four walls now around the relocated but displeasure with the new neighborhood were captured most succinctly in the respondents' wishes about alternative housing. Most of the relocated (57 percent) would rather have lived in a similar <u>new</u> apartment but in their <u>former</u> neighborhood.[7]

The next matter to be addressed was the possible relationship between the attitude of the respondents toward the government as a result of the relocation policy and their evaluations of their current environment. The sample was divided into three groups, depending upon the view toward government after relocation. The positivists were those who altered their feelings about political authority in a more favorable direction as a result of relocation. The negativists experienced a change in governmental perspective but in the other direction. Finally, the nonchangers were the respondents who did not switch their perceptions of the political system even though they were moved.

The pattern uncovered points to a clear correlation between attitude about the government following implementation of the relocation policy and orientations toward the new environs. The negativists were much more likely to criticize their relocated surroundings, especially as a good environment for youth, the police, transportation, and the overall neighborhood, than either the nonchangers or the positivists. On the average, 51 percent of the negative changers rated their new milieu as worse than their previous living conditions. The positivists, conversely, felt much more favorably disposed toward where they were moved. The nonchangers evaluated their new quarters somewhat between their positive and negative counterparts, but leaning somewhat toward the former.

The monotonic pattern between orientation toward the government and view of the environment was quite clear. Not unexpectedly, 87 percent of those negative about relocation preferred to be living in a structurally sound apartment in their former neighborhood, while only 41 percent of those positive and 56 percent of those who stood pat desired to move back into the previous *barrio*. Thus, while relocating did not affect everyone's view of government, for those altering their political views, a structuring of attitudes about the new living quarters was evident.

One objection to the argument presented so far is the suggestion that a switch in view toward the government as a result of the relocation policy <u>caused</u> positive or negative evaluations of the new environs. The methods employed in this study are not suitable to strictly investigate this type of causal relationship.[8]

However, an indirect test of this relationship is possible. The relocated were moved in various stages over the year before this study was conducted. By dissecting the respondents into four groups, depending upon the time of their move, we are able to analyze reactions to the government and the new surroundings, controlling for exposure to the latter. If feelings about the new living place were structuring attitude about the government, one would expect that the people living in public housing for the longest period of time would be the most likely to shift views toward the government and those moving into their new apartments more recently to be neutral in their political evaluations. Support for this argument was not found. Changes in governmental attitude, after relocation went into effect, were found in all groups of the relocated, regardless of how long they had been exposed to their new living conditions. Hence, there is little to suggest that affective ratings of the environment of the relocated structure feeling toward the government. We are left with a plausible case that a positive or negative view of the government, because of relocation, presaged evaluations of where the respondents moved.

A final factor that could contaminate the conclusion that reactions to the relocation policy influenced general social views is whether attitudes about either the government after this public policy or the new living environment are related to the demographic or attitudinal background of the respondents. The case for government intervention structuring overall orientations would be greatly weakened if there was any indication that certain segments of the study population appeared to be more affected by relocation or were more pronounced in their evaluations after displacement. The interviews secured an abundant amount of information pertaining to the social, psychological, and political terrain on which the tenants stood. There is little indication that these background characteristics clearly affected either evaluations of the government after relocation or of the environment once moved. Hence, none of the demographic factors of education, income, employment, sex, age, country of birth, or length of residence in the El Paso area,[9] or of the psychological dispositions measuring interpersonal trust and self-esteem,[10] or of the political feelings of interest or acts of participation,[11] show any significant relationship with views toward the government because of altering housing locale or the new neighborhood.

The only sign of a connection between past background of the respondents and their feelings about the government and their new surroundings occurred on our items measuring political efficacy. The more a person believed in his or her political competence, the greater the likelihood that he or she favorably evaluated the government and the new environment as a consequence of the relocation policy, and vice versa.[12] One could interpret this relationship as an indication that early learned feelings of political efficacy mediated reactions to the political system and the new neighborhood, thus vitiating the independent impact of the government decision to relocate on sociopolitical judgments. Yet it could also be argued that feelings of political efficacy are affected after relocation, with positive or negative feelings of political competence reflecting whether one is satisfied or not with the relocation policy. Our research design, since it was not a longitudinal panel study, cannot adquately test which of these interpretations best fits the data.

DISCUSSION

In many ways, the results of our study parallel previous work. This is clearest in our corroboration of the proposition that people, especially those from the lower socioeconomic strata, frequently exhibit negative appraisals of their new environment after governmental action (e.g., urban renewal, highway construction, or tenement eradication) forces them to change housing. Fried,[13] in commenting upon Bostonians relocated from the West End, notes that the majority of the displaced experienced a strong sense of "grief," that is, " . . . feelings of painful loss, the continued longing, the general depressive tone, frequent symptoms of psychological or social or somatic distress . . . the sense of helplessness, the occasional direct and displaced anger, and tendencies to idealize the lost place." While our study doesn't probe these displaced reactions in as great a depth, it does point in the same direction. In short, many of our respondents appreciated having a structurally sound new apartment while at the same time they exhibited a sense of estrangement from their new surroundings and a strong attachment to their former *barrio*. As one of the relocated in El Paso said in appraising her new living quarters: "It's a heavenly prison."

We attribute neighborhood dissatisfaction to unfavorable attitudes about the government during implementation of the relocation policy. In this regard our interpretation for estrangement in the wake of housing displacement emphasizes factors involved in the political decision of relocation. Other interpretations[14] of the reasons behind displacement alienation focus more on the social and personal disruptions caused by movement. The relocated, so this argument goes, find it difficult to adjust to the new living situation because the continuity of their lives, the solidarity of their living space, and their social relationships are abruptly disrupted. While we don't quarrel with this interpretation, we do suggest that more governmental concern for this loss of community and sense of self could assuage negative feelings about housing change.

Our underscoring the role of governmental action is prompted by our findings that those most negative about their new housing setting were those most critical of the government concerning relocation. Perhaps the reason why more of the relocated are not as dubious about both the government and their new milieu is because of some aspects of the program. Probably most welcomed by the relocated was the provision of public housing for the displaced. Also, in a rather fortuitous manner, the local officials of El Paso tended to condemn entire geographic sections containing tenements and relocate the tenants in a group. As a consequence, when asked, "How many of your previous friends now live near you in the public housing unit?," more than 90 percent mention at least some are still close by. Such actions most likely facilitate the transition and lower negative evaluations of the government and the new surroundings.

Conversely, a number of actions that were not undertaken by political decision makers in implementing the El Paso relocation program deserve consideration. For instance, the relocated very much would have desired the new dwelling unit in public housing to have been in their old neighborhood. They were given no choice as to where they were to be moved since availability of public hous- was the key to condemnation and relocation. Nor were they given much time between official condemnation and the deadline for entry into their new quarters--on the average, ten days elapsed. Nor were they given any financial or transportation assistance by local officials in the move; getting their possessions into the public housing unit was up to the relocated. Finally, no attempt was made to orient the tenants to amenities and facilities in and around the public housing unit. It may be that governmental officials involved in the program were severely bound by resources (legal and general political support, as well as financial). Indeed, interviews with the key political authorities associated with initiation and implementation of the program evince much concern with providing more assistance to the relocated and preserving their previous sense of community, but a frustration is evident among the leaders since, given available resources or the lack thereof, nothing could be done.[15]

On balance, we are left with the impression that, sincerity and concern on the part of the political authorities notwithstanding, the relocation policy in El Paso resembles similar programs in other areas and at other times in its lack of governmental activity that

244

might make the adjustment less pleasant. As Hartman, in
summing up studies of alteration in housing owing to government action in the West End of Boston and in other
jurisdictions, notes: "In city after city, one sees that
the great amount of time and effort spent in investigating and condemning housing conditions in the slums that
local authorities wish to tear down is in no sense matched by corresponding public and professional interest in
the fate of the displaced families once they have been
dislodged."[16]

NOTES

1. R. Dawson, Public Opinion and Contemporary Dis-
array (New York: Harper and Row, 1973); L. Harris, The
Anguish of Change (new York: W. W. Norton, 1973); W. E.
Miller and T. E. Levitin, Leadership and Change: The New
Politics and the American Electorate (Cambridge, Mass.:
Winthrop, 1976); G. Pomper, Voters' Choice: Varieties of
American Electoral Behavior (New York: Harper and Row,
1975).
2. P. Abramson, "Political Efficacy and Political
Trust Among Black Schoolchildren: Two Explanations,"
Journal of Politics 34 (November 1972): 1243-1275; F. C.
Arterton, "The Impact of Watergate on Children's Attitudes Toward Political Authority," Political Science
Quarterly 89 (June 1974): 269-288; J. Dennis and C. Web-
ster, "Children's Images of the President and of the Government in 1962 and 1974," American Politics Quarterly 3
(October 1975): 423-436; R. Sigel and M. Brookes, "Becoming Critical About Politics," in R. G. Niemi and Associates, The Politics of Future Citizens: New Dimensions in
the Political Socialization of Children.
3. Along this line, a recent study measuring the
impact of changing school policy (from one that maintained segregation inthe classroom to one that fostered desegregation) upon numerous attributes of the children involved can perhaps serve as an "ideal" model of the type
of research design necessary to evaluate the influence of
public policy on the orientations of those directly affected. This study does not include any political attitudinal variables, however. H. B. Gerard and N. Miller,
School Desegregation: A Long-Term Study (New York: Plenum
Press, 1976). Also pertinent as a methodological model
is the work (to be discussed later) by M. Fried, "Grieving for a Lost Home: Psychological Costs of Relocation,"
in J. Q. Wilson, ed., Urban Renewal: The Record and the
Controversy (Cambridge, Mass.: MIT Press, 1966).
4. The source of all information pertaining to the
housing situation of tenants before they were relocated
comes from the Department of Planning and Research of
the City of El Paso, Texas.

5. The reader might protest that the word "government" is too vague and that it might have been better to
solicit views about particular levels or agencies of government. In the pilot study, the original questionnaire
did contain items designed to measure evaluations of
various components of the government, from the federal
down to the local level, who played a part in the relocation program. The respondents found the detailed questions meaningless and redundant. All of the 36 tenants
in the pretest simply grouped all political authorities
involved in this program under the rubric "government."
Thus, in the final version of the questionnaire administered to the study sample, no attempt was made to gauge
the multidimensions of the "government" that decided upon
the relocation policy.
6. The format for each of the items in question was
similar in that the respondent was to rate various aspects of his or her new neighborhood as "better," "the
same," or "worse" than the same aspect in the previous
neighborhood.
7. The question asked the respondents where they
would rather live given the alternatives of moving back
into the old tenement, residing in public housing but in
their former neighborhood, living in public housing in
some other part of the city, or staying right where they
were.
8. The preferred methodology to uncover causal relationship would have been a panel study commencing before the relocation program was effectuated and continuing into the aftermath of the program. Timing and lack
of resources precluded implementation of this type of
research design.
9. Demographically, the sample contained diversity.
Although, overall, the respondents are very low in socioeconomic status, some range is evident. The mean education level is 5.2 years of formal schooling completed,
with 11 percent of the population finishing high school
and a comparable number not progressing beyond the
twelfth grade. Sixty-one percent of the sample is unem-
ployed; mean family income is $3,700 per annum, with 6
percent of the sample earning under $1,000 and 4 percent
topping $7,000. Seven of ten of the respondents are
females, not an unusual finding among the entire population in the general South El Paso area. The average age
of the relocated is 44 years old, ranging from a youth
of 19 to 88 for the oldest person interviewed. While
the largest percentage (over two-thirds) trace their immediate family ancestry to Mexico, only one-third of the
sample was actually born in that country. By law, all
the relocated are either citizens of the United States or
are legal resident aliens. The mean number of years of
residence in the El Paso area is 19, with less than 10
percent of the sample being recent arrivals (less than 5

years in the area) and more than 17 percent having been in the vicinity longer than thirty years.

10. Interpersonal trust was measured by asking the respondents if they had "confidence in other people"-- three-fourths do not. Self-esteem was tapped through two devices: one asked about plans working out as the respondent desired (53 percent feel that this happens), and the other inquired about whether the respondent felt his or her life would unfold as desired (55 percent say it will).

11. Political interest is suggested if the respondents pay attention to government (20 percent do "always," 37 percent "at times," and 43 percent "almost never"), follow politics in the media (22 percent do so "often," 33 percent "on accasion," 32 percent "not very often," and 13 percent "never"), or discuss politics with their friends (12 percent do this "very often," 39 percent "at times," and 40 percent "almost never"). Political participation consisted of voting in a national and/ or local election, campaigning for a candidate, wearing a campaign button, attending political meetings, or demonstrating, boycotting, or marching as signs of protest or support. The highwater mark in political participation is 25 percent voting in the last national election (1972). On the average, the other indicators of political participation never attracted more than 10 percent of the relocated.

12. Political efficacy was gauged through three questions: "Do you believe that you can have confidence in the government?" "Would you say that the government is run for the benefit of a few interests or for the benefit of all the people?" and "Do you believe that elections make the government pay attention to what the people think?" Inter-item correlations range from a low of .40 to a high of .65 (gamma), suggesting a modicum of structure to the three dimensions of efficacy. Hence, the respondents' scores on each item were summed to form a political efficacy index. The political efficacy index is related to whether the respondent is positive, neutral, or negative about the government after relocation, gamma=.46. An index that summarized feelings about the new neighborhood was also constructed by adding evaluations of various aspects of the environment together. Again, the more politically efficacious the respondent is, the more he or she favorably rated the new surroundings (gamma=.40).

13. Fried, "Grieving," p. 359.

14. Ibid.

15. Eighteen people serving in elected or appointed governmental positions were identified as being involved in the initiation, and/or development, and/or implementation of the relocation policy. Each was personally interviewed in the fall of 1974.

16. C. Hartman, "The Housing of Relocated Families," in Wilson, <u>Urban Renewal</u>.

12
Political Activation and the Socialization of Support for a Third Party: Mexican-American Children and the Future of La Raza Unida Party

Herbert Hirsch

INTRODUCTION

In the litany of political science, the two party system occupies a position somewhere between motherhood and apple pie. Despite the mythology of sacredness, data on public support for and perception of the two major political parties indicates they actually occupy a spot somewhat closer to Joe Namath and menudo. Dennis notes " . . . that the public has mixed and not highly supportive feelings about the institution of party."[1] At the same time, such venerable sources as The American Voter have amply demonstrated that most adults in the United States identify with one of the two major parties, and most of these tend to belong to the same party as their parents.[2] According to Page and Wolfinger, "only one in ten identifies with the opposite party."[3] They also note, "Almost three-quarters of adult Americans consider themselves Republicans or Democrats and an additional eleven to nineteen percent say they lean toward one party or the other."[4] Moreover, the parties' literature seems to imply third parties represent some deviation from the American norm. V. O. Key notes that "a large scale upthrust of minor-party strength is symptomatic of an incapacity of one or the other of the major parties to cope with the issues of the moment in a manner to maintain party unity,"[5] and Sorauf's major work on parties devotes only fifteen pages to the rise and fall of minority parties.[6] Most of this literature refers to third-party movements at the national electoral level. When one turns to state and local third-party movements, the neglect becomes even more evident. Key notes that " . . . the handful of minor parties of much consequence in state politics have existed independently on their local foundations rather than as branches or offshoots of one of the minor parties on the national scene."[7] Furthermore, "when a state or local minor party has no hope of becoming a majority, its leaders are under temptation to fuse with one of the major parties in return for whatever concessions may be wrested from the major party."[8] The consensus appears to be that third parties, acting in self-interest, are more concerned with having their issue positions adopted by one of the two major parties than in venting the frustrations of their members and providing an avenue for channeling of discontents. There have been few examinations of third-party movements in the local and state context.[9] At the same time, political socialization scholars have noted the tendency for young children to identify with the parents' party, although there appears to be some increase in those who identify as independents.[10] Greenstein notes that party identification plays an important psychological role in the child's development, making it

> . . . possible for him to both relate himself to, and distinguish himself from others. Therefore, one element in the earliness of party identifications, and in their subsequent stability, may be that they help maintain a sense of personal identity, as well as a link between the child, his parents, and other significant individuals and groups.[11]

According to Greenstein, "by the fourth grade more than six out of ten New Haven children were able to state whether their party preference was Republican or Democrat . . ."[12] A recent study by Connell, conducted in Australia, notes that most analyses of children's support for a political party have not inquired into the rationality of such adherence.[13] When he provided the children with a chance to identify with a party directly related to their concerns, he found they acted rationally.[14] This paper examines a circumstance which may be similar to Connell's: socialization of support for a third party among Mexican-American children in the community within which that party was formed.

MEXICAN AMERICANS AND THE MAJOR PARTIES IN TEXAS

That Mexican Americans have not been served by the major political parties is not readily apparent from the strong support they have traditionally given the Democratic party. McClesky and Merrill point out that as late as 1969 some 88 percent of Texas Mexican Americans expressed an orientation toward the Democratic party. It is important to note, however, that only 30 percent expressed a "strong" orientation. Hence, a majority of Mexican Americans have not been enthusiastic supporters of the party. These data contrast rather strongly with that for blacks, who have been shown to express nearly the same degree of orientation toward the party (90 percent) but only 27 percent are "weak" identifiers. Black Texans feel a stronger tie to the Democratic party than

do Mexican Americans.[15] The case regarding support for
the Republican party is molded by the basic fact that
Texas Republicans have virtually ignored Mexican Americans. Apparently convinced there was no way to draw
Mexican-American support away from the Democrats, Republicans made no attempt to do so. Consequently, in 1969
only 5 percent of Mexican Americans in Texas professed
support for the Republican party.[16]

When one considers that many of the most influential
people within Texas party structures are large ranchers
and farmers, it is not surprising that little in the way
of positive legislation aimed at improvement of Mexican-
American life has been forthcoming,[17] and Mexican Americans have never had a viable alternative. If Democrats
have been negligent, Republicans have been unconcerned.
If the Democrat politician in Texas can safely be labeled
conservative, the typical Republican must tip the reac-
tionary end of the scale. The Mexican American has had
little influence on selection of candidates for the two
major parties. Logistics of the nominating process, combined with exclusionary methods only recently invali-
dated, e.g., the poll tax, have served to virtually exclude the Mexican American from participation. For many
years the poll tax was sufficient to exclude a person
from trying to feed and clothe a family on less than
$3,000 per year. Moreover, since a large proportion of
the Mexican Americans are migrants[18] who leave for the
north in February and March and do not return until November, they are effectively denied the right to vote in
May primaries and June runoffs. If the migrant returns
in time for the general election in November, party nom-
inees have already been chosen. Finally, a factor which
has long been present but difficult to document, is in-
timidation of Mexican-American voters and potential candidates. Recently, Mexican Americans have seen two or
three candidates in one Texas county lose their jobs as a
result of their political activity.[19]

The two major parties have, therefore, failed to in-
corporate Mexican Americans into their respective organizations, and the Mexican American has remained on the
fringes of the parties. They have, for example, had the
lowest turnout rates of all Texas voters, both Anglos and
blacks having higher turnout rates.[20]

Unable and unwilling to rely on the Democratic and
Republican parties to satsify their needs, Mexican Americans have, in the tradition of creating their own institutions,[21] created their own party. Rather than making
demands directly on the dominant parties, creation of La
Raza Unida Party has provided a middle force focused on
fulfillment of the needs of Mexican Americans. Whether
this effort succeeds or not is largely dependent upon the
ability of La Raza Unida to recruit and socialize young

people to support the party and continue to avoid the two major parties.

LA RAZA UNIDA AND CRYSTAL CITY

The most immediate precipitating cause for formation of La Raza Unida was a student walkout in Crystal City, Texas, in the fall of 1969. Mobilized by the issue of populatity elections and other school-related problems, students walked out of the schools in early December. For an entire month, students remained out of school and worked at registering voters for upcoming school board elections.[22] This mobilization, largely catalyzed by students, created a situation within which students and their parents, along with emerging leaders, began to discuss the idea of formation of an independent third party. The idea was discussed at length during the walkout, and preparation was made to begin steps toward legal implementation. Finally, on January 17, 1970, the party was organized in Zavala County. Stories of the party's formation and legal battles involved are important but need not concern us here. The main point is that approximately one year after formation of the party, a team of researchers administered questionnaires to all seventh- through twelfth-grade students in Crystal City (N=726). These questionnaires form the data base for this paper, and provide an opportunity to take a rare look at the socialization process of support for an alternative party midst a climate of political change.

Political Activation: The Keniston Model

Most studies of socialization of party preference among children find strong relationships between the party of the parents and that of the children. Since, however, the situation in Crystal City is characterized by high politicization, it seemed logical to begin by first attempting to account for political activation and then try to examine how activation relates to support for La Raza Unida.
Rather than examining the numerous debates over different theories accounting for development of political activation among college students in the 1960s, this paper examines one model of activation to see if it accounts for development of political activation and support for La Raza Unida among this sample of Mexican-American youth. According to the Keniston model, radicalization or activation

. . . involves psychological continuity--indeed, a return to one's roots--at one level, and psychological change at another; it entails major confrontation with the unwelcome inequities in American society; and it leads to an activation and engagement whereby the individual comes to feel himself personally responsible for effecting radical changes and feels a part of a movement of others similarly committed.[23]

This process involves four steps. First comes confrontation. Prior to entry into the political movement, "most had been inarticulately dissatisfied with the options open to them, but they had lacked the vocabulary and, indeed, the perceptions necessary to formulate their dissatisfactions."[24] Contact with the political movement acts as a "structuring principle" providing the means necessary to perceive confrontation. This same situation prevailed in Crystal City. Following the school walkout, children and parents discussed the prevailing political situation which led to formation of La Raza Unida. It is likely that, prior to the walkout, the students and parents were "inarticulately dissatisfied with the options open to them" since options were severely limited by the dominant Anglo minority. The school walkout and eventual triumph undoubtedly gave expression to those dissatisfactions; thus, Keniston's second point should also follow.

Keniston's second step is disillusion with the "system" as a result of confrontation. As an example, he points to poverty programs of the late 1960s.[25] Crystal City respondents and their parents realized the simple act of walking out of school could meet with only limited success in achieving longer range goals. Thus, Keniston's third step, reinterpretation.

Keniston notes that when "concretely confronted with inequity and disillusioned with the system, the emerging radical tends to move toward a reinterpretation of the social and political world."[26] He goes on to note that a

corollary of the radical reinterpretation . . . is a progressive sense of estrangement from the mainstream. Although the radical's fidelity to most of the creedal values of American society remained firm, their sense of connection to the institutions and practices of our society became attenuated. As the young radical begins to reinterpret American society, he also redefines his own relationship to it.[27]

This sample of Mexican-American children does indeed adhere to the basic principle of American democracy, but is disillusioned with the specific operation as it applies to its group, and has reinterpreted in such a way as to see the need for collective political action to achieve its ends.[28] This process should lead to what Keniston calls activation and engagement.

According to Keniston's formulation these steps are

necessary but not sufficient to cause active radical-
ism.[29] Necessary for final activation is a sense of personal responsibility which emanates from early family experiences, especially a "family emphasis on 'stick-to-
itiveness,' and to the early acquisition of these qualities in childhood."[30] Not only is family involved as an
important agent of early socialization--a point congruent
with findings regarding socialization of party identifi-
cation--but models must be available for the incipient
radical.[31] The model should fit the present situation if
we include, as the ultimate measure of radicalization,
the child's own intention to support La Raza Unida.

It is important to note three caveats. First, Keniston's model was developed as a result of his experiences with and interviews of upper or upper-middle class
students involved in Vietnam Summer 1967, and data used
in the present study were gathered in a Mexican-American
community from a population of seventh through twelfth
grade high school students. Second, Keniston notes that
"to analyze the process of becoming a radical into aspects, stages, preconditions and end products is, of
course, to impose a conceptual framework upon an experience that is itself largely unanalyzed, whole, and in
many ways highly idiosyncratic."[32] It is possible,
therefore, that the Keniston model might not perfectly
fit the situation examined here. His formulations do,
however, provide a point of departure from which one
might proceed to construct a theory of activation and
support for a third party.

Dimensions of Activation

The Keniston model posits four steps in development
of activation: confrontation, disillusionment, reinterpretation, and activation and engagement. The major
problem with the model is that key elements are specified
in a most cursory manner which makes it very difficult
for researchers to operationalize the four elements. In
order to develop a more "rigorous" model, a series of
questions, which seemed as though they might tap some of
the Keniston dimensions, were factor analyzed. Four factors emerged which account for 53 percent of the variance
and did indeed seem to correspond to Keniston's stages.

The confrontation factor contained three questions
which measure the Mexican-American child's perception of
means through which to confront the "system." High factor loadings indicate there is general agreement among
respondents of a need to change government through means
involving public marches and demonstration. Frequency
distributions indicate 70 percent of respondents agree
the "best way to handle problems is to band together with
people like yourself to help each other out." Fifty-four
percent agree there is a need to change government, and

43 percent agree the best way to get officials to take action is to organize a public demonstration or march.

The disillusion factor involves four questions measuring presidential affect.[33] This factor is called disillusionment because Mexican-American respondents in this sample are much lower in affect for the President of the United States than other respondents. Eaton and Dennis hypothesize that presidential affect acts as a structuring factor influencing the child's later views of government and politics,[34] that the first thing that children learn about politics and government is affect toward key authority figures. These attitudes, in turn, influence development of later attitudes toward other dimensions of politics. We feel safe in calling this factor disillusionment because respondents generally display very low affect for the president.[35]

Reinterpretation consists of four questions. First, respondents were asked if it made any sense to form a third party to try to get new laws passed. The question was framed in the negative, and students were either neutral (26 percent) or disagreed (34 percent). A second question was asked regarding whether respondents believed they or their families could become political leaders. Again, a large percentage disagreed (43 percent). The last two questions involve whether respondents hear parents talk about government or politics (64 percent "yes"), and a series of questions forming a political knowledge index which asked respondents to identify local and state political figures (44 percent scored "high"). These seemed to indicate the students were likely to engage in reinterpretive activities.

Activation is represented by two questions. First, whether respondents perceive parents as active in local elections (68 percent "yes"), and respondents' own interest in politics (61 percent indicate interest).

Activation and Support for La Raza Unida Party

We have now seen that Keniston's model is correct in identifying four separate dimensions involved in the activation process. It remains to be determined whether the causal sequence runs in the direction hypothesized by Keniston. If his formulation is correct, development of activation should proceed as below:

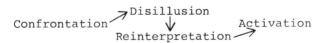

To examine the sequence, a path model was created and it appears that while Keniston is correct in specifying dimensionality, his estimate of the sequence involved does not accord with the present data. All path coefficients meet the basic criteria for inclusion in the model. All are at least twice as large as their standard errors and none of the paths can be dropped because the model does not reproduce the correlations.[37] Moreover, partial correlations are all relatively high and statistically significant. We have, therefore, an interactive model. However, if we were to simply take the highest path coefficients as sufficient to indicate occurrence of a path, Keniston's model would have to be altered in the following manner, where a confrontation with the "system" causes the individual to engage in reinterpretation which leads to disillusion and then to activation:

<pre>
                      Disillusion
     Confrontation   ↑   Activation
              Reinterpretation
</pre>

Moreover, if we are interested in accounting for total variance in activation, we may note that reinterpretation accounts for only .01 change in total variance, and confrontation accounts for only .05. Disillusion and confrontation together, however, accounted for .13 of the variance. Yet the path coefficient between confrontation and reinterpretation is .33, accounting for 10 percent of the variance. Hence, we cannot conclude that Keniston's model is invalid; on the contrary, the empirical data indicate the model is much more complex than Keniston originally supposed. Political activation would seem to be a product of confrontation, reinterpretation, and disillusionment, and the developmental path may follow either direction, although the higher coefficients would lead one to hypothesize the sequence running from confrontation to reinterpretation to disillusion is the most likely. On the other hand, it is possible that reinterpretation might be skipped completely and, though less likely as confrontation accounts for only 5 percent of variance in activation, the sequence could conceivably move directly from confrontation to activation. Finally, it is important to note that sex and ethnic self-identity (i.e., identification as Mexican American, Chicano, Latin American, or Spanish) were controlled and yielded insignificant coefficients of -.02 and .01 respectively. Parent's education was also controlled, but distribution was skewed so strongly to the lower categories as to yield no significant differences.

The ultimate concern of this paper is to ascertain factors involved in building support for La Raza Unida, and it was hypothesized that if the Keniston model were validated, it might be applicable to development of support for La Raza Unida Part. The activation dimension, as explicated in operationalization of the model, includes two variables, i.e., whether parents participate

in local elections and the student's interest in politics. While these created a separate dimension, it is
possible that this factor might more likely be labeled
"vicarious participation," because interest in politics
and perceptions that parents participate in local elections are not expressions of the child's predisposition
to engage in a political act. The question measuring the
child's party identification, however, asks: "If you
could vote, for which political party would you vote?"
This question measures an overt predisposition to engage
in a specific form of political behavior. In adapting
this to the Keniston model, what is evident is a strong
path between activation and intended party identification. Again, however, all paths, even the .07 from confrontation to party identification, meet minimum criteria for inclusion. The path criteria do not enable us,
therefore, to isolate one sequential model.

If, however, we perform a stepwise multiple regression using intent to vote as the dependent variable, and
add party identification of father and mother as perceived by the child, results indicate once again that the
primary determinant of the child's tendency to support
one party is party of the parents. If we examine raw
percentages, we find that 86 percent identify with the
party of their father and 89 percent with that of the
mother when that party is La Raza Unida.[38]

If we take out the first three elements of the Keniston model because of the small percentage of variance
accounted for in the child's party, we find that activation, father's party, and mother's party account for 43
percent of variance. This is further reinforced by partial correlations between the six variables. Partials
indicate that confrontation, disillusion, and reinterpretation do not intervene between activation and
child's party. However, controlling father's and mother's party causes the partial between activation and the
child's party to fall to a much lower, although still
significant, level. If we wish, therefore, to account
for variance in the child's party identification, we may
drop the first three portions of the model and are left
with variables which account for 43 percent of variance.
Moreover, we again controlled sex and ethnic identification and found little or no impact--Beta coefficients
were .09 and .003 respectively.

It is interesting to note the highest partial and
highest regression coefficient is between mother's party
and child's party. The main determinant of the child's
party and, therefore, disposition to support La Raza
Unida, is party of the mother. This finding parallels
closely more recent findings which also demonstrate
children of both sexes are likely to look to the mother
for political cues.[39] These findings are summarized by
Riccards to demonstrate that "there appears to be little

evidence to support the notion that children receive more of their political cues and issue orientations from their father."[40] This is interpreted as being "due to the greater emotional attachment and closer relationships mothers have with their children."[41] In the present case there are additional reasons. Women in Crystal City have been in the forefront of the political and social process during and after the school walkout. During the walkout, moreover, mothers of the students became engaged and activated earlier than fathers. It is obvious that " . . . it seems that the mother is a much more valuable asset for either party than is the father."[42] Present findings substantiate this conclusion. This assumes even greater importance because the future of La Raza Unida depends to a large extent upon the party's ability to recruit new members. The powerful role of the mother seems to indicate that Raza Unida will continue to meet with success in this area because it is building upon strong family ties which already exist in the Mexican-American culture.

CONCLUSION

        Prior to examining the implications for La Raza Unida's future, it seems appropriate to review the main findings. First, Keniston's model of political activation was operationalized and found to contain four separate empirically defined dimensions. Second, elements of that model were used to ascertain causal sequence. This demonstrated that Keniston had oversimplified his model for, in actuality, activation was accounted for by complex interaction of confrontation, disillusionment, and reinterpretation. Third, we attempted to ascertain whether the activation model acted as a set of intervening variables leading to the child's party identification. It was found that the model was largely unnecessary and that activation, and parent's party, accounted for 43 percent of variance in the child's party identification. This indicated the social-psychological variables in the model were less influential upon the child's party choice than direct effects of modeling and activation. Therefore, we have again substantiated that party identification is learned within the primary environment of the family.

        Implications regarding the future of La Raza Unida in Texas and the Southwest undoubtedly depends on more than success of recruiting new members--although this is certainly an important element. Data presented here would seem to indicate the party has a bright future in the sense of continual recruitment of additional Mexican Americans to rally to its cause. Strength of the family in Mexican-American communities and importance of parents

as agents of socialization of support for political parties indicates the ranks of the party should continue to
swell. Whether Raza Unida meets with political success
across the broader context of Texas and the Southwest depends upon additional factors. Raza Unida ran statewide
candidates for the first time in 1972 gubernatorial elections in Texas and garnered 6 percent of the total vote.
Whether it gains more votes depends upon some of the
following.

First, moblization of resources. Money and manpower
have been hard to come by. Financial contributions have
been mainly small and come from individuals. The Mexican
American population has a median income of less than
$3,000 and cannot afford to donate money to a political
party. Moreover, party activists have been primarily
volunteers.[43]

Second, demographic characteristics of the Mexican-
American population demonstrate it is becoming largely
urban and located in the northern part of the state.[44]
Areas of the state losing population are southern counties. Tactics and cost of mobilization may make it difficult to catalyze large scale organization in urban and
northern areas.

Third, if a large bloc of liberal Democrats suddenly gained power and formed a coalition in Texas, this
might drain Anglo support from Raza Unida. This is tied
to the important possibility of forming a coalition with
blacks and liberal Anglos which could give La Raza Unida
the balance of power. This coalition, of course, is a
long way off.

Fourth, incumbent Mexican-American politicians have
been reluctant to embrace La Raza Unida. If this continues, it could have disastrous effects upon the party's
future. In the long run, however, this paper demonstrates what can occur within a political community which
has become activated. If nothing else, it is safe to assume that the future of La Raza Unida in this particular
area is probably secure. Having once tasted the fruits
of victory and unity, it is unlikely they will be willing
to give them up.

ADDENDUM

Not long after I wrote these optimistic words, my
predictions were proven to be completely wrong. Chicanos
of Crystal City have, in fact, given up both their unity
and victory. How and why it happened provides a fascinating case study of the "rise and fall" of a third party
to observers of U.S. and Southwestern politics. The complete story remains to be told elsewhere; for now, it is
important to briefly update events as they relate to the
present paper.

Raza Unida in Crystal City foundered for two

reasons: first, external interference by the state and, second, internal disagreements exacerbated by interference of those outside forces. A rival faction formed and split off from Raza Unida. Called the "Barrio Club," this faction accused Raza Unida leaders of authoritarian leadership and lack of concern for the people. At the root of these criticisms was a dispute between leaders of the two factions over distribution of the spoils. Members of the Barrio Club were concerned lest their lucrative "drug trade" be disturbed either by Raza Unida or state officials. Rumors have it that the state encouraged the Barrio Club to oppose Raza Unida in city elections. In exchange for active opposition, the drug trade would be allowed to continue.

Forces of the state of Texas also took less covert action in its attempt to destroy what it perceived as a "radical" third party. The governor issued repeated denunciations of Raza Unida and succeeded in getting the federal government to delay program money initially marked for Crystal City. Both federal and state intelligence agencies also attempted to disrupt Raza Unida activities and gather information which might eventually lead to indictment of party leaders. Failing this, the state was left with the recourse of clandestine support of forces opposing Raza Unida and with outlandish statements condemning Raza Unida, which were issued on several occasions by the governor.

While all this external interference was in motion, leaders of the party were not without fault for their eventual defeat at the polls. The very fact that people in Crystal City turned against them is at least indicative of the fact that Raza Unida began to be perceived as simply another elitist group out to line their own pockets. Leaders lived in fine homes and drive big cars while the situation for the majority of the people, although better than under the previous Anglo domination, had not improved enough to persuade people to continue to support the party.

What finally resulted was that Raza Unida lost control of the school board and city council, although they still control county government. Many reforms instituted by the party were immediately undone, e.g., Chicano studies programs were eliminated from the schools. This was to have profound effects upon the process of political socialization within Crystal City. Leaders of Raza Unida contributed to their own defeat; their greed gave the opposition the chance they needed to attempt to secure for themselves some of the spoils of office. The opposition was supported by the state and emerged victorious. What is most disheartening about this situation is that once again it is the vast majority of the people who are left to suffer. They lived in miserable poverty before Raza Unida came upon the scene and live in virtually the same conditions now. As with political parties in general, it is not the leadership that suffers. Since political parties are basically elitist institutions dominated by business classes, they do not hesitate to forget about the people as soon as party leaders have a chance to "make it" for themselves. Sadly, Raza Unida proved no exception.

Interestingly, I would maintain this does not invalidate my previous examination of political activation and socialization of support. If party identification is learned within the primary environment of family, then it depends upon what long-term identification is being inculcated by the family. Since the situation in Crystal City has become so chaotic it is likely that Chicanos will take one of two directions. They will either turn back to one of the two major parties or they will eschew party politics entirely. If the period described in this paper had any impact upon the children examined, my guess is that they will adopt the latter rather than the former. After years of domination by the Anglo-run Democratic party, Chicanos of Crystal City are not likely to look to them to correct the very abuses originally created and supported by the Democrats. Now Chicanos carry the added burden of observing their own party leaders acting much like "Gringos" of the Democratic party. They are left with only frustration.

Finally, the success of Raza Unida depended on much more than recruitment of new members. In all four areas discussed above, the party failed. Thus, it was unable to generate money and manpower. In a recent abortive attempt to raise money to run for Congress, one former leader could generate little money or support. Second, Chicanos continue to flock to urban areas of Texas and Raza Unida has experienced no successes in politically organizing in the cities. Third, election in 1976 of a "liberal" Democrat, Jimmy Carter, seems to have drained Anglo support away from Raza Unida. There is little or no Anglo support for the party and no coalition has been formed with the blacks. Raza Unida has been, consequently, isolated, and likelihood of such coalition-forming is now close to zero. Fourth, incumbent Mexican-American politicians have rejected the party and it has had the predicted negative impact upon it.

What remains of all this hopeful and important activity is a small group of determined and committed people. This is necessary but not always sufficient to generate the necessary energy and insight to build a successful third-party movement. To all extents and purposes, there is no more Raza Unida party and there will not be another until internal dissension and greed are confronted and exorcised.

NOTES

1. Jack Dennis, "Support for the Party System by the Mass Public," American Political Science Review 60 (September 1966): 613.

2. Angus Campbell et al., The American Voter (New York: John Wiley and Sons, 1960), pp. 146-149; Benjamin I. Page and Raymond Wolfinger, "Party Identification," in Raymond Wolfinger, ed., Readings in American Political Behavior (Englewood Cliffs, N.J.: Prentice-Hall, 1970), pp. 289-99; Herbert McCloskey and Harold Dahlgren, "Primary Group Influence on Party Loyalty," American Political Science Review 53 (September 1959): 762-70.

3. Page and Wolfinger, "Party Identification," p. 296.

4. Ibid., p. 290.

5. V. O. Key, Jr., Politics, Parties and Pressure Groups (Thomas Y. Crowell, 1958), p. 309.

6. Frank J. Sorauf, Party Politics in America (Boston: Little, Brown and Co., 1972), pp. 43-58.

7. Key, Politics, p. 302.

8. Ibid.

9. Two interesting examinations of third parties are: James Weinstein, The Decline of Socialism in America, 1912-1925 (New York: Vintage Books, 1969); and Norman Pollack, The Populist Response to Industrial America (New York: W. W. Norton, 1962).

10. M. Kent Jennings and Richard G. Niemi, "The Transmission of Political Values from Parent to Child," American Political Science Review 62 (March 1968): 173.

11. Fred I. Greenstein, Children and Politics (New Haven: Yale University Press, 1965), p. 74.

12. Ibid., p. 71.

13. R. W. Connell, The Child's Construction of Politics (Melbourne: Melbourne University Press, 1971), p. 81.

14. Ibid., p. 81.

15. Clifton McCleskey and Bruce Merrill, "Mexican-American Political Behavior in Texas," Social Science Quarterly 53 (March 1973): 785-98.

16. Ibid., pp. 785-98.

17. Clifton McCleskey, The Government and Politics of Texas (Boston: Little, Brown and Co., 1969), especially Chapter 4, pp. 68-118.

18. Estimates of the number of migrants range from 15 to 40 percent of Mexican Americans engaged in seasonal labor. Scholes has written, "The Texas Mexicans leave the rural areas in Texas in overwhelming numbers to move north with the cultivating and harvesting seasons. Towns such as Asherton in Texas may have a population of 2,000 people in January and a population of 10 or 20 people in July, when everyone has moved north for the harvests." Rev. William E. Scholes, "The Migrant Worker," in Julian

Samora, ed., La Raza: Forgotten Americans (Notre Dame:
University of Notre Dame Press, 1966), pp. 67-68. See
also, Hearings Before the Senate Subcommittee on Migra-
tory Labor (Washington, D.C.: U.S. Government Printing
Office, June 19, 1963).
    19. Armando G. Gutierrez, "Institutional Complete-
ness and La Raza Unida Party," in Rudolph de la Garza,
Z. Anthony Kruszewski, and Tomas A. Arciniega, eds.,
Chicanos and Native Americans: The Territorial Minorities
(Englewood Cliffs, N.J.: Prentice-Hall, 1973). Gutierrez
notes, "It is hardly a coincidence that the King Ranch in
South Texas had never witnessed a split in its workers'
vote until 1968, when the first poll watcher was allowed
on the ranch."
    20. McCleskey and Merrill, "Mexican American Politi-
cal Behavior," pp. 785-98.
    21. Gutierrez, "Institutional Completeness," p. 7;
and Miguel Tirado, "Mexican-American Community Political
Organization," Aztlan (Spring 1970): 53-78.
    22. On Crystal City, see: Michael V. Miller and
James D. Preston, "Vertical Ties and the Redistribution
of Power in Crystal City," Social Science Quarterly 53
(March 1973): 772-84; Armando Gutierrez and Herbert
Hirsch, "The Militant Challenge to the American Ethos:
'Chicanos' and 'Mexican Americans,'" Social Science
Quarterly 53 (March 1973): 830-45; and John Shockley,
"Crystal City: Los Cinco Mexicanos," and "Crystal City:
La Raza Unida and the Second Revolt," in Renato Rosaldo
et al., eds., Chicano: The Evolution of a People (Minne-
apolis: Winston Press, 1973), pp. 314-26.
    23. Kenneth Keniston, Young Radicals: Notes on Com-
mitted Youth (New York: Harcourt, Brace, Jovanovich,
Inc., 1968), pp. 110-11.
    24. Ibid., pp. 125-26.
    25. Ibid., pp. 127-28.
    26. Ibid., pp. 129-30.
    27. Ibid., p. 130.
    28. Gutierrez and Hirsch, "Militant Challenge,
pp. 830-845.
    29. Keniston, Young Radicals, p. 133.
    30. Ibid., p. 134.
    31. Ibid., p. 135.
    32. Ibid., p. 145.
    33. These items have been used in a number of stud-
ies, first developed by Easton and Dennis, and used most
thoroughly in David Easton and Jack Dennis, Children in
the Political System (New York: McGraw Hill, 1969). For
a dissenting view, see Dean Jaros, Herbert Hirsch, and
Frederick J. Fleron, Jr., "The Malevolent Leader: Political Socialization in an American Sub-Culture," American
Political Science Review 62 (June 1968): 564-75. The
presidential affect measures have been subject to a great
deal of criticism. See, for example, Reid R. Reading,

"Is Easton's Systems-Persistence Framework Useful? A Research Note," Journal of Politics 24 (February 1972): 258-67.
34. See Greenstein, Children and Politics, pp. 45-46; David Easton and Robert D. Hess, "The Child's Political World," Midwest Journal of Political Science 6 (August 1962): 229-235.
35. Frequency distribution on the four variables are: "How hard do you think the President works as compared with most men?"

Harder	53%
As hard	21%
Less hard	26%

"How do you view the President's liking for people as compared with most men?"

Likes almost everybody	31%
Likes as many as most	38%
Doesn't like as many	31%

"How do you view the President's knowledge as compared with most men?"

Knows more	46%
Knows about the same	39%
Knows less	15%

"How do you view the President as a person?"

Best in the world	8%
Good person	65%
Not a good person	27%

36. For explication of a similar process: Norman Nie, Dale H. Bent, and C. Hadlai Hull, SPSS: Statistical Package for the Social Sciences (New York: McGraw-Hill, 1970), pp. 226-27.

37. Kenneth Land, "Principles of Path Analysis," in Edgar F. Borgatta, ed., Sociological Methodology (San Francisco: Jossey-Bass, Inc., 1969); Otis D. Duncan, "Path Analysis: Sociological Examples," American Journal of Sociology 72 (July 1966): 1-16.
38. Distributions are as follows:

Party	Father-Child Agreement	Mother-Child Agreement
Republican	83%	68%
Democrat	63%	63%
Raza Unida	86%	89%

When percentages are viewed to demonstrate agreement of parents with child's party, they become lower.

Party	Father-Child Agreement	Mother-Child Agreement
Republican	54%	66%
Democrat	66%	66%
Raza Unida	72%	69%

39. M. Kent Jennings and Kenneth Langton, "Mothers versus Fathers: The Formation of Political Orientations Among Young Americans," Journal of Politics 31 (May 1969): 339-340.
40. Michael P. Riccards, The Making of the American Citizenry: An Introduction to Political Socialization (New York: Chandler Publishing Company, 1973), p. 45.
41. Ibid., p. 44.
42. Ibid.
43. Gutierrez, "Institutional Completeness," passim. This last section draws heavily upon Professor Gutierrez's stimulating paper.
44. Harley S. Browning and S. Dal McLemore, A Statistical Profile of the Spanish-Surname Population of Texas (Austin: Bureau of Business Research, University of Texas, 1964), p. 13.

Afterword
Territorial Minorities:
Some Sociopolitical and International
Aspects and Their Possible Implications

Z. Anthony Kruszewski

In the multicultural panorama of the contemporary American nation, Southwestern society basically is composed of three major segments: Anglos, Chicanos, and Native Americans. This does not strike a casual observer (or even a researcher studying ethnicity in general) as very complex or different from any other part of this country inhabited by the descendants or recent immigrants stemming from upward of hundreds of different roots.

Although the multinational roots of the American nation have been generally acknowledged, its vast and varied dimensions have not been, until recently, properly documented, especially in any exhaustive work. This was remedied by a pioneering first--the publication of the Harvard Encyclopedia of American Ethnic Groups. The fact that the publisher is one of the most prestigious American universities assigned a special importance to that work which, although not definitive, is bringing together (in one volume) the story of at least 106 ethnic groups which participate in the continuing saga of the American nation.

But what even this sorely needed encyclopedia did not bring out adequately and clearly for the readers to understand, relates to the typology of ethnicity in the contemporary United States, which has a direct bearing on the Southwestern society. It is a fact that both Chicanos and Native Americans share characteristics which are not shared by any other American ethnic group--that of territoriality. These two groups, which are an important component of Southwestern society, are the only American territorial minorities. Both these ethnic minorities and their territories were incorporated into the American nation through expansion of U.S. borders and through conquest. This involved all the American Indian lands being incorporated into the new nation as well as half the original territory of Mexico (including most of the West as well as the Southwest) under the terms of the Treaty of Guadalupe-Hidalgo of 1848 and the Gadsden Purchase (or the Treaty of Mesilla) of 1853.

These treaties guaranteed the Mexican Americans cultural autonomy, land rights, and other privileges they possessed before the cession of the Southwest and West by Mexico and its acquisition by the United States. The provisions of these treaties and many Indian treaties have resulted in the creation of both legal and psychological situations setting these two American ethnic groups apart from other ethnic minorities catalogued in the Harvard Encyclopedia of American Ethnic Groups. These facts are still, amazingly enough, not well-known or realized even by persons familiar with the American ethnic scene of the 1970s. And their importance is crucial to the understanding of what it entails for Chicanos and Native Americans vis-a-vis other ethnic groups and the American nation at large.

As territorial minorities, both Chicanos and Native Americans acquired and perpetuated their attachment to the land which was theirs before the arrival of the Anglo colonists in the Southwest and West in the 1840s and later. The original Mexican population was sparse (approximately 75,000 people in the vast areas acquired following the United States-Mexico War of 1848) and the Indian population was both sedentary and that of hunters. In both cases, however, land rights were claimed either under the original patents of the Spanish kings or the tribal Native American law. (There are still some 170 tribal Indian groupings in the United States today.)

Out of the conflict with the Anglo immigrants over the acquisition of land, which clashed with the traditional land claims, the problems were created which were not ameliorated in the nineteenth century with the creation of the reservations for the Indians nor through the reissue of land grants by the new American authorities after the 1840s. Some of these problems still are with us. The Tijerina land grant movement in New Mexico or law suits being entered in many courts on behalf of Native Americans all over the country are examples of such problems.

Thus territoriality and linguistic separateness of both these Southwestern ethnic groups have been established since the beginning of the "Manifest Destiny" and the American annexation of these territories. The fact that these ethnic groups had such binding ties to the land and separate identities has been a reality ever since. The subsequent vast wave of Mexican migration across the Mexican-American border, especially after the turmoil of the Mexican Revolution of 1911 and since, was greatly helped by the prior existence of the Mexicans "on this side" of the border (as it's called in the Spanish Borderlands), mostly having Spanish or Mexican names, and their familiarity with the area in a long stretch of history dating back to the early 1700s in the whole upper Rio Grande Valley (Santa Fe was established before the arrival of the Pilgrims at Plymouth Rock!).

The prior hold on the land, linguistic separation, and the subsequent discrimination of Anglos against the Mexican Americans in their own land (as they perceived it) laid the foundation of the territorial minority character of the contemporary Chicanos. They mostly lived separately, and although they occasionally mixed with the Anglos, they were not really encouraged at all to participate in the concept of the "melting pot," as propounded at the turn of the century and since. Large and persistent waves of subsequent migrants did not come into a foreign land peopled by different strangers over the distance of thousands of miles (and, psychologically important, over the ocean, which obviously necessitated ever looser contact with the "old country"), but over much lesser distances into a historically familiar land which in the collective psyche of the people was theirs until fairly recently (as the history of nations go!), peopled to a large extent with their compatriots. But even more important was the possibility, and indeed the reality, of going back and forth between the Southwest and Mexico. Intermarriage, extended family linkings, and now new waves of the undocumented cousins (however much resented now for job competition) have created a situation quite different from that of many American ethnic groups which, although replenished by subsequent migratory waves, as a rule have been linguistically Americanized at least by the second generation.

The advent of radio and television and bilingualism in schools (which especially in the 1920s and 1930s was strongly objected to and actually suppressed in the ethnically predominant schools of the Midwest and Northeast to the point of actual eradication of the knowledge of the immigrant languages) have only recently reinforced the territorial minority characteristics of the Chicanos since it provides them with direct, frequent, and permanent contact with the Spanish language and its cultural heritage. Whereas among other ethnic Americans, such contact, although quite evident in American cities, is usually limited to recent immigrants. With the Chicanos it resulted, because of the above described reasons, in the fact that Spanish is the *lingua franca* of a large segment of the population along the border (25-30 percent), if not a majority (as in the Texas cities of San Antonio, El Paso, etc.). Only in Southern California was the "melting pot" syndrome, so well-known to other "white ethnics" (e.g., giving up their native language, even at home), successfully implemented. In a curious twist, some of these Mexican Americans are re-learning Spanish on the wave of *chicanismo*.

Thus by missing an important "melting pot" chapter in U.S. history, the Mexican Americans, constantly reinforced by the influx of new immigrants from across the

southern border, have established themselves as territorial minorities (next to the Native Americans, who were
always treated as such by the larger society). The consequences of this fact are not yet fully researched, at
best not even fully appreciated, if not totally realized
or misunderstood. It is especially true of the Anglos in
the Southwest and even more true of other "Sunbelt" immigrants streaming into the Southwest in the 1970s, with no
end in sight. A better understanding, analysis, and appreciation of this fact would avoid future tensions and
problems for both sides. It should be added here for the
non-Southwestern reader that in the peculiarity of social
relations on the folkloric level, our society is divided
neatly into Anglos and Chicanos (or Mexican Americans).
Thus both the blacks and the Polish-born author of this
essay find themselves, to their astonishment, to be
"Anglos." It is also the greatest shock for the white
ethnics who "melted in" to discover the Mexican-American
bilingual/bicultural community and their territorial
characteristics. These Americans especially do not understand or condone linguistic minority status since they
gave up their own immigrant languages and clutural identity.

The creation of the Southwestern territorial minorities has not yet really been noticed by the society at
large, even in scholarly journals. This is largely due
to the fact that the terms and experiences are largely
foreign to the American history of nation building, which
has stressed amalgamation rather than perpetuation of
fragmentation of the society since its colonial beginning. Israel Zangwill's "melting pot" concept was only
its more recent manifestation. The perpetuation of the
territorial minorities in the Southwest, even if negatively perceived by the larger society, has become a fact
we have to cope with. Although the Anglo society does
not notice it, largely because of historical reasons, the
concept is very familiar to vast areas of Latin America,
Asia, Europe and Oceania, hence spanning all the "worlds"
from the First to the Third. The revival of ethnicity,
the linguistic divisions, and other regional "homeland"
groupings is now an acknowledged phenomenon not only in
the new and developing nations, but suddenly in Old
Europe as well (Belgium, Brittany, Wales, Scotland,
etc.)

That perpetuation of fragmentation is often ascribed
to twentieth century alienation and technological pressure sweeping familiar structures and old quaint customs. The nostalgia for past traditions and heritage
brought forth in many countries an ethnic revival not
even suspected a few years ago. Although our Southwestern experience with the territorial minorities might be
considered peripheral by the society at large, especially
in such a vast nation of continental dimensions, it would

be beneficial to analyze some of the characteristics, trends, and possible implications for the nation. This is especially true not only since the new influx of the undocumented aliens, but especially because the demographic trends will undoubtedly increase the visibility of the Southwestern society within the national context in the 1990s and beyond. These observations, now not quite noticed, will become self-evident because of the growing shift of the population toward the Southwest and West and their economic opportunities. Within the context of growth of the region, the importance also of the Chicano territorial minority in the Southwest will be undoubtedly noticed.

Thus whereas a relatively new type of multicultural social relationship does exist in the Southwest now and will increase in the future, other segments of the Chicano population, now migrating for the first time in a large-scale movement to the Midwest or Northeast, might be affected by different pressures and different societal patterns of the older established "melting pot" traditions. It remains to be seen how different the Chicano society of the Southwest will be, if at all, from, say, the Midwest (e.g., Chicago now has close to 500,000 Chicanos), and whether the multicultural pattern (obviously shorn of territorial minority characteristics) is going to be preserved there. It soon will call for the serious attention of ethnic scholars and research of these issues.

The polyarchic and pluralistic characteristics of the contemporary American society clearly favors the maintenance of the multicultural mold of *chicanismo* in contradistinction to the anti-immigrant and anti-East/ Southern European immigrants and, in particular, the attitude prevailing in the 1910s, 1920s, and 1930s (not to say anything about the blacks or Asians). It will be interesting to observe if this nation in the future will be more tolerant to non-English-speaking Americans and accept the multilingual posture toward its citizens. There are some trends suggesting quite a polarization on the issue of bilingualism in the American schools which, not only across the country but amazingly enough, is totally misunderstood in the bicultural Southwest where acceptance and need for the knowledge of Spanish among the Anglos is minimal, if not practically nonexistent, in the larger segment of the population. The truly bilingual members of the society continue to be only the Mexican Americans.

The reinforcement of the societal strength of the Southwestern Mexican-American community, through the more recent influx of immigrants and the highly favorable demographic trends still being maintained, was not limited only to its numbers or its tenacity to maintain its language. The receding of the long-standing

discrimination directed at that group, the recent enlarg-
ing of the scope of the equalization of opportunities,
and growing upward mobility also have been important factors in the new-found strength. The awakening of *chicanismo* and its growth, regardless of obvious polarization
within the Mexican-American community about the means,
not goals (or not all the goals), has made a considerable
impact in the recent past. The "resolution of rising
expectations" and the socioeconomic impact of slowly
rising levels of education is already visible. The new
generation of leaders, lawyers, and activists trained in
the 15 years since the emergence of *chicanismo* is already
assuming new roles, placing new social demands, and providing different inputs into the political system. The
partial transformation of the roles of the traditional
Mexican-American organizations is to be observed (e.g.,
LULAC) with the acquisition of new sociopolitical roles
on many popular issues previously not eschewed.

This gradual but accelerating tempo of change within
the Chicano community is further aided by the growth of
the college-age Mexican-American cohorts. It will be
even further accentuated in the future since the ratio of
Anglo vs. Mexican-American college graduates is still unfavorable for the latter. And the rate of unemployment
among the Mexican-American teenagers and the school drop-
out rate and high school successes are inversely related.
Hence, in the Mexican-American community the concentration of attention in the future will be, next to economic
opportunities, on quality of education. If it succeeds
in influencing the political system on the local level,
it also will have a large and far-reaching impact on the
role of that minority within the larger Southwestern
society.

Increased awareness and higher level of education
has traditionally been reflected in other American ethnic
groups, rather rapidly within a generation, in upward
mobility and in the contribution and impact of that particular group on the society as a whole. Similar trends
can be observed in the Chicano community as exemplified
in recent times in higher professional visibility and
voting potential, still not fully realized, however. The
only difference in the overall American pattern will be
preservation of cultural and linguistic heritage.

The new inputs into the American political system
and demands of the Chicanos will be progressively maxi-
mized in the changing sociopolitical circumstances. The
recent quest for redistricting, which will increase the
community's political and hence economic power, has been
supported in several court cases. The voting patterns
are changing, however slowly, and they will be helped by
these developments; it can only translate into further
growth of the political power of the Mexican-American
community. Hence the trends are there, although changes

are slow and gradual, largely because of the relatively slow raising of the level of consciousness of the community and its voting patterns which affect political inputs and outputs. The fundamental changes, both within that community and in its role in Southwestern society, are already observed by researchers. The concommitant quest for upward mobility, social and economic, and the increase in the political power of the community, once achieved will bring a new political phenomenon--the impact of ethnic/linguistic identity on American politics, both local and regional, if not national.

It is only on reaching that stage in its community/group development that when some of the questions currently fascinating only to researchers can be addressed. To what extent, then, will the well-established and political influential community affect and change the American concept of an integrated, monolingual, and unicultural (on the official, not "family heritage," level) nation? The trends do not offer us a clear vision since there are too many variables which still can affect the Mexican-American community within the United States in the near future and change the directions of developments (e.g., future tenacity of the linguistic and cultural identity vis-a-vis societal, technological, and conformistic pressures in the society at large, which influences Americans of all ethnic backgrounds).

If one is allowed to project some possible scenarios, the possible perpetuation of the territorial minority characteristics within the Chicano ethnic community will have a far-reaching future impact not only on internal American politics, but even more in international dimensions. The very fact of the area of habitation along the border with the growing and dynamic neighbor to the south, ethnically akin to that American territorial minority, will bring both challenges and dilemmas to future American foreign policy makers. The issue of minority rights and treatment, if removed from the scene, will by its absence serve as a bridge to the south, but at the same time the growth of the Mexican-American ethnic pressure group will increasingly affect future American foreign policy toward not only Mexico, but the whole of Latin America as well.

Such trends are now observable as indicated by the budding development of the Chicano inputs in the American foreign policy making and, however slow, of realization of those developments by the powers that be. Once released from the burden of economic inequality, if not racial discrimination, in effect a juxtaposition of socioeconomic and ethnic cleavages that Karl Deutsch calls the "double trouble" syndrome, the Mexican-American community of the United States will play a full and well-earned role within the American nation. Furthermore, the new concept of ethnically and linguistically distinct and

274

fully developed territorial minority with all its economic, social, and political dimensions, will test, enrich, and challenge the American integrative national model. Only time will tell what such a symbiosis will bring for the Southwest and the American nation.

SELECTED BIBLIOGRAPHY

Acuna, Rodolfo. Occupied America: The Chicano's Struggle Toward Liberation. San Francisco: Canfield Press, 1972.

Andersson, Theodore and Mildred Boyer. Bilingual Schooling in the United States: History, Rationale, Implications, and Planning. Vol. 2. Austin, Texas: Southwest Educational Development Laboratory, 1970.

Barron, Milton L., ed. Minorities in a Changing World. New York: Alfred A. Knopf, 1967.

Castro, Tony. Chicano Power: The Emergence of Mexican America. New York: E. P. Dutton and Company, Inc., 1974.

Dahl, Robert A. Modern Political Analysis. Third edition. Englewood Cliffs, N.J.: Prentice-Hall, Inc., 1976.

De La Garza, Rudolph, Z. Anthony Kruszewski, and Tomas A. Arciniega, eds. Chicanos and Native Americans: The Territorial Minorities. Englewood Cliffs, N.J.: Prentice-Hall, Inc., 1973.

Fishman, Joshua A. Language and Nationalism: Two Integrative Essays. Rowley, Mass.: Newbury House Publishers, 1972.

Garreau, Joel. The Nine Nations of North America. Boston: Houghton Mifflin Company, 1981.

Gomez, Rudolph, Clement Cottingham, Jr., Russell Endo, and Kathleen Jackson, eds. The Social Reality of Ethnic America. Lexington, Mass.: D. C. Heath and Company, 1974.

Gordon, Milton M. Assimilation in American Life: The Role of Race, Religion, and National Origins. New York: Oxford University Press, 1964.

Grebler, Leo, Joan W. Moore, and Ralph C. Guzman. The Mexican-American People: The Nation's Second Largest Minority. New York: The Free Press, 1970.

Hedrick, Basil C., J. Charles Kelley, and Carroll L. Riley, eds. The Mesoamerican Southwest: Readings in Archaeology, Ethnohistory, and Ethnology. Carbondale, Ill.: Southern Illinois University Press, 1974.

Litt, Edgar. Ethnic Politics in America: Beyond Pluralism. Glenview, Ill.: Scott, Foresman and Company, 1970.

Mackey, W. F. Le Bilinguisme: Phenomene Mondial. Montreal: Harvest House, Ltd., 1967.

Mackey, William F. Bilingual Education in a Binational School: A Study of Equal Language Maintenance Through Free Alternation. Rowley, Mass.: Newbury House Publishers, 1972.

McWilliams, Carey. North from Mexico: The Spanish-Speaking People of the United States. New York: Greenwood Press, 1968.

Neighbor, Howard D. City Council Districting in the 1980s. New York: National Municipal League, 1980.

Novak, Michael. The Rise of the Unmeltable Ethnics. New York: Macmillan Publishing Company, Inc., 1973.

Olson, James Stuart. The Ethnic Dimension in American History. Volumes 1 and 2. New York: St. Martin's Press, 1979.

Ryan, Joseph A., ed. White Ethics: Life in Working-Class America. Englewood Cliffs, N.J.: Prentice-Hall, Inc., 1973.

Schaefer, Richard T. Racial and Ethnic Groups. Boston: Little, Brown and Company, 1979.

Schermerhorn, R. A. Comparative Ethnic Relations: A Framework for Theory and Research. New York: Random House, 1970.

Smith, Anthony D. The Ethnic Revival. Cambridge, England: Cambridge University Press, 1981.

Sowell, Thomas, ed. American Ethnic Groups. The Urban Institute, 1978.

Thernstrom, Stephan, Ann Orlov, and Oscar Handlin, eds. Harvard Encyclopedia of American Ethnic Groups. Cambridge, Mass.: Harvard University Press, 1980.

Tyler, Gus, ed. Mexican-Americans Tomorrow: Educational and Economic Perspectives. Albuquerque: University of New Mexico Press, 1975.

Weber, David J., ed. Foreigners in Their Native Land: Historical Roots of the Mexican Americans. Albuquerque: University of New Mexico Press, 1973.

Weed, Perry L. The White Ethnic Movement and Ethnic Politics. New York: Praeger Publishers, 1973.

About the Contributors

Zbigniew Anthony Kruszewski. Ph.D. The University of
Chicago. Professor of Political Science and Director of
The Cross Cultural Southwest Ethnic Study Center at The
University of Texas at El Paso. Member, Center for
Inter-American and Border Studies Advisory Committee, The
University of Texas at El Paso. Former Chairperson,
Department of Political Science, The University of Texas
at El Paso. His interests lie in the general field of
cross-national political institutions and behavior, and
the specialized fields of social and economic stratification, international politics, political development and
modernization, and ethnic politics. Dr. Kruszewski's
research activities have included communication research
at The University of Chicago, Human Relations Area Files
research on area monographs, and socioeconomic research
as a visiting scholar in the Center of Sociology and History of Culture of the Polish Academy of Sciences. His
writings include books, monographs, and articles on socioeconomic and cultural change and political development. He also directed a four-year National Endowment
for the Humanities which developed the Interdisciplinary
Humanities Border Studies project at The University of
Texas at El Paso.

Richard L. Hough. Ph.D. The University of Illinois at
Urbana-Champaign. Sociologist. Associate Research Pro-
fessor, Department of Psychiatry and Biobehavioral
Sciences, School of Medicine, Neuropsychiatric Institute,
The University of California at Los Angeles and Adjunct
Associate Professor, Division of Behavioral Sciences and
Health Education, School of Public Health, The University
of California at Los Angeles. He is concurrently Chief,
Health Services Research, Brentwood Veterans Administra-
tion Medical Center, Los Angeles and Co-Director, Mental
Health Epidemiology and Evaluation Research Training
Program, The School of Public Health, The University of
California at Los Angeles. His primary research inter-
ests and numerous publications include field studies of

276

life stress, change, coping, and illness, particularly in
culturally heterogeneous environments. His teaching interests concentrate on psychiatric epidemiology, social
stress, and coping behavior and evaluation research.

Jacob Ornstein-Galicia. Ph.D. Ohio University. Professor Emeritus of Linguistics and Modern Languages at The
University of Texas at El Paso. He was co-founder and
co-director of the Cross Cultural Southwest Ethnic
Study Center at The University of Texas at El Paso. His
area of expertise is Socio-Linguistics and applied and
Theoretical Linguistics. He is an experienced specialist
in language teaching methodology and socio-linguistics
as applied to bilingual/bicultural education. He conducted extensive research on Southwest Spanish and bilingualism. A prolific and continuous writer, he has become
internationally known through his several hundred
articles and more than a dozen books, authored or co-
authored. A "Festschrift for Jacob Ornstein: Studies in
General Linguistics and Sociolinguistics" was published
in 1981 in his honor by his colleagues.

Everett D. Edington. Ph.D. Professor of Educational
Management and Development, New Mexico State University.
Director of the Eric Clearinghouse for Rural Education
and Small Schools at New Mexico State University. His
major research interests are in the areas of rural education and educational change processes. His most recent
publication is "Educational Change a Prerequisite,"
Educational Considerations, Winter 1981.

David B. Eyde. Ph.D. Associate Professor of Anthropology, The University of Texas at El Paso. His interests
are in Southwestern pluralism, Mexican and Mexican-American society and culture, from both social structural and
symbolic perspectives, and Melanesia. A recent publication is "Orozco as Myth: A Structural Analysis," Proceedings of the 29th Annual Conference, Rocky Mountain Council on Latin American Studies, Lincoln, Nebraska, 1981.

Paul W. Goodman. Ph.D. Associate Professor of Sociology
at The University of Texas at El Paso. His interests are
in the sociology of education, borderland studies (twin
plants), and the sociology of poverty. A forthcoming
publication is "System-Environmental Adaptation: Corporations in a U.S.-Mexico Border Metropolis," Studies in
Comparative International Development, co-authored with
Julius Rivera.

Herbert Hirsch. Ph.D. Professor and Chairperson, Department of Political Science, Virginia Commonwealth University. His publications include The Right of the
People: An Introduction to American Politics (1980);

Learning to be Militant (1977); Violence as Politics (1973); Comparative Legislative Systems (1971); and Poverty and Politicization (1971). He is currently at work on The Dialectic of Obedience: An Inquiry into the Causes of Genocidal Behavior.

Clark S. Knowlton. Ph.D. Professor of Sociology, University of Utah. Former Director of the Center for the Study of Social Problems, University of Utah, and former Director of Social Research and Development Division, American West Center, University of Utah. Apart from sociology, his other interests are political science, anthropology, archaeology, and natural resources. Author of one book and forty-five articles, among his his more recent publications is "Rural Ethnic Minorities, Adaptive Response to Inequality," a chapter co-authored with Thomas J. Durant, Jr. in Thomas R. Ford, ed., Rural U.S.A. Persistence and Change (Ames: Iowa State University Press, 1979).

William P. Kuvlesky. Ph.D. Professor of Sociology, Texas A&M University. He is a past president of the Southwest Sociological Association and the Association for Humanistic Sociology. He has written widely on minority youth, rural minority groups, and intergroup relations, and has served on the Citizen's Advisory Committee on Equal Opportunity for the U.S. Department of Agriculture.

James W. Lamare. Ph.D. Lecturer, University of Canterbury, Christchurch, New Zealand. Formerly Associate Professor of Political Science at The University of Texas at El Paso. His previous publications include numerous articles on the political socialization of Chicano children residing in the Southwest and he is the author of Texas Politics: Economics, Power, and Policy (St. Paul: West Publishing Company, 1981).

Mary Steffey Lamare. A graduate of and former teaching assistant at The University of Texas at El Paso, she currently resides in Christchurch, New Zealand.

Manuel A. Machado. Ph.D. Professor of History, University of Montana. His publications include Listen Chicano! An Informal History of the Mexican American (Chicago: Nelson-Hall, 1978) and The North American Cattle Industry, 1910-1975: Conflict, Ideology, and Change (College Station: Texas A&M University Press, 1981).

Dennis Medina. Medina was a research assistant in the Department of Rural Sociology, Texas A&M University at the time the study was done.

Michael V. Miller. Ph.D. Assistant Professor of Sociology, The University of Texas at San Antonio. He has published various articles on Mexican Americans (the family, career orientations, political action, e.g., Crystal City, and ethnic identification) and the border (poverty, economic development). His most recent publication is Economic Change Along the Texas-Mexican Border: The Case of Brownsville, Texas (Austin: Bureau of Business Research, The University of Texas at Austin, 1982).

Victoria P. Morrow. Ph.D. Having taught sociology at Chabot College, Hayward, California, since 1975, she is serving her second two-year term as President of the Academic Senate of that institution. She was selected for the 1982 "Leaders for the 80's" program for administrative training, sponsored by the American Association for Women in Community and Junior Colleges. Her 1978 dissertation was entitled "Bicultural Education: An Instance of Cultural Politics."

Fernando Peñalosa. Ph.D. Professor and Chairman of the Department of Sociology, California State University at Long Beach. His interests are in sociolinguistics of U.S. Hispanics, Chicano sociology, world system theory, and language and sociohistorical development of the Macedonian Slavs. He has published thirty articles and four books, including Chicano Sociolinguistics (1980) and Introduction to the Sociology of Language (1981).

F
790
.M5
P64
1982

Politics and society
in the Southwest

DATE			